The Vested

Interests

ⅬⅬⅬⅬⅬⅬⅬⅬⅬⅬ

⊐⊓⊐⊓⊐⊓⊐⊓⊐⊓⊐⊓⊐

Books by Edward Ziegler

Men Who Make Us Rich

The Vested Interests

⊐⊓⊐⊓⊐⊓⊐⊓⊐⊓⊐⊓⊐

THE VESTED INTERESTS

Their Origins, Development

and Behavior

EDWARD ZIEGLER

The Macmillan Company, New York
Collier-Macmillan Limited, London

[1964]

Copyright © Edward Ziegler 1964

All rights reserved—no part of this book may be reproduced in any form without permission in writing from the publisher, except by a reviewer who wishes to quote brief passages in connection with a review written for inclusion in magazine or newspaper.

First Printing

THE MACMILLAN COMPANY, NEW YORK
COLLIER-MACMILLAN CANADA, LTD., TORONTO, ONTARIO

Library of Congress catalog card number: 64-10251

Printed in the United States of America

DESIGNED BY RONALD FARBER

For My Parents
Vinton Edward Ziegler
and
Beatrice Skelton Ziegler

Contents

エⵊⵊⵊⵊⵊⵊⵊ⌐

Introduction

ЛЛЛЛЛЛЛЛЛЛГ

A vested interest is an institution with economic power that seeks profit and is under private control. There is nothing new about vested interests. They have been visible for as long as the Republic has existed. James Madison noted in *The Federalist* that "a landed interest, a manufacturing interest, a mercantile interest, a moneyed interest, with many lesser interests grow up of necessity in civilized nations." He also noted that "the regulation of these various and interfering interests forms the principal task of modern legislation, and involves the spirit of party and faction in the necessary and ordinary operations of the government."

As in Madison's day, so in ours. The quest for relative advantage among the various interests continues to influence politics and economics as well as cultural and social forms. This book is concerned not only with the vested interests themselves but also with the principal beneficiaries of those interests. It is concerned with the insiders—the Americans who have the desirable jobs, who lead "the good life," who hold and enjoy the lion's share of the wealth.

This work concentrates on showing how these vested interests came to be the way they are, how they spice the flavor of everyday life, and how they and the classes who populate them shape and guide national affairs.

EDWARD ZIEGLER

The Vested

Interests

⌐Π_⌐_⌐Π_⌐_⌐

O N E

Vested Interests

and Sound Thought

ՄՆՄՆ

I begin with a loaded term when I set out to describe "vested interests," as the phrase alone makes them seem worse than they probably are. Yet no other label will do. I am not trying to sketch merely a view of American industry, or of corporate enterprise, or of profit-making business. They are subjects of interest, but they are not the principal focus. That center of attention is broader than a single group of institutions. A vested interest, as viewed in this book, is a whole basis of economic organization. Hence, at one stage in this nation's development, agriculture represented the vested interest, the principal end for which society was arrayed. At later stages, finance, manufacturing, or other interests have enjoyed predominant influence over society, as following chapters will try to demonstrate.

Contemporary vested interests have several distinguishing traits: a public rhetoric or style of discourse; preoccupation with financial stability; skillful use of specialization; secular piety; an intricate ceremonial mode; tolerance of some dissent; a static view of the universe; cultivated indifference to outsiders; and continuity of administration. A vested interest is a tyranny, of sorts, al-

[1]

though its arbitrary and despotic exercise of powers is hedged around with scented smokescreens emitted by skillful public relations. Nevertheless, as the following chapters attempt to show, the powers of the vested interests are and always have been considerable.

As the succeeding chapters try to show by repeated citations of historical examples, vested interests have always sounded as if they were endowed by God with perfect moral elevation. As an example, the manufacturing interest in the United States wishes to keep its costs as low as possible, and it always has tried to do so. One effective way to keep costs low is to oppose on a systematic basis any government expenditure or labor settlement likely to raise taxes or wage costs. Systematic opposition from a plateau of moral excellence is more public service than private pleading, and thus the manufacturer will invoke "incentive," "individualism," or "constitutionalism," to drive off those who would vex him with higher taxes or wage payments.

The vested interest tends in every era to have close association with capital. Either a given interest creates capital itself or maintains and manipulates someone else's capital. Machines, factories, transport networks, real estate—these are the raw stuff of capital, and these have historically been the basic concerns of the ranking interests. Order and stability thus are the great goals. Financial security, as it happens, can be won only at the cost of something else. Often it appears that this "something else" is the acute discomfort of workers or others outside the vested interest's central concerns. However that may be, financial stability will be maintained if a vested interest continues to have its way, and usually the interest does have its way.

To say that a vested interest encourages specialization and skillfully uses specialists is really to say no more than that the reign of modern vested interests has grown more noticeable with increasing industrialization. The narrow skill deeply applied has been essential to the spread of systematic economic endeavor, whether it be agriculture or manufacturing. Once a task (take housebuilding) is broken down into a series of separate steps (excavating, foundation-laying, framing, plastering, roofing, and so on) organizers can realize great efficiencies, buyers great economies, workers great increases in wage income. On the plane of economic advantage, everyone benefits.

Secular piety, another of the characteristics that I have ascribed to vested interests, is that large inventory of slogans and slogan-like thoughts that make up the standard words and ideas of the American middle class. These slogans, these sound thoughts, are concerned basically with conferring honor and distinction on the American middle class and upon the industrial institutions that keep the middle class and its betters solvent. Bestowing honor on oneself, then, is the essential goal of secular piety. The vested interest honors itself in like fashion, because that is one of *its* functions. If the leaders of the ranking interests did not proclaim themselves archangels of well-being, a new vested interest might soon constitute itself, expropriate the symbols of authority, and proclaim itself the source of solvency and public welfare. (The attitude of secular piety will be examined fully in the succeeding pages, as will the closely associated subject of sound thought.)

Ceremonial luxuriance is in many ways the most interesting aspect of the contemporary vested interest, as corporate ritualism has much of the flavor of group magic. For want of a better term, I have advanced the phrase "sacerdotal bureaucracy" to describe the new look in corporate chambers, the new private visage of the vested interest. The implication of the rapid growth of sacerdotalism (that is, priestly behavior) in the corporate world is that it represents an organized quest for love by middle managers of uncertain status. Such ritualism of necessity poses problems for productively oriented managers in industry, because they find themselves more and more limited by the veto powers of their fellows who are not so interested in productive as in ritual labors.

To its credit, the American vested interest still is capable of tolerating dissidence. There is some evidence that the periodic turnover in top management is one great assurance that the love of stability and risklessness will not entirely stifle the innovative urges in corporate bureaucracies. The limits of tolerance are nevertheless fairly well defined, as will be made clear.

The large capital investment in plant and equipment that is represented by American industry occasions a stylized outlook shaped in most respects by the implicit fear that something is going to erode that capital base and that it must be watched vigilantly.

It may be said that the vested interests' indifference to the one-third of the populace that is outside its employ or its primary markets is the first mark of a growing enclave mentality. Something similar in many ways to the enclosure movement of the fifteenth to nineteenth centuries in Great Britain is operating in the American economy. In the British experience, the great landowners "enclosed" their lands by planting hedges or building fences around them. Thus the poor could no longer gather firewood or graze their sheep and cattle on what had been common land.

In the twentieth century enclosure movement, America's prime vested interests have been pursuing policies that also threaten to build impregnable walls in society—walls that hopefully keep those outside outside, those inside safe from economic adversity. The middle and upper classes thus are effectively insulating themselves from the lower classes, or so they think. Examples of the emerging enclave mentality in the United States are provided by various mass magazines that, despite their large circulations, avoid the poor masses as readers and thereby concentrate their readership in the middle classes. Thus situated, they use their editorial space to cluck tongues at the poor. Chapter Nine explores this phenomenon in detail.

· 1 ·

The intellectual milieu of the vested interests derives from their economic and political goals. They play three distinct roles. They are in one sense pools of wealth; in another sense they are procreative organisms; and in a third sense they are ideological beacons. Each of these roles depends on the others for support and amplification. Without a pool of wealth to supply capital, expansive production would be impossible. Without expansive production, no new capital would be created. Without the ideological beacons, the leaders of the interests fear that certain dark forces in America would somehow efface large corporations or entire classes.

What the interests offer in pursuit of their goals is a philosophy with two objects: to preserve the wealth already in hand and to equate this wealth with virtue. The label "sound thought" applies to this philosophy.

Other elements of sound thought seem to flow from the bottom belief: avarice is far from being a sin but is on the contrary a benign and ennobling attribute. Another element is that riches owned by an individual may and perhaps should be infinite. A third element is that an elite of wealthy and powerful persons is the proper group to look after the affairs of a nation such as this one. A fourth element is that institutions are merely vague aggregates of all human goodness and meanness, nobility and churlishness, and therefore if there are such things as social problems, they have their proper remedy in individual reform.

The historical foundation of sound thought is a principle with distinctly religious overtones, the principle of the deserving rich:

Since time began there have been two types of people, the hard-working savers and the shiftless spenders. The savers have always been ascetic and have denied their desires to spend. The spenders have always been voluptuaries, powerless before each new temptation to spend. The savers have been strong and the spenders have been weak. Because the savers have saved, they are rich. Because the spenders have squandered their substance, they are poor. The principle also gives retroactive service: The rich have saved and that is why they are rich. The poor have spent, and that is why they are poor. The principle therefore confers or withholds sanctity: To save is good, to spend is bad. Therefore those who have been good are rich, which is very nearly the same thing as saying that to be rich is to be good. As John D. Rockefeller, Sr., said, riches are "a gift from Heaven signifying, 'This is my beloved son, in whom I am well pleased.'"

This law of society found expression when Mr. Cobden, about 1850, told the workingmen of Huddersfield, England, "The world has always been divided into two classes—those who saved and those who spent—the thrifty and the extravagant. . . ." It found more recent expression in one of the aphorisms that the *Saturday Evening Post* runs. In the January 20, 1962, issue appeared this version of the law (softened a bit for the times): "The haves and the have nots can often be traced back to the dids and the did nots."

· 2 ·

This brief glance at sound thought and its diction does not pretend to be complete, but rather to suggest what the succeeding chapters will attempt to establish—namely, that a particular kind of thought distinguishes our vested interests and that the consequences of that thought are often noxious to the economic health of the nation. In the past, sound thought may well have been a positive necessity, particularly when the nation was building its industrial plant between 1870 and 1914. But beginning about 1914, and continuing to the present, sound thought has more often been injurious to the economic health of the nation than not, and that is one of the things the succeeding chapters seek to prove.

Sound thought's temporal goal is to make America safer for investment capital. Safer than what? one might ask. Safer than whatever degree of safety prevails at the present moment. Investment capital needs to be needed. It needs to bask in good wishes and exclamations of affection or it may just waste away, and it does not hesitate to say as much.

This kind of life-view thus creates its own public pressures that coalesce in the politics of sound thought, the legislative art of making America safer for the very rich.

One of the most highly visible examples of the power of the

vested interests' public philosophy is provided by the history of the progressive income tax. As Chapter 6 will describe in some detail, the progressive features of the Federal income taxes have been very nearly nullified. Furthermore, increasing wealth equalization has been reversed since 1946.

Still further evidence of the remarkable potency of sound thought as a public philosophy is provided by the observation that the poor don't seem to care much about the relative attenuation of the progressive ideal in taxation. Poor Americans, that is, tend to accept their present poverty, so long as it doesn't get worse. The tales of the lower-middle-class Americans preferring to slip into the upper fringes of the lower class rather than give up their "freedom" during the Depression by accepting aid from an active Federal government suggests how deep the roots of sound thought go.

The have-nots seem to fall into three attitudes. The largest number of them no doubt accepts the standards of sound thought and tries to emulate the feats not so much of the big rich but of the middle-class, junior-executive group. A second group in effect renounces the present world for the next through a return to fundamentalist religion like that of the Pentecostal Holiness or Jehovah's Witnesses sects. The third group of the poor adopts a class-consciousness and looks to institutional remedies for its problems in the hopes of winning security against economic adversity. Although this group may at times hold ascendancy, the emulators rather than these militants seem more typical of the American poor. Even the militance of the Negro serves the ultimate cause of emulation, not revolution. Far from wishing to tear down the country-club walls or plow up the putting greens, the Negro poor merely wish to use the bus-terminal lunch counters on equal footing with their financial peers.

Given this forbearance on the part of the poor, the politics of sound thought enjoys great scope in conferring new distinctions on the holders of accumulated wealth and on high-income earners. To return to our income-tax example, Treasury Department figures indicate that the average effective rate of payment of income taxes for Americans filing as man and wife and earning $1 million or more a year is 24 percent. If the recommendations of the National Association of Manufacturers were put into effect, these same people might well be paying 35 percent. So deep is the thralldom to sound thought, in fact, that the N.A.M. sets out to slay a 91 percent dragon that has long since been dead—if it ever was alive. (It really wasn't. There is a statutory prohibition against taking more than 87 percent of a man's income in taxes.)

The elements of the politics of sound thought, then, may be listed in this rough order of importance: The government must sustain incentive for those who contribute most to the economy, the investors; to fail in this objective is to invite national disaster. The government must not interfere in private business affairs, for to do so is to restrict personal freedom. The government must not adopt an antibusiness attitude, for to do so constitutes a psychic tax on the reigning leaders of the interests, the archons of industry.* The government, therefore, should levy lightly on the archon's tangible income, not at all on his psychic income, and it should not even hint at any restriction of his personal freedom.

· 3 ·

One of the major paradoxes of the contemporary vested interests is that while they enjoy a concentration of power into units more dense and centralized, they at the same time find their new power less than absolute because each unit of wealth-producing power grows more and more dependent on its environment. Still, in many particulars, the interests seem more able than ever before to shape that environment to their own wishes and needs.

To phrase the point more concretely: at the same time that the corporation grows more dependent on the purchasing power of the mass market, it gains new power to dictate, at least in some degree, the behavior of the mass upon whom it depends for its

---

* Archon: a ruling or presiding officer; from the Greek ἄρχειν (archein), to rule.

survival. By means of improved technology, this relative power to influence and even to dictate to the mass market may well enjoy a great refinement. Given a simple device like a negative ion dispenser (attached to air-conditioning units), which according to its makers can cause a profound change in one's mood, the possibilities at retail seem endless. Given additional skillful conditioning by means of psychologically programed music piped into the marketplace and into the factory, and the vested interests can help cause a dissenting frame of mind to vanish. Given inexpensive and widely available tranquillizers, even the angry and frustrated become more agreeable.

· 4 ·

The nucleus of the vested interests is the modern corporation, and most specifically the large manufacturing corporations, which in a real sense rule this nation, set the tone of its culture and daily life, control the broad outlines of government action, maintain a virtual veto right over Federal monetary and fiscal policy, act to decide how the relative shares of income shall be distributed, inform our national attitudes, and create our wealth.

There can be little question that the corporation is in fact the prime institution in America, nor can there be much doubt that the top executives within these corporations today enjoy the rights and privileges of property even though the property itself no longer maintains its traditional concrete form. These top executives, then, owe their eminence and power to the fact that they control the means of production and finance without actually owning those means. Who, then, does own those means? The question is becoming difficult to answer, for a significant portion of the stock of these corporations has passed into the hands of still other institutions, whose "owners" in turn have suffered a severe diminution of their ownership rights in return for security. Mutual funds, pension funds, investment trusts, and other institutions that invest the funds of many people collectively are gathering up a significantly large percentage of corporate common stock and are thereby making the question of "ownership" far less significant than that of control.

America's early agrarian leaders sensed that the huge aggregates of liquid-wealth power that corporations represent could work a fundamental and to them undesirable change on the illiquid-wealth of agriculture that then was the basis of the new nation's structure. Agriculture looked forward to the rise of manufacturing with trepidation. Jeffersonian beliefs assumed a nation of smallholders prospering by agriculture, and such belief recoiled at the thought of vast concentrations of power that would enjoy the legal privileges of a person yet remain a legal fiction. As A. A. Berle, Jr., has written:

. . . the Federal government was specifically denied the power to create corporations [by the Constitutional Convention]. This was to be left to the states and it was assumed that they would not exercise this power or, if they did, would exercise it only as a means of carrying on government. This doctrine survived less than 15 years [that is, until 1791]. . . .

Berle goes on to point out:

Corporations did do, have done and are doing exactly what our forefathers worried about. . . . [The result has been] the highest concentration of economic power in recorded history. Since the United States carries on not quite half of the manufacturing production of the entire world today, these 500 groupings [that is, corporations]—each with its own little dominating pyramid within it—represents a concentration of power over economics which makes the medieval feudal system look like a Sunday School party. In sheer economic power this has gone far beyond anything we have yet seen.[1]

As stewards of vast amounts of wealth-creating power, the archons of industry play a central role in maintaining or upsetting the wealth-accumulation of their countrymen. Each of us, to an extent we hardly comprehend, depends upon the decisions made

[1] Footnotes appear on p. 267 and thereafter.

in the executive suites of our largest corporations. Let the top executives decide that their vast liquidity should be withheld from capital investment, as they did decide in 1953, 1957, and 1959, and as their predecessors decided *in extremis* in 1930, and the result is a drought of liquidity: retrenchment, diminished consumption, unemployment, and wasted human resources—a desert of purchasing power created almost by mistake (as it often seems).

This restrictive, parsimonious attitude evidenced periodically by the industrial leadership represents the ascendancy of the institutional precaution motive over the more normal speculation motive. Or is it really the "more normal" motive among our industrial leaders? Perhaps not.

Financial manipulation under the cumulative power it feels from an archon's decision puts the interests of capital most obviously at odds with the interests of the mass of potential consumers among the poor. The manipulation of inventory (in which everyone tries to get the way station before him on the pipeline to assume the costs: the auto dealer, the factory; the auto factory, the steel warehouse; the steel warehouse, the steel mill; the steel mill, the ore supplier; and so on) is just one example of the power of executive decisions.

Such inventory juggling has been singled out by congressional Joint Economic Committee research investigators as the key to several of the postwar recessions, as the volatile fuse that has set off business slumps by over-restricting sales and therefore inhibiting production.

It is perhaps the ultimate irony of the modern corporate interests that the major distinction in the effects that the various activities of the archons have in the present political climate is to cause the rapid unemployment of many workers or to cause the somewhat slower loss of jobs by these same workers. Let financial-precaution motives predominate, and the result is recession, in which as many as twenty of every hundred unskilled workers is out of work. Let speculation-innovation motives predominate, as usually occurs after a bout with finance-precaution (1955 being the prime example), and automation and mechanization manage to expel the same stratum of worker from the plant, albeit somewhat less dramatically than under a campaign of retrenchment.

The unskilled have no real hope of seeing their circumstances improve unless they gain a somewhat bigger slice of an expanding pie; they have virtually no prospects of gaining an improvement if the pie is static or shrinking. Therefore the ascendancy of the innovation spirit is apparently an essential ingredient for heightened economic growth, and represents a greater hope to the unskilled than does its opposite, the precaution spirit. But even at that, this "greater hope" is at most the promise of intermittent unemployment rather than chronic unemployment, and as such it is the less bad of two unattractive alternatives.

· 5 ·

This rather abstract exploration of some of the elements of sound thought, vested interests, and the modern enclosure movement will be pursued in more concrete form in the succeeding chapters of this book. My object is not only to attempt an examination of the economic effects of the vested interests but their political and social effects as well. I have tried to pursue these matters with an eye to their historical development, their present status, and their direction of change. Lastly, although I know it is probably vain work, I have done what I could to expunge the hidden value judgments that customarily give books of this type their pretensions to disinterest in the presence of bootleg moral philosophy. If any bootlegging is going on, let the deed be done in full view.

The Evolution of Interests

꠲꠲꠲꠲꠲

A vested interest does not come into the world strong and dignified. In spite of its decorous bearing when mature, its origins have probably been rowdy. Mayhem and bellowing have accompanied the birth of almost every one of them.

Some interests have grown weak and toothless with advancing years, and cannot stand against newer interests. Commercial agriculture provides an outstanding example. Other interests, such as commerce and transportation, have succeeded agriculture and have had their crests of power. They in their turn have made way for more powerful interests, specifically manufacturing and finance.

The rise of advertising-consumerism in the twentieth century suggests that this new interest may go on to preeminence of its own within the next few decades, unless the acquisitive habits of consumers fall into neglect. Whatever the future may hold, the present and the past are of more immediate concern here.

· 1 ·

The progress of America from the lowest form of economic interest, hunting and gathering, to the subsistence stage of agriculture was, for the most part, finished business within about a century of the founding of Jamestown, or by about 1700. Thereafter the issue was hardly in doubt, despite the occasional Indian uprisings that continued into the nineteenth century.

After 1700 the succeeding years may be described as follows:

Commerce was in flower within another few decades, with American shipping interests rising rapidly along with the fur, lumbering, and fishing industries. Under the stimulus of active overseas trading, as noted above, commercial agriculture also developed, but commerce began to outshine agriculture well before the culmination of agriculture's powers. The point is perhaps more clearly made by noting that New England, as the commercial region of early eminence, and the South, as the great agricultural region, found their interests more and more in conflict after 1750. Meanwhile, America's commercial interests suffered from their continual collision with their British counterparts, especially because of Britain's economic (and hence military) power, which created and enforced mercantilist policies unfavorable to the colonial commercial interests. The ultimate clash of these vying national interests was played out in the American Revolution, a rebellion that in spite of its rhetorical ornaments was nevertheless colored by practical market rivalry as much as by anything else.

Within a few years of independence came manufacturing industry on a significantly large scale. Hitherto, Britain had discouraged industrial self-reliance in its colonies. These territories were supposed to supply raw materials for British mills and markets for finished products. The first rapid industrial growth in the new nation was in textile manufacturing, and soon thereafter, behind the sheltering tariff walls, other manufacturing began to flourish. For the next hundred years, the new nation busied itself with the accumulation of capital—expanding westward and taming new land; building a transportation network of canals, turnpikes, and railroads; and improving its financial and monetary system. The government was unwilling to involve itself in the issue of currency, after its bad experiences with the scrip issued by the Continental Congress. Therefore private banking under government charter was to be the rule. An early concentration of financial power in the Second Bank of the United States threatened to elevate finance to a position from which it could exert harsh pressure on agriculture and commerce alike. But the day of concentrated finance had to wait for a more pliant and tolerant government and people. In the 1830's, farmers and small merchants had their tribune in Andrew Jackson, who vetoed the renewal of the bank's charter.

Agriculture was not yet an unequivocally second-rate vested interest, as these events, and the later events preceding the Civil War, demonstrated. Once that war was over, however, there remained no doubt of the primacy of manufacturing industry run for the benefit of concentrated financial interests. The first victors of the war, in the sense that they reaped the first great spoils, were certain young men who stayed far back of the lines. These men among themselves fashioned a gigantic new vested interest of finance. They have come to be known as the Robber Barons, and their era was from about 1870 to about 1910, or roughly those years of greatest activity of their prototype, John D. Rockefeller. He and J. P. Morgan, the elder, were the economic supernovas. Near these brilliant stars of avarice and efficiency rose many others of lesser magnitude: Gould, Drew, Harriman, Carnegie, Fisk, and Vanderbilt.

The clashes of the titans of finance were viewed with apparent approval for many years, but at length the public and the government grew weary of them. Their era faded with the panics in Wall Street that followed such huge contests as that of May, 1901, when Rockefeller and Morgan fought to a standoff for control of the Northern Pacific. In that financial crossfire hundreds of smaller investors were wiped out. The laboring classes, meanwhile, began to grow restive, particularly after the effective end of free land in the West—which until 1880 had been a safety valve for the malcontents who found life in the factory-dominated East intolerable. Through the 1880's and into the 1890's, labor began to phrase its demands for better wages and working conditions with a more powerful voice.

The lords of manufacturing and finance still had a large residue of public approval, particularly among the native-born Americans, who did not find themselves ground down in quite the way that the waves of immigrant laborers were. Most Americans seem to have approved the new grandeur of scale that the Robber Barons brought to industry and finance. The embryo unions, meanwhile, came more and more to be identified with "foreign" elements and with the alien faith of radicalism. In response to the clamorous and often violently enforced demands of labor, the captains of industry called out private armies to do battle with the unruly strikers. Often enough the regular army would save the industrialists the cost of hiring their own warriors. In any event, the lines were fairly well drawn between the rights of property and the rights of labor. The law was clearly on the side of the new vested interests.

Nevertheless there was an element of unrest in public opinion that began to crystallize about 1890 and found some expression in the Administration of Grover Cleveland. Cleveland told the Congress in 1893: "The wage earner relies upon the ventures of confident and contented capital. This failing him, his condition is without alleviation, for he can neither prey on the misfortune of others nor hoard his labor." In spite of Cleveland's views, the courts began about the same time to strike out at the new unions as "conspiracies in restraint of trade." Thus, as Matthew Josephson has written, "the very laws which for long years it was found impossible to enforce against collusive combination or conspiracy among the industrialists were invoked with remarkable promptness and effectiveness against the associations of laborers." [1]

Theodore Roosevelt also grappled with the trusts, but the damage he did to the reigning financial and industrial interests was limited more to psychic levies on individual Robber Barons than to absolute restrictions of the interests' powers. In view of the behavior of the two outstanding men of the era, it may have been that the withdrawal of public approval from the builders of concentrated industry had at least some visible and immediate results. Rockefeller retired to philanthropy shortly after the courts demanded the breakup of Standard Oil. He retained public-relations help, began giving away dimes to poor children, and

bent every effort to gain the good wishes of a nation. The elder
J. P. Morgan, meanwhile, after a hostile probing of his banking
methods before the Pujo Committee, retired to Rome where he
died in 1913, some say from a heart broken by the Vatican's re-
fusal to sell him the Sistine Chapel.

The real effects of trust-busting, as it was called, were slight
in the degree that they stemmed the inexorable concentration of
productive and financial power. The great barrage of publicity
seems to have done small lasting injury to the financial interests
themselves. What real injury they would face would be self-
inflicted. Their bad times were still a few years off.

The epitaph for the era was delivered by George F. Baer, president of the Philadelphia & Reading Company, a leading coal company: "The rights and interests of the laboring man will be pro-
tected and cared for—not by labor agitators, but by the Christian
men to whom God in his infinite wisdom has given control of the
property interests of the country."

· 2 ·

The condition of the workingman from the time when he first
organized for wage bargaining until the end of the great wave of
immigration, about 1914, was unhealthy. Although the economy
was growing rapidly, the increase in real wages was small. Some
say there was no real increase at all. The Progressive Era (from
about 1901 until 1916) made possible a rather widespread series
of institutional changes that served to weaken the relative power
of finance and to reduce the power of a single man over the economy. The first legislative encouragement of unionism came at this
time, as did graduated income tax and the Federal Reserve
Banking System. The voters were making ready the way for a
more equitable distribution of the wealth.

The years 1920–1929 were the balmy days for the new rulers of
the financial interests, the soft-spoken heirs of the Robber Barons.
The banker became the most respected member of the community,
and the stock market became a wondrous machine that created

wealth for everyone. Manufacturing, also, enjoyed enormous scope, especially in automotive and related fields, which in this period were growing with dazzling rapidity. These were the peak years in the forty-year period that saw auto production rise 180,000 percent. At the same time manufacturing was scoring sustained victories over labor. The advances that were turned aside by bayonets and writs in the 1890's were again turned aside in the 1920's by accusations of radicalism as the real basis of the unions' campaigns. The Great Crash of October, 1929, and the subsequent paralysis of constructive thought by the business leaders represented the virtual abdication of responsibility by the financial interests. A nation waited three years to let individual initiative and local relief take hold. In essence, nothing happened. Unable to reform themselves, the reigning interests made inevitable the rapid rise of government initiative.

A new administration under Franklin Roosevelt took immediate action to revive the nearly prostrate banking system. The Emergency Banking Act of 1933 was credited with saving the financial interests from the utter ruin that they seemed to be courting. For eight more years a virtual vacuum of constructive action marked the industrial leadership. It was not until World War II that the economy was back nearer to normality. Manufacturing rose anew to prominence in the 1940–1945 period as, with the advent of war, no one any longer objected to massive government expenditure or to nationalized investment. Central direction of the most exacting and comprehensive kind at last eradicated the Depression.

That same war provided the means by which unionism became established throughout industry, and it provided the certainty that given their new strength, the unions would use it. That is exactly what they did in a series of major strikes in 1946 and 1947. Manufacturing was not without resources of public support, however. Its friends were busy making capital on the bumptiousness of the unions, with the result that the Taft-Hartley Law came into being. The Eightieth Congress had been readying other balm, as well. A new tax law restored a great deal of confidence among investors and controllers of accumulated capital.

The 1950–1960 decade saw an increasing influence for the industrial interests, a trend especially in evidence after the election of General Eisenhower, and the new rewriting of the tax laws in 1953—once again to the advantage of industry and accumulated wealth in general.

The evidence at hand suggests that 1957 may have been the years in which advertising-consumerism at last began to enjoy a more or less unassailable position as a major force in the American economy. The recurrent awareness of overcapacity obliged more than one top executive to enroll a reverence for advertising in the canons of sound thought. General Electric, for example, was described by one of its directors as primarily a marketing, no longer simply a manufacturing, organization. In 1958 American industry gave its wholehearted support to the loud advertising exhortations to consumers to "buy our way out of the downturn." President Eisenhower told one of his press conferences during the year that the way to cure the recession was to buy. "Buy what?" came the question. "Anything," was the response. These and other signs indicated that there was increasing awareness that industry had virtually solved its production problems; that the effects of automation were beginning to be felt in a large way; that the failure (or inability) of the consumer to do his required share of consumption was causing severe and unwelcome problems.

· 3 ·

These events were in large part a sophisticated new manifestation of the age-old jockeying for advantage between the haves and the have-nots. The history of that conflict may be seen in the apparent cycles of income distribution in the past one hundred years in the United States. The series of peaks and valleys indicated by a glance at the various periods of economic and political activity may be taken as the crests and troughs of influence of the vested interests. Without exception in the past century, these interests have stood for the enhancement of the powers of accumulated capital, if necessary by the restriction of income equalization. This is the rough pattern that suggests itself:

1865–1900, rapid growth of income inequality; 1900–1916, growth of equality; 1916–1932, growth of inequality; 1932–1946, fairly rapid growth of equality; 1946–1963,* growth of inequality. The first period (1865–1900) was the period of trust formation and the creation of enormous fortunes and highly concentrated wealth. The reaction period was 1900 to 1916, the Progressive Era, which saw the coming of regulatory legislation like the Pure Food and Drug Act, the progressive income tax, the Federal Reserve Bank System, the first official encouragement of labor unionism, and the apparent breakup of certain of the trusts. The years 1916 to 1932 were the World War I period, followed by Normalcy and the New Era, with sharp rebuffs to labor and welcome relief for the wealthy—the Mellon tax-reduction schemes and other methods of heightening inequality. The years 1932 to 1946 were the period of Depression, of the New Deal, and of World War II, and of rapid postwar wage increases and inflation. These, together with social security, increased government spending, and various pieces of social legislation promoted income equalization. The last period (1946–1963) was the era of repeated tax relief for accumulated capital under the guise of improving incentives for investment; 1947, 1953, and 1963 were all years in which Congress softened the burden on high-income earners and on the wealthy with almost as much diligence as shown by Secretary Mellon between 1921 and 1928 (as Chapter 6 will demonstrate in some detail).

One last theme worthy of note here is the future relative power of manufacturing and advertising. Manufacturing owes much of its present eminence to its close association with the military and to the government commitment to increasing national defense spending. The Kennedy Administration's rapid expansion of national defense outlays had the effect of carrying the nationalization of investment forward, of cementing the manufacturing interests' strong identification with the military, and thereby of na-

---

* I list 1963 here because that was when this was written, not because the tide turned that year.

tionalizing an important part of consumption as well. There was every reason to believe that this stress on national defense and space expenditure would continue throughout President Johnson's term of office, also. In this sense, then, a part of the tension between manufacturing and advertising perhaps may be seen as the pull between nationalized, military consumption of goods on the one hand and individualized, domestic consumption on the other hand.

· 4 ·

The discussion above has the obvious defect of description by aggregates. Broad categories such as I have tried to use always leave a number of unanswered questions or somewhat artificial glosses on reality. What these broad categories tend to ignore is people. People did make these changes, after all.

What of these people? What set of attitudes helped America grow to its present eminence? If there were a single phrase to sum it up, that phrase might be "holy parsimony" leavened with relapses into hedonism. The people were impelled by that curious mixture of general piety and specific irreverence for tradition that goes under the label of "Protestant Ethic." They worked hard, to be sure, but what may have been equally important, they worked in isolation—geographic and temporal. They had no predatory neighbors to invade and harass them, nor had they repressive priests to interfere with their commercial instincts. Inspired as they were by their Calvinistic beliefs to work here and now to "the glory of God," and equally bemused by the ideal of frugality, they created a productive spirit perfectly suited to exploit the immense natural wealth of their land and to capitalize on their good luck in finding such a continent in the first place.

It may have been their isolation from their more tradition-minded former countrymen, the bracing climate, or their belief in their "calling"; whatever the exact reason or combination of reasons, there flowered such an excellence of purposeful greed that in scarcely more than a century of independence, Americans had elevated their nation to primacy in economic power. The combination of the related spirits of workmanship and chicane provided the psychology of progress. Until the productive apparatus was built, the proximity of two such different qualities caused little notice. The spirit of chicane was no doubt of key importance in accumulating the original stock of capital. Once conditions of near maturity had been reached in the economy, however, the speculative fever (the common manifestation of the spirit of chicane) disclosed a malignant ability to paralyze production. The old kind of greed proved in panic after panic that it was no longer invariably constructive. Hence one might say that the old style of greed had simply outlived its usefulness and had to be repressed by a new (and as yet unperfected) type. By historic parallel, the greed of the Persian bazaar was superseded after many centuries by the greed of the Protestant Ethic (which will be explored in detail in Chapter 8). As Max Weber has suggested, with the Persian style of personal avarice, the Industrial Revolution would probably have been impossible. Instant greed, that is to say, made way for prudent greed. Prudent greed's successor has yet to reveal itself.

As for the land, it lay in unexampled richness for the people to plunder, and that is what they did with it. Its lumber and fur, its rich soil, its fuels and minerals, and its virtual emptiness all combined to provide an opulence that had never before been approached. The people used their natural riches to produce scores of millions of automobiles, and to throw an asphalt shroud over an area as big as New England. They built skyscrapers and bridges. They also made guns out of which to shoot a part of the Mesabi Range and Butte Lode at Château-Thierry and Belleau Wood, at Iwo Jima, at Cassino, and at Pusan. They converted their petroleum into miracle drugs, synthetic fibers, and versatile plastics, and they turned it into clouds of carbon monoxide. They turned their water on arid land and they turned their waterways to sewers. Their land they made into scientifically plowed fields and geometrically perfect suburban subdivisions, as well as graveyards for old cars.

The catalyst to all these reactions was the accumulation of the stock of capital that financed the expansive development of these higher forms of enterprise. Slave labor helped commercial agriculture get its stock of capital assembled. Farther north, virtually enslaved immigrant labor brought here under contract and put into squalid company-town shacks provided cheap and docile manpower for the lords of the railroads and factories, and helped them accumulate their capital.

The institutional engine that made possible these vast concentrations of power was the corporation. This one instrument has set the pattern of the culture more than any other except the Constitution. From the beginning of the corporation as a fictitious man, the real men learned to invent trusts and trade associations and tax laws marvelous for their asymmetry. They also learned somewhat late how to cultivate an air of benevolent concern for those who were injured in their drive to power.

· 5 ·

The peculiar characteristic of a corporation is that its owners are not required to meet all their obligations should they fail in business. That is to say, their liability is limited to their investment. Their other recources cannot be seized by creditors in satisfaction of their claims. Given that floor under possible losses, American enterprise became able to attract many investors of limited means with the promise of great rewards at limited risk. Begun as an essay in risk limitation, the corporation soon turned its attention to risk prevention, and more recently has begun to enjoy a status of virtual risklessness, given a certain size—say $160 million in annual revenue, for an approximation.

As for the men who direct and control such institutions, there seems to be a fairly clear evolutionary pattern that reflects the growing ability of business organizations to avoid risk. The early-model precorporate enterpriser was the merchant trader, who had to play for possible gains that resulted from conditions beyond his control. As Veblen phrased it, ". . . the work of the business man was rather to take advantage of the conjunctures offered by the course of the seasons and the fluctuations of demand and supply than to adapt the course of affairs to his own ends." [2]

With the growth of the corporation in the United States, and in the wake of liberalized chartering procedures for "associated wealth," the promise of vastly reduced risk created radically new conditions. No longer did a prayerful merchant-trader eye the horizon with his spyglass to see how his fortune would turn; he instead began to lay plans to capture an entire productive apparatus and thereby a hold on the market. He became less a supplicant to the trade winds and more a maker of his own trade winds. As the Hepburn Report in the New York Assembly of 1879 said of the new climate of enterprise: "The history of this corporation [Standard Oil] is a unique illustration of the possible outgrowth of the present system of railroad management in giving preferential rates, and also showing the colossal proportions to which monopoly can grow under the laws of this country. . . ." [3]

The more recent pattern of corporate enterprisers has been that of the archonic executive, a professional administrator, whose basic task is to keep the gate of an organization someone else built. With few exceptions—and those fairly well limited to military-goods production—the giant corporations that have come into existence in more recent years are not in any real sense procreative organisms. They are usually more the outward evidence of some subtle maneuver for tax preferment. The Land Camera and the International Business Machines interests do provide contrary examples within the fairly recent past, but such examples are not easy to find. With a few such exceptions, the rule seems to be that the archonic enterpriser is principally interested in precaution and accretion, not adventure. He keeps the pools of wealth undefiled and the ideological beacons lustrous. He mans battlements thrown up by his predecessors. He says the old words, but says them with better diction. In reality he runs a benign private government good to its constituents because it balances their loyalty with its ability to confer security.

The transition from what might be called the aristocratic-dynastic interests of feudal-style agriculture to the archonic-corporate interests of modern industry has not been complete so far as the old habits of mind are concerned. But so far as the effects on individualism are concerned, a banker fairly well summed it up in 1933. Russell Leffingwell of the Morgan bank told the Pecora Committee of the Congress, "The growth of corporate enterprise has been drying up individual independence and initiative. . . . We are becoming a nation of hired men, hired by great aggregates of capital." [4]

As is indicated above, the transition from aristocratic to archonic regimes is not complete. An illustration of the durability of one element of the vested interest is provided by the token of fealty past and present. The ancient vassal took this vow: "I become your man from this day forward of life and member, and of earthly honor, and to you shall be faithful and true. . . ." [5] The modern vassal for the most part need not render such ceremonial fealty. Archonic-corporate interests usually rest easy with tacit vows, no weaker for being unspoken. But there are exceptions. International Business Machines Corporation, for example, requires of its sales executives a rendering of the corporate anthem "Ever Onward," from time to time. The second chorus goes like this:

> EVER ONWARD—EVER ONWARD!
> We're bound for the top to never fall!
> Right here and now we thankfully
> Pledge sincerest loyalty
> To the corporation that's the best of all!
> Our leaders we revere, and while we're here
> Let's show the world just what we think of them!
> So let us sing, men! SING MEN!
> Once or twice then sing again
> For the EVER ONWARD IBM. [6]

THREE

America's Major Interests

⎣⌐⎦⌐⎣⌐⎣⌐⎣⌐⎣⌐⎦

Because it provides about a third of the national income in a year, manufacturing industry naturally occupies a position of predominance in this society. The leaders of the manufacturing interests consequently enjoy many of the marks of a ruling class.

A ruling class with staying power knows something about defending itself. One effective method of defense is to cause potential attackers to misdirect their fire. In this respect, the skills of the contemporary industrial leadership are highly developed and worthy of close scrutiny.

This defensive skill has many similarities to the art of the conjurer. The magician guides your eye to the empty hand by looking at the empty hand himself. He talks constantly about irrelevancies. He directs your attention to that corner of the stage in which nothing is happening. To compound his skill and your wonderment, he has confederates in the audience who really don't look like confederates at all. A ruling class, then, seems to enjoy maximum potential power in proportion as it can direct attention to irrelevant symbols.

To illustrate the function of such a symbol, consider the phrase "free enterprise," and the image that it summons: the eighteenth century entrepreneur. When archonic leaders talk of business affairs, they usually speak in terms that let your mind's eye conjure up a group of daring men congregating on some quay, waiting uneasily to see if their ships have survived a stormy crossing. They seem to tremble at the prospects of sudden ruin or enrichment—mostly ruin. They humbly petition for the goodwill of powerful and independent consumers. They jockey for some small advantage in a fierce competitive melee. In sum, the corporate archon directs attention not to himself so much as to his great-great-grandfather. That is only part of his act, however, and hardly the best part, at that.

Viewed as a whole, the act is a sustained illusion that combines many elements of the magician's art: levitation, appearance, disappearance, and transformation. For levitation, manufacturing raises its own interests to a symbolic apex of an entire society. For sudden appearance, it adduces its concern for public welfare and lets it be known that its own private goals are not at all in conflict with public welfare but are in essence the same thing. For disappearance, it denies that it exerts any special political or cultural influence or that its financial power is in any way remarkable. It is therefore seen as a somewhat feckless whipping boy, deserving of sympathetic consideration. For transformation, it converts its own hierarchic, highly concentrated corpus into a democratic, hotly competitive semblance. Monopoly thereby is seen as free, competitive enterprise.

To reiterate, manufacturing interests, like their predecessor ruling classes, know how to keep themselves secure. The grand strategy is for this one part of society to represent itself as symbolic of the whole.[1] Thereby, this small fragment is in a position "to be defended as though it were the state itself." That is why manufacturing industry in large measure, and lower forms of business enterprise in lesser degree, can claim identity with "The American Way of Life." Daily life, therefore, is one of ledger books, tax-loss carry-forwards, turret lathes, expense accounts, rediscounting, committee meetings, loss-leaders, quality control, subassemblies, and "sell-a-thons." Nonbusiness as well as business activities are therefore "American" to the extent that they support or supplement this symbolic package. Render tribute to a professor and you will say he has "a fine business sense," to a minister that he is a "good administrator," and to a professional athlete that he is a "money player." This symbolic fortress owes its stout walls to the general support these views command. There is a consensus that endows these values with the key honorific term, "sound and practical." Furthermore, this symbolic fortress makes any general criticism of business seem to be an attack on the United States of America, its Constitution, its traditions, and its ideals. It is for that reason that the leaders of the vested interests and their advocates can say without much contradiction that most general criticisms of business are in reality subtle attacks on the whole nation and are therefore subversive and probably are inspired by some foreign power.

· 1 ·

The firm equation of the United States of America and the manufacturing interests did not come about by pure legerdemain. There is good reason for this consensus, and that reason is the commitment to production that is typical of almost every element in this society:

On the importance of production there is no difference between Republicans and Democrats, right and left, white or colored, Catholic or Protestant. It is common ground for the general secretary of the Communist Party, the Chairman of Americans for Democratic Action, the President of the United States Chamber of Commerce, and the President of the National Association of Manufacturers.[2]

But one may wonder what lasting power such a preoccupation has if no steps are taken to increase the ability of the poor to consume. One may wonder what durability it can have when all forces combine to inspire greater incentive for investment capital so that production may increase; when one of every sixteen workers is out of work; when 15 percent of the population is on the edge of subsistence; when poverty is a daily fact of life for some thirty million Americans. He may muse over the relevance of such a preoccupation when about one-sixth of productive capacity lies unused year after year.

The vested interests will explain in a somewhat roundabout way that the big task facing the economy is to take better care of our dollars; if we do, all the people will inevitably prosper. That is the solution to the problem. Thus the conjurer's sleight-by-appearance has established that private goals and public goals are really the same thing.

More instructive, perhaps, is the technique of rapid transformation whereby it is seen that the big problem facing the nation is neither unemployment because of automation nor underconsumption because of unemployment but foreign competition (and therefore the integrity of the dollar). In this instance, a useful and attractive device in an unimportant corner of the stage is gold bullion. The performer may draw attention to it merely by gesturing absently. He need hardly embellish his patter. While motioning to it, the domestic problem of unemployment and widespread hard-core poverty is whisked out of sight and in its place is foreign competition.

An example of this particular kind of dexterity was provided in 1962 by the president of the United States Steel Corporation. The president did not rely merely on a straightforward sequence of sleights but on a combination of them.

The president said that manufacturing industry needed higher profits to protect the national gold supply and to compete successfully in international trade. "Our situation," he said, "is one where we have been 'costed out of the market,' if I may use such a term." (By "our situation," he meant the situation of American industry, presumably. There is no other ready interpretation to put on the words, although if challenged, the president might say that he was really talking about U.S. Steel alone. That possibility will be explored below.) The president did not mention automation. Unemployment, he suggested, arose from the inability of American industry to compete with foreign manufacturers. The whole problem came down to a "dwindling supply of investment capital." And investment capital was dwindling because corporate after-tax profits had been "squeezed down" in the 1950–1960 decade. He concluded his statement by noting, "If all our gains must be used to cover higher employment costs and higher government costs, then nothing is left to stimulate more investment or consumer demands through better profits and lower prices. Nothing is left to help us grow as a nation, to increase employment opportunities for our increasing population or to meet our international challenges."

Although explanations of sleight-of-hand techniques almost invariably are anticlimactic, the above does require some annotation. To take the major statements one by one:

"We have been 'costed out of the market' . . ." "We" presumably means United States industry. Although it may mean merely the steel industry, the context suggests the first interpretation. In any event, it is an argument disembodied from any factual base. The merchandise balance, as it is called, had been highly favorable to American industry in the years directly before the president's talk. The balance at the time he talked was also favorable. By general agreement, the balance-of-payments deficit in those years was the result of America's military expenditures and grants overseas and to massive movements of private American capital overseas, the short-term money that flits where the interest payments are highest. Far from being at a disadvantage, United States industry enjoyed a good competitive position. Even at that, there was an escape hatch built into the statement. If one were to have challenged it, the speaker would have had the option of saying that he was talking of the steel industry alone, in that particular context. If pressed still further, he would have had yet another out. He might ultimately have said that he was speaking solely for U.S. Steel, and specifically about the trend in tenpenny nails or some other arcane submarket. Thus symbolic manipulation can be a flexible exercise.

"Investment capital is 'dwindling' because corporate after-tax profits have been 'squeezed down' in the 1950–1960 decade." The talk here shifts into the higher legerdemain, tax accounting. Profits did indeed fall in the 1950–1960 decade, but not because of sinister outside forces. They fell because industry asked for a new tax law to encourage capital investment. Early in that decade,

1953, the Congress responded to industry's demands and a new tax law came into being. The result was that some of what used to be called "profit" began to be called "depreciation reserves," and became tax-free. The result was that "cash flow," the amount of retained earnings plus depreciation reserves available to American industry, climbed steeply during that same decade. The statement, then, that there isn't enough profit to attract or create enough investment capital is better seen as a skillful but essentially diversionary patter. There was indeed a profit squeeze in 1950–1960—a squeeze invited by industry and accepted as one inevitable effect of a new tax law written to encourage capital investment.

"*If all our gains* . . ." It is worth repeating here the entire peroration as an illustration of the conjurer's art of disappearance. The key qualifier "if," is what vanishes. Therefore what begins in a conditional vein ends up at the brink of certainty: "If all our gains must be used to cover higher employment costs and higher government costs, then nothing is left to stimulate more investment or consumer demand through better profits and lower prices. Nothing is left to help us grow as a nation, to increase employment opportunities for our increasing population or to meet our international challenges."

This statement has been examined here in such tedious detail not because it is exceptional in any way but because it is typical of the vested interests in action. No matter what public-relations ingenuity may have been at work, it is still a matter of meeting the needs of the symbolic apex. It is still a matter of assuring that The American Way of Life be preserved by means of support for one segment of the nation, if necessary, to the detriment of other segments.

As it later became clear, the comments of U.S. Steel Corporation's president were the first salvo in one of the most memorable skirmishes of the 1960's, the Steel Pricing Affair. In retrospect, it became clear that the speech examined above was directed in large measure at the Federal government, which had taken an active part in wage negotiations that were then going on. The government wanted steel management and labor to reach a non-inflationary settlement.

Such a settlement came in the spring of 1962, and a proud President Kennedy expressed his pleasure at the outcome. Directly thereafter, in clear violation of the tacit understanding among management, labor, and government, U.S. Steel announced that it had to raise prices of its products an average of $6 per ton to restore a more equitable cost-price relationship. The response of the Executive Branch of government was swift and unequivocal. In a celebrated contest of economic pressure, U.S. Steel and the other large companies that had followed suit in raising prices rescinded their raises. The victory seemed to go to government. Yet not five weeks later, Wall Street went into a state of deep shock, climaxed by Blue Monday, as it came to be called (May 28, 1962). Almost $21 billion in paper valuation disappeared in that one day alone. It took the better part of a year for the bulk of lost valuation to be restored to the stock-market lists.

Federal government in collision with a leader of manufacturing industry found growing hostility to government among businessmen and investors. The concerted anger of the latter demonstrated how contagious the views of archonic leadership can be. As the events leading up to Blue Monday demonstrated, the sounds of the vested interests do not suffer for want of amplification. Their views and aspirations, their alarms and judgments, their discoveries and enthusiasms move swiftly from their board rooms through the major media and into the lowest tributaries of the communications ganglia (as Chapters 9 and 10 will attempt to describe). In nearly unanimous deference, a national consensus listens to what the ruling class has had to say, and having heard it, understands more about the pressing needs of the times. In this instance, steel got its price increase a year later.

· 2 ·

It is fitting that a ruling class should be made up of the best people in a society. With some qualifications, in fact, "best" and "leader" mean very much the same thing. For that reason, it will be worthwhile to examine how the leaders of the vested interests as a ruling class came to be the way they are, and how the consensus in this nation regards those who lead.

The present-day archon has two historic predecessors, the entrepreneur of the eighteenth century and the Robber Baron of the nineteenth century. The early entrepreneur owed his success, according to the sound thought of his day, to certain personal qualities, most important of which were thrift, ambition, and hard work. He prospered because of these qualities, and it was thought a near certainty that given those talents, any man could succeed.

The business leaders of the era of the Robber Barons prospered because of personal qualities in part, but also because of the business climate of their day. They, then, had to share with the system of capitalism part of the glory of their ascent.

The present-day corporate leaders owe a great deal to the system, and do not hesitate to say so themselves. The modern leader is not notably associated with the early characteristic of thrift, although he still is linked with ambition and hard work in the public mind. He is seen as a man who is able to survive long years of slow upward progress in the corporate substructure and is consequently notable more, perhaps, for his ability to get along with his fellows than for any other trait.

It is a paradox of the contemporary consensus that the archons by common consent owe their preeminence to the system but that the poor and the unemployed owe their lowly position to some personal failing. Therefore, the rich of the eighteenth and nineteenth centuries were rich because of personal qualities predominantly. In more modern times, the rich have their wealth because of the free enterprise system. The poor, on the other hand, are and always have been poor basically because of ineptness, not because of any system.

The question of personal qualities associated with wealth and poverty is of interest because the principle of the deserving rich bears directly on it. It is a matter of common observation that solvency confers an aura of excellence on a person and that many people of uncertain pecuniary power will go to great lengths to convey an impression of substantial solvency. Such activities are not only for window dressing but also for the purpose of attracting good wishes. The very idea of goodness, in fact, is closely associated with wealth (and to a lesser degree with income).*

The best people in the sense that they are most productive of good and most worthy of emulation tend to be closely associated in some way with manufacturing or finance, either as owners of stocks or as controllers of managerial power. The good people are those who most nearly succeed in emulating the standards of consumption and thought set forth by the best. The bad, on the other hand, are those who cannot or do not accept the norms of their superiors.

These bad people, in fact, confirm their badness in many ways. They smell, for one thing. For others, their crime rate is high, they tend to be depraved, they tend to idleness, and they become drains on the public treasury. Only in so far as the poor work hard and without complaint are they known as worthy poor. The suspicion will not down, in any event, that they really prefer to while away their time in immoral pursuits.

Therefore, in the parlance of secular piety, pecuniary power and moral goodness are near synonyms. And hence the ruling class can at one time speak for the preservation or enhancement of its own position and rest assured that it thereby throws a new buttress on the walls of public goodness. It is in this light that "Make America safer for investment capital" appears as a philanthropic sentiment. In reality, it is a sort of creeping sanctimony.

· 3 ·

The geography of America's vested interests deserves attention both for what it may suggest about the channels of economic

---

* The holiness ascribed to money at rest is greater than that ascribed to money in motion for reasons difficult to assign. Whatever they may be, great *wealth* bespeaks "background," while great *income* may indicate nothing more than cleverness, or maybe luck.

power in this country and for what it may reveal about the centers of that power.

Since 1929 manufacturing industry has been producing about a third of national income a year. If contribution to national income is a reliable index of relative power (and it should be), manufacturing industry—including mining—occupies an unchallenged first position, followed by these other interests: commerce (accounting for about 27 percent of national income); finance (10 percent); construction (5 percent); agriculture (5 percent); and transportation (4.5 percent), according to Commerce Department figures.

The manufacturing interests are dominated, in turn, by the 500 largest corporations. As it has become commonplace to observe, these 500 account for more than half of sales revenue. They hold almost 70 percent of all manufacturing assets and they produce more than 75 percent of all manufacturing net profits. In their turn, these 500 are in some measure dominated by the three-dozen corporations whose annual sales total $1 billion each or more. It is from such industrial giants as General Motors, Standard Oil, General Electric, U.S. Steel, du Pont, Union Carbide, and IBM that the natural spokesmen for American industry rise. The words spoken by one of these leaders carry weight not so much because of the man himself but because of the financial power that he represents. Not only is such power immense; it is also broadly based. It is a typical mark of these enormous corporations that they are diverse in their activities. Thus General Motors makes not only automobiles, trucks, locomotives, and heavy machinery for its own plants, but is involved in consumer finance, textiles, rubber, and defense contracting. Its competitor, Ford, branches out in similar fashion, even to the extent of making about half of its own steel in its own mills.

The decision-making power of these massive interests and their smaller competitors and satellites is concentrated geographically to a large degree. The leaders favor the large cities almost in direct proportion to the population of those cities. A geographic listing of the 3,000 largest corporations shows New York—as would be expected—with by far the most listings, followed by Chicago and Los Angeles. The others, in rough order of eminence, are Detroit, Philadelphia, Pittsburgh, Cleveland, St. Louis, Boston, and San Francisco.

As for the relative influence of various industries, it is worthwhile to note that some industries, particularly petroleum and steel, require great amounts of capital investment per worker, while others, notably textiles and leather products, do not. Therefore, the number of companies competing in a given field depends in large measure on the ease with which a corporation can enter that field. American manufacturing industry tends to be dominated by those single industries like petroleum, automobiles, and primary metals that represent extraordinary aggregates of capital under the control of a relatively small group of corporations. The billion-dollar group includes ten oil companies; four automotive, four metal, and four aircraft-missile companies; two chemical and two rubber companies; and a miscellany of mercantile, package-goods, processed foods, and tobacco companies.

Given this concentration of financial power within industry, and the peculiar authority of the billion-dollar corporations as natural spokesmen for American industry, it should not come as a surprise that the leader of the giant corporation is an investment taste-maker. If he proclaims that his company plans a large investment in new plants and equipment, the mere announcement is sometimes enough to cause all of manufacturing industry to follow suit. In 1954, when there was hesitation among industrial leaders as to whether or not to invest, the chairman of General Motors announced his corporation's intention to invest more than $1 billion in new equipment in the coming year. As it happened, that decision coincided with consumer decisions to buy new cars in unprecedented qualities. It may have inspired consumer confidence, for that matter, and thereby hardened the resolve of buyers while reviving the hopes of investors. The year 1955, at any rate, was a boom year, and a national magazine bestowed its man-of-the-year citation on the General Motors chairman for inspiring the spirited round of production and consumption.

When two or more great corporate leaders concur in their public announcements in a year, a pattern of investment psychology may soon make itself felt. Not since 1955, however, have corporate optimism and consumer optimism come together in the mixture that assures an uninhibited boom. The subject is mentioned here in passing and will be pursued below after a brief examination of the dynamic climate in which such corporate-investor psychology operates and which it in large measure helps to create.

· 4 ·

The 1960 decade that promised to begin with great *élan* did not perform as expected. Some said an untimely relapse into pessimism was at fault; others, that a sustained "rolling readjustment" was under way. Still others saw the trouble in the shackles that government locked on the limbs of businessmen.

The 1960's saw the beginning of a new economic climate in the United States, whatever the precise cause may have been. For the first time in the country's history, there was a long-range promise of an excess of private-sector capital *and* an excess of private-sector labor. Never before had there been such a clear surplus of both factors of production in times of normality.

The slow encroachments of self-operated and self-controlled machines were visible enough, but new events had to be described as best a defective and obsolescent vocabulary could describe them, which wasn't very well. New realities had to fit into pigeonholes long since built. If the new realities really didn't belong where they were filed, no one seemed to mind. There was no crisis. That was clear enough. And if there wasn't one, no perversity could invent what practiced eyes failed to see. There was no crisis and there would not be one, for American institutions had proved themselves flexible enough to accommodate almost any change in the past. (Yet these remarkable changes afoot seemed certain to test and strain—if they would not destroy—the established patterns of thought.)

For one thing, the industrial hourly worker was simply a vanishing American. He grew less and less able to compete with labor-saving machinery. If he were a coal miner, he could see for himself what continuous strip-mining devices could do. If an auto worker, he could watch automatically cast and machined engine blocks come down a conveyor by the hundreds of dozens. If he were a petroleum worker, he could see huge refineries run by computers better than men could run them. And even if he were a textile worker, he could watch a weaving shed where a half-dozen battery hands oversaw seven hundred looms, and he could figure out for himself how the trend was going. He could sense what was happening and so could his unions.

His unions were feeling the pressures of declining membership; they were feeling the new rigidity of management when the two sat down to bargain. They were feeling the slow effects of lost vitality and lost public sympathy, as well. These union bulwarks of the more privileged American workingmen were slowly losing their power as machines simply made obsolete the productive contributions of semiskilled workers. For the workers without union representation, the future looked even less bright.

As for the corporations, they were outfitting themselves with wholly new central nervous systems so sensitive in perception and so deftly quick in operation that the accounts-receivable clerk could suspect that the day she left to get married would be the last day any person held her job. A spindle of magnetic tape would take her place. She wasn't alone. Some managers accustomed to the comfort of relatively easy tasks performed in a virtual vacuum of accountability would find themselves at a forked road. The brightest would move up into more responsible positions. Others might sink into semitechnical oblivion where they would take their orders from electronic masters. Above—far above—the top executives were growing in power, as many of the deterrents to their authority began to recede. An increasingly attenuated unionism and a satisfied middle-class constituency began to make ready the way for a measure of autonomy for the topmost executives undreamed of a few years before. Next in importance to this archon rose the scientist-executives. Given enough money, any productive miracle seemed easy under their guidance.

Meanwhile, in the Bureau of Labor Statistics, the figures were showing a greater residue of unemployment after each postwar recession, despite "full recovery." This residue rose from 3 percent in the early 1950's to nearer 6 percent ten years later. No longer did the White House say that 3 percent would be the target, irreducible minimum of unemployment; 4 percent was to be the figure, or perhaps 5 percent. But even at that, some of the more vocal partisans of the manufacturing interests were saying that unemployment wasn't that much of a problem. If the United States counted its unemployed the way Great Britain or Sweden counted *theirs*, the problem would assume its proper perspective. (This point will be examined in some detail in Chapter 7.)

Manufacturing industry maintained that greater growth would come about by increasing capital investment, which could in turn come about if government provided more incentive. A vice-president of the Ford interests spoke the mind of industry when he said that it was a dangerous thing to blame unemployment on automation. He said that automation in fact was increasing employment, and the more automation, the more jobs:

If the solutions to our nation's unemployment problems are adopted and pursued on the false premise that unemployment is inherent in automation, then we may very easily kill the goose that lays the golden eggs of industrial growth and development.

The vice-president added that the nation had too much unemployment because there had been too little automation, not enough technological progress, and insufficient business investment. It wasn't a completely one-sided argument, however. He did add: "I think that we have probably done too little in many ways to help those individuals and groups who have lagged behind the industrial and educational progress of the nation as a whole. . . . But to say all this is a far cry from saying, as some are, that automation is making a whole large segment of our popula-

tion redundant." The solution to all the problems, he said, would
be to stimulate economic growth by union forbearance on wage
increases, by government policies more understanding to business, and by "a tax program to encourage savings and investment. . . ."

· 5 ·

"The American economy," the *Economist* of London observed
at about the same time, "no longer offers a job to any willing pair
of hands, as was its tradition, or even to hands that have not quite
got the right sort of skill."

The nation faced the prospect of seeing 26 million new workers
enter the labor force in the 1960's, of whom about a third would
never finish high school and would therefore be virtually unem-
ployable.

There were plans afoot for massive retraining programs and
for extended vocational schooling, both of which pointed to aid
for that sector of the economy that needed scant aid, production.
No plan of substantial dimension seemed to address itself directly
to the problem of promoting the other, forgotten, sector: consumption. There seemed to be real difficulty in mustering even a
modest minority opinion to subscribe to an axiom laid down by
Adam Smith. Smith's central indictment of mercantilism (an indictment that applies with equal force to corporate capitalism)
was just that—that no one looks out for the consumer:

> Consumption is the sole end and purpose of all production, and the
> interest of the producers ought to be attended to, only so far as it may
> be necessary for promoting that of the consumer. . . . But in the
> mercantile system the interest of the consumer is almost constantly
> sacrificed to that of the producer; and it seems to consider production,
> and not consumption, as the ultimate end and object of all industry and
> commerce.

Quite aside from the well known effects of unemployment and
subsistence consumption on the dignity of the poor and on their
ability to play a full role as citizens, there was the less well under-

stood problem of economic psychology. This problem bore directly on the basic optimism that has always been a distinguishing quality of the American nation. This optimism, this belief in progress and an improving standard of living, underlies much of the willingness of consumers to buy automobiles and other durable goods on the installment plan. Behind their purchase decision is an unspoken but real feeling that things are going to improve for them financially and therefore that they may have confidence in the future and in their ability to pay off their debts.

Surveys conducted by the University of Michigan Survey Research Center have demonstrated the force of this optimism on the economy. Although consumer attitudes are not nearly so changeable as investor attitudes, the slight ups and downs in optimism and buying plans can cause investors to hesitate, with unpleasant results. As Professor George Katona has written:

> . . . prosperity requires self-reinforcing optimistic attitudes based on sound reasons. The economy must derive dynamic forces from a widespread and strong conviction that more and more is obtainable.[3]

The question then arises, How durable can such a cheery outlook be if more and more workers are out of work, are putting in only part-time, or are working at tasks paying less than they need to live? One may wonder how impregnable and how resilient optimism is when faced with persistent adverse evidence. There are no precise answers to such vexing questions; not yet, anyway. Events nevertheless have a way of upsetting the most durable and solidly based habits of mind, and as the 1960's progressed, the historic optimism of the American found less reinforcement from events year by year.

The manufacturing interests, meanwhile, moved gracefully and spoke pleasantly onstage. Flashes of lycopodium powder, sparkling bullion, and audience confederates combined to keep fresh the skills of the conjurers, and to make the real problems seem to disappear.

FOUR

How the Interests Work

⎍⎍⎍⎍⎍⎍

A vested interest, like a swain in springtime, has well defined objectives. It knows what rights it would like to enjoy and what responsibilities it would like to evade. When the public heeds the blandishments of the interests, it does so at risks as great as those the trusting maid assumes when she takes the young man's word that nothing is going to happen.

The seduction of the public by the vested interests is carried out not so much on the promise of marriage in the future as on the assurance that common-law marriage is already in effect (the goals of industry and of the nation are one and the same).

· 1 ·

A full catalog of economic seducers and their professional methods would make a repetitive treatise. More useful would be a profile of a limited number of interest groups. Therefore a look at two interests that respectively represent the yokel and the city-slicker schools of lawful ravishment ought to suffice. For the first, the textile industry will give good service; for the latter, the petroleum industry.

Each deserves a brief general description to begin with. The textile industry fairly represents the hayseed seducer because its methods and its milieu are relatively primitive. Its mental processes are straightforward: unweighted by subtlety, unconcerned with nicety. It is furthermore an older lothario that sometimes— in spite of the new mores—betrays a crotchety bent. The petroleum industry, on the other hand, is suave and well kept. It speaks charmingly and deferentially to its quarry. It is extremely well connected with any number of important people in any number of capitals in every nation in the free world. Its method and its milieu, in short, are sophisticated, modern, international. Its mentality, consequently, is a marvel of nuance and flection. Although its forebears were confirmed ravishers, it is far too assured of success ever to resort to force. Immense and liquid assets make seduction less a test of skill than a perfunctory calisthenic.

· 2 ·

The textile industry was the first large-scale manufacturing interest in the United States. From its inception it has had a tradition of individualism and relatively low concentration of productive power. Even as recently as 1957 the 50 largest companies accounted for somewhat less than 50 percent of sales and owned less than 10 percent of the mills in operation.

It is a debatable question as to how much lasting influence a single man can have on an industry. Some would argue that accidents of personality can hardly have a durable effect. Others, with as persuasive argument, see institutional forms and collective attitudes following the early channels that caprice or circumstances laid out. If the latter interpretation has any validity, the "father of American manufactures," Samuel Slater, would provide a fit subject for study. In Slater's accomplishments there is much to foreshadow later developments in manufacturing industry in general; more directly, there is some precedent for the condition of the contemporary textile industry.

Slater's talent, as his biographer has pointed out, was mechanical skill combined with marked gifts for organization, promotion, and financial administration. Slater's great mechanical feat was to emigrate from England with his head full of plans for the Arkwright carding machine and spinning frame. The year after he arrived in America he had set up and was in charge of the first practical American cotton mill. It began operation in Pawtucket, Rhode Island, on December 20, 1790. The workers were seven in number, two girls and five boys. None was older than twelve or younger than seven. Slater himself proved a kindly manager, given loyalty and diligence in his work force. He may occasionally have had to use his cane on an errant mill hand, but, as his biographer notes, "this with no hard feelings from the parents, for Samuel Slater was fair in his discipline." [1]

Slater had marked solicitude for the welfare of those who were dutiful and helpful in his cotton-manufacturing ventures. He had, in fact, well formed views on the proper function of charity and on the employer's responsibilities to his workers. As the *Providence Journal* noted in his obituary in 1835, Slater made no "pretension to high-wrought philanthropy":

"Direct charity," he has been heard to say, "places its recipient under a sense of obligation which trenches upon that independent spirit which all should maintain. It breaks the pride, and he soon learns to beg and eat the bread of idleness without a blush. But employ and pay him, and he receives and enjoys, with honest pride, that which he knows he has earned, and could have received for the same amount of labour from any other employer." [2]

Therefore in that day as in this it was fairly well established that the indirect charity of employing a worker helped sustain independence of mind and action. Such independence occasioned another important step in Slater's lifework, the founding of what was perhaps the first Sunday school in the nation.

On their first day off, which was Sunday, a group of Slater's boy employees were plotting a raid on a neighboring apple orchard when Slater overheard their discussion and suggested that they come to his house instead. He would supply all the apples they wanted and they would learn something worthwhile while they were at it. The boys seized on his suggestion, and the Slater Sunday School directly became a fixture of Pawtucket mill life. Slater was able to ignore complaints by the gentry that he thereby dishonored the Lord's Day. Slater himself did most of the teaching, using five Webster spellers and three Testaments as texts. As the years went on, the school became somewhat more secular.

Thus the career of the first great manufacturer in the United States presaged much of manufacturing growth, behavior, and belief in succeeding years. No inventor himself, Slater was instead a gifted imitator and an inspired mechanic. His organizational and promotional skills helped him erect an industrial empire vast for its day. It spread from Rhode Island into Connecticut, Massachusetts, and New Hampshire. In spite of their size, the Slater interests were still dependent on a loyal work force. Occasionally, with apparent regret, the master had to punish those whose work or attitude proved defective. But he was like a father to those who were faithful, and he let his philanthropy show by fulfilling an employer's obligations, not in ostentatious distribution of his wealth. In fact, useful charity, in his view, consisted largely in promoting that spirit of self-reliance that accompanies the diligent discharge of such duties as spindle doffing or loom tending.

· 3 ·

From the beginning, the textile interests depended on child labor as an important part of their work force. By the late 1800's, however, that condition had largely disappeared in New England, where the new industry had centered. With gathering speed after 1870, the cotton mills began to move south. What made Southern textile manufacturing more profitable than New England production was proximity of raw materials in part and child labor in part. Some argue that the latter advantage was the decisive one.

Professor C. Vann Woodward has pointed out that in the 1890's, women along with children between ten and fifteen years of age made up 65 percent of the work force in the four leading textile states of the South. As he has suggested, the "New South" program of industrialization was in some measure a program to get children out of the fields and into the mills.

In 1911 the Tulsa *Daily World* reported that "just a few years ago there were 87,500 children under 10 years of age . . . in the cotton mills of Georgia," and they worked a sixty-hour week. "Slaving their baby lives away," was the *Daily World*'s description of their labors. The paper added that the going wage was between a cent and a cent-and-a-half an hour—or 60 to 90 cents a week.

In the New South, the millowners enjoyed many of the conditions that used to typify a feudal society: a tradition-minded, pious, and docile work force without much education and without the excessive zeal for progress that marked the Puritan strains of New England. Given a climate congenial to a strict hierarchic society, the textile industry wasted little time in creating and enforcing feudal methods of control. As will be shown shortly, these methods are still very much in use in the 1960's.

These hierarchic attitudes hardened as the fresh winds of the Progressive Era began to blow. By the 1910's, the National Child Labor Committee began in earnest to campaign for a restriction on child labor. The committee's wrath and the public support behind it swung onto the textile interests.

The response of the industry to this threat provides an excellent case history of the way a vested interest attends to its own welfare. The first necessity in such circumstances is to adopt a stance of moral superiority. Thus, the chief apologist for the textile interests, a North Carolina trade-journal owner named David Clark, could write: "We do not claim that mill conditions are ideal and we do not expect that perfect conditions will ever be reached before the end of time.

"We do believe that there is less discontent and less real suffering among the cotton mill operatives of the South than among the employees of any other industry.

"The mill owners and managers almost without exception take a great interest in the welfare of their operatives and many mills are spending large sums on welfare work." [3]

As the child-labor campaign grew in intensity, the American Cotton Manufacturers' Association passed a strong resolution in opposition to Federal interference in private affairs. But, in Clark's words, "I had seen enough of those behind the measure to realize that there must be organized opposition." Thus came into being the executive committee of the Southern Cotton Manufacturers' Association, whose crusade and reason for being was to fight enactment of any child-labor legislation; to challenge the constitutionality of any law passed; and to defeat any attempt to pass a child-labor amendment to the Constitution.

The Progressives were moving strongly in 1916, and the Keating-Owen Child Labor bill got through its Judiciary Committee hearing. As Clark wrote, "We put on a number of witnesses, including prominent doctors, but very little attention was paid to their testimony and within a month the House passed the bill by a vote of 337 to 46."

Then the fight swung to the Senate, but again the textile interests were bested. As Clark wrote, the advocates of the bill "induced Woodrow Wilson to go to the capital [Capitol] and demand, of the Senators, that it be passed, and in August I sat alone in the Senate gallery while a thunderstorm raged without and heard the bill pass 52 to 12."

The manufacturers did not rest there. They directly began work to overturn the law. Clark, in behalf of the textile interests, retained a skillful panel of attorneys and set out to test the law in the courts.

"I asked the attorneys to decide the kind of test case that would be most effective and with that information spent weeks in search of the exact type of case. . . .

"Roland Dagenhart, who was working at Fidelity Mills in Charlotte, had two sons, one 13 and the other 15, and was very much opposed to the 13-year-old boy having to leave the mill and the 15-year-old boy being limited to eight hours.

"My attorneys prepared an application for an injunction to prevent the Government from interfering with the Dagenhart boys, and Dagenhart gladly signed same."

Shortly thereafter, a Federal District Court issued an injunction and declared the Keating-Owen Law unconstitutional. As the case moved up to the Supreme Court, the textile interests began a public-relations program in earnest: "Realizing that a great deal of criticism of the cotton manufacturing industry of the South was due to lack of information, we conceived the idea of publishing a 'Health and Happiness Number,'" Clark wrote. The magazine issue was "filled with photographs of our mills and their welfare work and it was sent to members of Congress. . . . it attracted much favorable comment."

The case finally was at the point of decision. The industry had hoped for a 5–4 decision favorable to its stand, and that was just the vote. The majority stood with the textile interests. As Justice Day concluded for the majority, in *Hammer* v. *Dagenhart*, as the case was known, ". . . if Congress can thus regulate matters intrusted to local authority by prohibition of the movement of commodities in interstate commerce, all freedom of commerce will be at an end, and the power of the states over local matters may be eliminated, and thus our system of government be practically destroyed." It was, as one observer noted, the technique of *argumentum ad horrendum*. And thus, in 1918, the first child-labor legislation was struck down and the children were again free to work sixty-hour weeks.

Congress came back directly with a second bill, and Clark with another stratagem. "We had an amendment drawn placing the enforcement of the new law under a special bureau in the Treasury Department.

"We managed to get this adopted and Miss Grace Abbott and her Children's Bureau cohorts were not able to get their claws on any of the funds appropriated for the enforcement of the law.

"I got about as much pleasure from leaving Miss Abbott and her parasites out in the cold as they did from the passage of the law, and I was confident that the law would be declared unconstitutional." Clark's confidence was well founded. The second law was struck down by an 8–1 vote.

Advocates of child-labor legislation came back once again, this time with a plan for a constitutional amendment. By June, 1924, Congress passed the proposed amendment and sent it on to the states for ratification. Eight years had passed in fruitless attempts to halt child-labor abuses. The 1920's dragged on, and by the end of the decade only five states had ratified the proposed amendment and over three-fourths had rejected it. The textile interests had won, despite the massed force of public opinion expressed by Justice Holmes in the first Child Labor case: "[I]f there is any matter upon which civilized countries have agreed . . . it is the evil of premature and excessive child labor."

As Clark summed up his efforts in behalf of the textile industry, "I played a part in breaking the back of a great effort to centralize power in Washington and to eventually destroy our system of Government."

And thus, with uncommon clarity, a vested interest put its case: to legislate against child labor was in fact merely a convenient method of accomplishing the darker goal—the destruction of "our system of Government."

It was not until 1938 that child-labor legislation finally came into being with the passage of the Fair Labor Standards Act, which was subsequently upheld by the Supreme Court. By then, of course, the great preoccupation of the textile interests had swung to the problem of rebuffing unionism's planned advance on the textile industry. But before detailing that story—as a case history of a contemporary vested interest in action—a further word on the feudal nature of the textile interests is in order here.

A document of strange poignancy was the Mamie Burns Testament, the personal credo of a young woman mill hand. It was more or less of an extended oath of fealty and chastity by a wage serf to her lords. As a comparative document to a 1961 statement of lordly beneficence, it helps illuminate the curious but real bond between docile workers and responsible employers in the cotton-manufacturing industry.

Mamie Burns's comments were delivered in front of her employers at the Southern Textile Association meeting in 1911, but were cast as if they were addressed to her co-workers. Thus they served the purpose of showing what a good employee thinks. Her comments further suggested a massive problem of unseemly female behavior in the mills. After explaining that she began as a wage earner at age twelve, Miss Burns said that nothing was more of an ornament to the industry than a pure mill hand. "The reason so many women are failures, is because they shrink from, and are ashamed of, their employment. Nothing is more disgusting than to see a woman evade truth concerning her circumstances in life. . . . I have sincere pity and compassion for the girl who will wilt and droop in the face of honest toil.

"Because your lot is cast as a mill girl, do not shrink from your labors, or hesitate to openly, truthfully proclaim your honest station in life. Rather blush for duties left undone and strive with a determination of stability to rise above all that does not measure up to your standard of idealism. And as you rise above detrimental impediments, by self-improvement, put forth every effort with womanly purity and perseverance to improve, and bring out all the higher latent traits of character of those with whom you daily labor."

The peroration went like this: ". . . try to grasp the fact that you are part and parcel of this, the South's greatest industry, and upon you rests the responsibility to help it grow and expand into broader fields, and upon a higher plane. Measure yourself, your life, your work, and set your standards, remembering you cannot place your ideals beyond attainment if you embody them in purity, courage, and reliance in the right."

It was no doubt a similar phenomenon that occasioned the observation that the Bible is a great enough and big enough book to meet everyone's needs. Employers may live by the Old Testament, employees by the New.

· 4 ·

It was a kindlier world for working people in 1961 than it had been in 1911, but feudalism still held its attractions for employers and employees alike. The Comer interests (Avondale and Cowikee Mills) were substantial employers in Alabama. Over six thousand people worked for them, and more than $50 million in revenues came into company coffers in a year. The chairman of the company occupied a place similar to that of benign royalty in that he contrived to share his daily life, his tours and cruises, and his thoughts with his employees by means of weekly letters that appeared in the company newspaper. The chairman's words suggested not only *noblesse oblige* but a democratic disposition as well. It must have been flattering for a slasher-hand to read that the chairman and his wife "are back in Bonita Springs and we did quite a little traveling since we left. I . . . went over to Boston for the American Mutual Insurance Company Directors Meeting. . . . I wanted to go visit Mr. J. A. Erickson, President of the Boston Federal Reserve Bank, but I was just too late. . . . We did, however, have the pleasure of visiting our friends at the Shawmut Bank. . . ."

Thereafter came a discursive description of a visit to the Carter Underwear Company's president, a call on a relative (oldest son: dean of admissions, Harvard College; daughter: on tour of Iran; second son: Unitarian minister in Denver), another Federal Reserve Bank (this one in Atlanta), and a cruise of the Florida waters in the chairman's one-hundred-foot yacht, *Gomol*. Management men from various mills made the cruise with the chairman, and the company newspaper editor was on hand to take pictures, thus rendering the trip a type of symbolic cooperative consumption of the chairman's yacht by all the employees. Not only were management travelers featured in large pictures, but a full description of two explorer scouts from Sylacauga, who were invited along by the chairman, was included. Also, pictures and descriptions of the yacht skipper, first mate, cook, and the chauffeur, who kept up with the yacht and met it at each port of call, filled page after page of the company house organ.

In an age in which impersonality was too much a rule, personal, open sharing of an interesting life no doubt struck a responsive chord in the Comer interests' work force.

· 5 ·

Thus far, little of the irascible side of the bucolic ravisher has shown, except for the brief flashes of anger in the child-labor battles. The anti-union campaign of 1946–1961, and its historic precedents in the 1920's, demonstrate in fuller dimension something of this less benign side of the textile interests. Espionage, racial incitement, financial intimidation, firings, denials of free speech and freedom of assembly, and mill closings have been recurring themes in the textile industry's successful campaign to frustrate unionization.

The 1929 strike at the Marion Manufacturing Company in Marion, North Carolina, was a particularly bitter affair. The workers were averaging $11 a week for a seventy-hour workweek. Some of the women employees were making less than half that much. A strike began in July, after the mill president had refused the workers' demand to lower the working shift to ten hours. In September the union seemed to have gained a concession, owing to the intervention of the state governor as mediator. The workers won a fifty-five-hour week, at corresponding reduction in pay, while the owner won the right to fire fourteen of the strike leaders. The owner fired 102 union members, instead. The workers went back on strike—despite the presence of armed deputies within the mill. In an ensuing skirmish, six strikers were shot dead, all in the back.

The millowner took the news equably. As the Asheville *Citizen* quoted him:

I understand sixty or seventy-five shots were fired in Wednesday's fight. If this is true, there are thirty or thirty-five of the bullets accounted for. I think the officers are damned good marksmen. . . . I read that the death of each soldier in the World War consumed more than five tons of lead. Here we have less than five pounds and these casualties. A good average, I call it.[4]

The ferocity of feeling suggested by those observations had not entirely disappeared from the textile industry in succeeding years. Although no longer expressed with such vigor, the anti-union views of the industry leaders continued to be effective: somewhat less than a third of the industry was unionized by 1960, according to the Textile Workers Union.

Of particular use to the industry in the postwar years was the enactment of the Taft-Hartley Law, especially those sections dealing with third-party interference. By lifting the limitations on such third-party activity, the Congress gave the partisans of the employers' point of view new scope for aid to millowners. These partisans performed a peculiar function that had no exact parallel elsewhere in the United States. Near parallels had existed in such places as Butte, Montana, which was run as a branch office of the Anaconda Copper interests for many years. Mount Pleasant, Michigan; Corning, New York; and Harlan, Kentucky, had provided other instances; but in all cases by the advent of the postwar period the employers' potential powers no longer were used to the fullest. In more typically agrarian settings, however, things were different. Porterdale, Georgia, is an example.

The Bibb Manufacturing interests controlled Porterdale closely and used their powers without hindrance in 1946 when an attempt was made there to unionize the mills. The National Labor Relations Board described the feudatory status of Porterdale in 1949 (82 NLRB 338). The Board said:

. . . All of its property, excepting a railroad right-of-way and churches, which the respondent [the company] donated to the various religious congregations, is owned by the respondent. All of Porterdale's utilities and public services, excepting police protection and education, are controlled directly by the respondent. In this setting, the relationship between the respondent and the police department, as set forth below, establishes a significant pattern of conduct.

Town officials were in effect company employees. The mayor was "house agent" of the company and was in charge of the police. The town recorder was the company paymaster and treasurer. The town attorneys were company attorneys.

Given such an interlocking arrangement, it surprised no one when the campaign to organize the Bibb workers for collective bargaining failed. Police kept union organizers under twenty-four-hour surveillance, with particular attention to the home of employee Walter Reynolds, which the organizers used as their headquarters. As the NLRB examiner wrote:

By this 24-hour watch over Reynolds' home the police were able to know when the organizers were in town and to follow or trail them throughout the town while they were calling upon employees of the respondent [the company]. As soon as the organizers left the house on foot or by vehicle, the police followed by police car. If two organizers started out together and then went separate ways, there would be a policeman following each of them. Everywhere the organizers went, the police were sure to follow. For at least the above period of time [July 10, 1946, to August 10, 1946], there was a policeman within 60 to 75 feet of any organizer who was in Porterdale.

Such painstaking police work made the employees uneasy about talking to union organizers, and it contributed materially to the collapse of the union campaign.

In 1954, in Elkin, North Carolina, the Textile Workers Union began organizing at the Chatham Manufacturing Company's blanket mill. The union discovered it could find no place in town to hold a meeting. The YMCA was closed to it. The union then tried to rent a vacant school building for its meeting. A school official explained why it would not be possible: "Chatham contributes a sum of money each year to our school lunch program. Knowing how Chatham feels about the matter, I personally can't make a decision that might take away the children's lunch and milk program." [5]

Later a school in an adjoining county was made available for the meeting, but on the night before the meeting the principal told the union that he was withdrawing permission. Therefore about three hundred workers had to meet in the open in a wooded grove fifteen miles out in the country. As workers drove up to the meeting they were stopped by police who examined every driver's license. It was a "road check," the police explained.

Occasionally, union workers met with open violence, as was the case when an organizer returned to his hometown of Alexander City, Alabama, and began to collect signatures from workers. He was under constant surveillance for some months. The police chief summoned the organizer to city hall to tell him that if he didn't leave town he would no doubt be "mobbed." The police chief added that he could get the organizer drafted, if the other warnings did not impress him. The chief did not have to point out the power of the employer whose interests he represented. The Russell Manufacturing Company ran three cotton mills and also owned the principal bank, a woodworking plant, a gristmill, a creamery, the hotel, and the town water supply. The organizer finally paid for his continued defiance. He was severely beaten up by two employees of the cotton mills in sight of a police officer, who told twenty shopkeepers witnessing the affray that he would "make cash bond for anyone who beat up a union organizer." [6]

If violence does not dissuade the union, appeals to the prejudices of the workers sometimes will make the union campaigns impossible. The key element in such appeals by the textile interests is that the union organizers are "outsiders," and that they represent radicalism and racial "mongrelization," if not Satan himself. One company newspaper, under the headline "Labor's Worst Enemies," said:

> The worst enemies that labor have [sic] today are the professional radical agitators who are preaching class-hatred, strife and discord, and creating malice and suspicion between the worker and his employer.
> We are told that Satan often appears as an angel of light. Likewise, the red, radical agitators come under the guise of being the friends of the workers and the common people. . . .

A pamphlet issued by another company showed a Negro union leader's picture. Next to the picture were the words: "Do you want the C.I.O. after seeing this? Do you know the 'Distinguished Gentleman' shown above? . . . C.I.O. Believes in This. . . . Do YOU?" Another broadside showed a white woman at dinner with a Negro. The headline read: "Don't let this happen to you or your family! . . . Defeat the C.I.O. . . ." Another publication suggested that CIO officials were mere "carpet baggers." It added a listing of the birthplaces of labor leaders, thus documenting its charge that they were "foreign-born propagandists."

These tactics were most typical of the smaller companies, at least by common repute. Large, national corporations did not participate in such blatant appeals to prejudice. Or did they? Consider the case of Burlington Industries, the largest single textile company in the United States, with more than 50,000 employees in over 100 plants and gross revenues in excess of $1 billion a year. As recently as 1955, the Textile Workers Union campaign to unionize the still-unorganized southern plants of the company resulted in a countercampaign of considerable virulence. At the company's Steele Mill in Cordova, North Carolina, a reprint from the *American Nationalist* was distributed to workers. It showed Walter Reuther handing a $75,000 check to NAACP President Arthur Spingarn, "the Jew who has headed that trouble-making organization since 1939." It exhorted "white Americans to take action if this Jew-inspired program for compulsory mongrelization is to be defeated." A cartoon distributed at the company's Hunt and Altavista, Virginia, mills showed a carpetbagger saying, "The NAACP sent me down here to desegregate you trashy bastards."

As the TWUA argued: "Word-of-mouth use of the racial issue by Burlington supervisors was discovered during TWUA's campaign in a pattern strongly suggesting central direction."

Another method of discouraging workers from signing up with the union organizers had similarities to the feudal practice of forfeiture—the withdrawing of a privilege granted by the lord if the vassal fails to perform his duties or maintain his fealty. Thus firing for union activity was not the worst of the terrors facing a mill hand. The related step of eviction from his company-owned house was an effective refinement. Eviction has been a common practice throughout the cotton textile manufacturing areas, the TWUA reported. An instance of forfeiture was provided by Pacific Mills in Rhodiss, North Carolina, which discharged an employee sympathetic to the union and helpful to it in signing up other workers. As the NLRB trial examiner reported:

. . . . I believe the respondent's plan to rid itself of Hamby [the employee] included not only his separation from the payroll but separation from the right to occupy the company house. Not only was it calculated to impress on Hamby, but also to impress on all others employed by the respondent and living in company-owned homes, the disastrous effects of engaging in union activities.[7]

A variant of this device has been organized pressure on workers by their creditors. Thus, in Jackson, Alabama, when Clark Mills was fighting the union, grocers called on their charge-account customers among the mill hands to urge opposition to the union. Car dealers, landlords, bankers, and town merchants—all of whom had a real stake in keeping the union out—repeated the procedure with their mill-hand debtors. The school principal called on former students with a similar admonition to withdraw from the union campaign "for the good of the town."

Such tactics are not limited merely to after-the-fact maueuvering. Some towns promise prospective employers that there will be no union trouble. The Chamber of Commerce in Wilson, North Carolina, for example, prepared a brochure in 1956 listing its attractions to industry that might wish to relocate in that town:

.... Our working people are from 100% American stock, from rural areas, used to hard work, and, for the most part, are independent. The majority of workers are between 20 and 40 years and most of them have secondary education. This accounts for the lack of enthusiasm for unionization.

The Chamber will actively fight any attempt by union organizers to bring a union into the local industries. A smaller city like Wilson has the advantage of combating unionization if requested to do so.

The textile interests have a final weapon at their disposal, which they have occasionally used. In 1956 the Deering Milliken interests closed their Darlington, South Carolina, mill after the workers had voted for unionization. Five hundred workers were thrown out of jobs and the community suffered severe hardships. Within a few months the mill fixtures and machinery had been auctioned off. Newspapers in the area chose to denounce the workers and their union for tampering with established economic order and bringing ruin on themselves. No successful prosecution of the Milliken interests was possible.

As the above descriptions suggest, the bucolic ravisher enjoys a wide range of outlets for his passions. Nor does he scruple to use every advantage that fate has provided him. In spite of his great successes in keeping wages down, in avoiding costly improvements in work conditions, and in maintaining the good wishes of his neighbors, he is in many ways a saddened old rakehell.

His profit margins shrink, his inventories all but bleed him dry, his overseas competitors cause him to totter on the brink of penury.

He announces his poverty with particular eloquence at the midwinter meetings of such organizations as the American Cotton Manufacturers Association that he attends each year at Boca Raton, the Cloister at Sea Island, or the Grand Ballroom of the Waldorf-Astoria.

· 6 ·

The petroleum industry came into prominence at just the time when the American Industrial Revolution was driving to completion. In the decade after Colonel Drake's well came in, in 1859, western Pennsylvania blossomed with oil rigs. The industry grew rapidly thereafter to a position of primacy among the extractive industries.

A century later, ten major oil companies and a dozen smaller organizations (of great size by almost any standards but those of the petroleum industry) dominated the field. From their beginnings the petroleum interests have had a reputation for conspiracy and enforced cooperation. These interests have been haunted by the specter of uninhibited competition.

The great organizing genius of the early petroleum industry was, of course, John D. Rockefeller. In contrast to Samuel Slater, a great deal has been written about Rockefeller. Therefore the highlights of his business career need be repeated here only in briefest form.

His monument (quite aside from his many private benefactions) was an orderly industry from which the recklessness of youth had been purged. Rockefeller in effect took a mob of rowdy boys, banished most of them, and made those whose talents seemed useful into the staid cabinet of a private government: the

Standard Oil Trust. The Trust laid and collected taxes, concluded treaties, raised small armies, negotiated with foreign nations, and occasionally waged war.

The industry that Rockefeller made his own had a volatile beginning, as suggested above. It had enough experience with wild price fluctuations to jade its taste for free enterprise. In 1859 oil was fetching $20 a barrel. In 1861 the price was $0.52. In 1863 it had gone to $8. In 1865 it was less than $3. The erratic price pattern was caused by the sudden discovery of new wells, the abrupt exhaustion of established ones, the momentarily effective pacts of well owners, and the subsequent collapse of their amiable conspiracies.

Rockefeller bought into the industry in 1862 with $4,000 he had saved from a commission grocery business he had started a few years earlier in Cleveland. That $4,000 was capital enough to establish the young bookkeeper as an oil refiner. (Refining was a simple enough operation then, and required no vast or expensive equipment.) He prospered. In 1870 he formed the Standard Oil Company with two partners, and under the charter of a defunct corporation that he and his partners got from the Pennsylvania State Legislature, there grew a federation of refineries with a secret weapon. The weapon, as Henry Demarest Lloyd named it, was "the smokeless rebate." Under this scheme, Standard Oil paid just $1.50 a barrel to ship crude oil from Cleveland to New York. Its competitors paid $2.56. With endless variations, that remained the essential device that concentrated between 70 and 90 percent of the petroleum business in Standard Oil's hands by 1900.

In vain the Congress thundered, "a gigantic and daring conspiracy." To no effect the Chamber of Commerce of New York called the rebate a means of "deliberately making the rich richer and the poor poorer. . . ." Equally ineffective were the probes and questions of the New York and Pennsylvania legislatures and the dissolution order of the Ohio Supreme Court. Combination swept everything before it. Immensely concentrated oil power stood unassailable—and no small part of its impregnability was its ability to serve an international market efficiently and at a reasonably stable price. From well to wick the oil flowed in orderly and predictable measure. To be sure, the field was littered with those who got in the way of the Trust. The master businessman had embittered most of a nation by eliminating so many redundant businessmen.

At last the muffled cries of outrage had effect. The Supreme Court split up Standard Oil; but no financial damage of consequence followed. John D. Rockefeller by then could retire to contemplate the Hudson from his solitude in Pocantico Hills. He could devote himself to philanthropy and the placid stewardship of a fortune of perhaps a billion dollars, undiminished by income taxes. (He had seen to that some years earlier: his attorney pointed out to the Supreme Court that the income-tax law fell afoul of the Constitution. Federal government had no business levying direct taxes on property, he argued, and the Court agreed.)

· 7 ·

Despite the protracted lesson in discipline, the oil interests had not quite purged themselves of their inherent flamboyance. The new discoveries in the Southwest and the Far West produced a new and uninhibited crop of millionaires. They had considerable scope in the 1920's, and unlike their more discreet mentor, some got caught more or less red-handed.

Teapot Dome is a name that summons memories of a President mysteriously dead, a suddenly affluent Secretary of the Interior, a bundle of registered Liberty Bonds, and a few prominent oilmen brought to a kind of justice.

Warren Harding died suddenly on August 2, 1923, on his way back to Washington from an extended Alaskan tour. He had been morose for months. He had been haunted by the knowledge that his friends in his Administration had dishonored him.

The President was supposed to have contracted ptomaine poisoning from eating crabmeat on the boat trip from Alaska, but no such food was aboard, and no one else on the ship was taken ill. The poisoning went into pneumonia and the pneumonia into a fatal stroke of apoplexy. He died as his wife read to him. Whether the dark rumors of deliberate poisoning (later reiterated by the oblique hints of a Justice Department detective) had substance, there was little question that Harding died weighted by the knowledge of his friends' betrayal. Although death came at the peak of his reputation, his name suffered posthumously as the extent of his friends' avarice slowly emerged to public view.

As the story came out, it proved to be a tale of private oil interests able to corrupt a great part of the Executive Branch of the government. The tale began to unfold in the fall of 1923. By early 1924 it was apparent that private oil interests had been enjoying a gigantic windfall from the friendly actions of Secretary of the Interior Albert Fall. Also involved, if indirectly, were Postmaster General Hays, Navy Secretary Denby, and Treasury Secretary Andrew Mellon, the last of whom owned Gulf Oil Company.

These events had their beginnings in 1912, when the United States Navy began converting its ships from coal to oil. Fears of potential oil shortages were marked enough for Presidents Theodore Roosevelt, Taft, and Wilson all to endorse the plan to set aside certain oil lands as naval reserves for use in times of national emergencies. One such reserve was at Teapot Dome, Wyoming.

The policy of holding such reserves under government control had been repeatedly attacked by oilmen as being contrary to the spirit of free enterprise. Time and again they tried to lay hands on the rich reserves. Time and again they were rebuffed. As Woodrow Wilson's Secretary of the Navy Josephus Daniels said, "I have been compelled to fight almost every day of my incumbency in office to prevent the dummy entrymen and illegal operators from taking the Naval Reserves. . . ." Daniels fought well, but not his successor. Control of the naval reserves was transferred from the Navy Department to the Interior Department less than three months after the Harding Administration took office. On

April 7, 1922 (a year after the new Administration had come in), the new Secretary of the Interior, Fall, secretly leased Teapot Dome to Harry F. Sinclair's Mammoth Oil Company. Eight months months later he leased another naval reserve, Number 1, at Elk Hills, California, to Edward F. Doheny's Pan American Company. Both companies had ties with Standard Oil of Indiana, and each company expected eventual profits of about $100 million from the deals.[8] Because both leases were granted under color of national emergency planning, their secrecy could be maintained for a time. But rumors of irregularities apparently reached the ears of President Harding himself. Nothing came from the whispered reports until some months after his death. His taciturn successor, Calvin Coolidge, was unmoved by spoken words. It took the findings of Senate investigators to budge Coolidge. Then he empaneled a bipartisan body to investigate. The probers did not have to look long or hard to discover a huge fraud against the people of the United States.

Although it was a complex tale, it bears retelling, if for no other reason than to suggest the great resourcefulness of the oil interests in pursuing an object that they imagine to be a worthy one. (As will be shown below, the same interests were up to very much the same sort of high-level maneuvering thirty years later in their similar thrust for favorable administration of the "tidelands" oil areas.)

On November 17, 1921, in the Vanderbilt Hotel in New York, a conference took place among Colonel E. A. Humphreys, who owned the Mexia oilfield, and four others: Colonel Robert Stewart, chairman of Standard Oil of Indiana; Harry F. Sinclair, owner of the Sinclair Consolidated Oil Company; Harry Blackmer of the Midwest Oil Company; and James O'Neil of the Prairie Oil Company. At the meeting Colonel Humphreys heard a strange proposition: Would he sell 33,333,333 barrels of oil from his wells at $1.50 a barrel to the Continental Trading Company, Ltd., of Canada? But he had never heard of the Continental Trading Company. Nor had anyone else outside that room. No matter. Sinclair and

O'Neil would vouch for the *bona-fides* of the Canadian company if Humphreys would just sell the oil. Very well, Humphreys would most certainly sell the oil.

Thus began the deal that would enrich Albert Fall by about $400,000. The way it was to work was that the Continental would resell the oil at $1.75 a barrel to Sinclair and O'Neil's respective companies. The Continental company, in turn, would buy Liberty Bonds with its profits—which ultimately mounted to $3 million —and kick back some of the profits in the form of bonds to the various gentlemen in the room at the Vanderbilt that afternoon, excepting Humphreys. He, after all, had just made a $50 million deal, which would be good enough work for any November afternoon.

Sinclair got about $750,000 in bonds; O'Neil, $800,000; Stewart, about $760,000; and Blackmer, about $760,000. Sinclair in turn gave Interior Secretary Fall $260,000 in bonds. A while later, Doheny (who was working on the Elk Hills naval reserves) "loaned" Fall $100,000 without security. A mere "bagatelle," as he later explained to congressional investigators.

The Senate heard about these strange goings-on later—much later. Meanwhile, other actors drifted onstage, and their names need concern us here but briefly. Sinclair also had made a "loan" of $185,000 in bonds, plus a $75,000 gift, to the Republican National Committee. The "loan" went to Harding's Postmaster General Will Hays, who was also national party chairman, and sometime Sinclair attorney. Of this money, $100,000 eventually shuttled back to Sinclair. Meanwhile, Hays had quit as Postmaster General to go to Hollywood, where he turned his talents to suppressing immorality. (His new job was to uphold the standards of the motion pictures, and he gave his name to the Hays Office. Among the rules he laid down were prohibitions on filmed shots of the insides of ladies' thighs, and a ban on couples being photographed lying on or in a bed. At least one foot had to be on the floor.) From Hollywood, Hays sent the bonds Sinclair had given him (to reduce the Republican deficit from the 1920 campaign) to various rich men. In return, the rich men sent back untraceable money, which was then applied to reducing the party deficit. Sinclair's generosity thus went unremarked. It wasn't until 1928 that investigating Senator Walsh of Montana, who had been plodding along for almost seven years, had a moment's exhilaration. The winding trail of the hot bonds that had its genesis in the Vanderbilt Hotel pact of November, 1921, at last led to the most august man in the Harding or Coolidge Administrations (with the possible exception of Herbert Hoover), Andrew Mellon, "the greatest Secretary of the Treasury since Alexander Hamilton."

Yes, said Mellon, now that you mention it, there were some bonds back in 1923 that someone had sent. "When Mr. Hays called shortly thereafter, he suggested . . . that I hold the bonds and contribute an equal amount to the fund [to reduce the party deficit]. This I declined to do." Mellon sent the bonds right back to Hays along with a check—an outright gift—for $50,000. He had no idea at all that there was any connection with the Teapot Dome affair.

In those same years, the Vanderbilt Pact signatories were equally reticent. Sinclair, O'Neil, Blackmer, and Stewart took none of their directors or company officers into their confidence. Sinclair, of course, had had the bad sense to scatter his bonds about rather freely. But the others kept their bonds and held their peace. When the Senate went looking for the quartet in 1928, Blackmer was in Europe, and happy enough to stay there. Sinclair was uncommunicative, and ultimately he went behind bars briefly for contempt of Congress, and for contempt of court— for hiring detectives to trail jurors. O'Neil also favored Europe. Stewart, on the other hand, found Cuba more to his liking. He came home to face the investigators only when John D. Rockefeller, Jr., ordered him to do so. (The Rockefellers later cast Stewart out of his position at Standard Oil of Indiana, but he went with his pension, at any rate.) Fall, after being convicted and fined for accepting a bribe, went to work as an oil consultant; Denby left public office under fire; and Doheny lived to boast that he found some of his most useful advisers to have been Cabinet members. He had hired no fewer than four of Wilson's—Interior, Treasury, Justice, and War.

Although the Supreme Court held the leases fraudulent and null, the private oil interests had enjoyed profitable access to the reserves for over seven years. No law did more than disturb their powers. As Senator George Norris noted sadly in his autobiography, "under the American system of jurisprudence it is very difficult, if not impossible, to convict one hundred million dollars."

· 8 ·

The very same year that the Teapot Dome scandal began, 1921, saw the first outlines of the great "tidelands" oil fight begin to take shape. That is a case history of the oil interests waging far more skillful and rewarding war for private privilege. The offshore oil campaign, unlike the Teapot Dome scandal, *was* more like a war. It lasted thirty-two years. Teapot Dome was more the minor skirmish—the initially successful attack on a few isolated outposts. It lasted only seven years. Furthermore, in the tidelands fight, there was no provable illegality. In fact, it was the first demonstration of the perfection of the art of ventriloquism as practiced by the modern vested interests. From the time that the campaign became a matter of major importance, in 1937, there was scarcely an oilman to be seen, hardly a direct thrust visible from the oil industry itself. Almost the whole debate was carried out on the gaseous plateau of "states' rights."

Nevertheless, as a demonstration of raw power, the drive of the oilmen for offshore oil under terms most favorable to their interests was strong enough to override fifteen years of fixed Federal policy, two presidential vetoes, and two Supreme Court decisions. It was enough to support a new political party in one campaign (1948) and to ensure the defeat in another campaign (1952) of the candidate whose views conflicted directly with those of the oil interests. When General Eisenhower came to office, the oil interests did not have long to wait. He came in

January, 1953. In May of that year he signed into law a bill that the *New York Times* called "one of the greatest and surely the most unjustified give-away programs in all the history of the United States." The history of that campaign by the oil interests illustrates the increasing sophistication of those interests, their system of alliances, their dogged pursuit of their objectives, and their well founded confidence in their ultimate triumph.

In the first place, the mere phrase "tidelands oil" represents a small victory accomplished by skillful conditioning of the public psyche. As the term suggests, tidelands are those lands overrun by flood tides and exposed by ebb tides. Were these the lands that caused all the ballyhoo? Were these thin slivers of territory —a few hundred feet wide at most—what the oil interests wanted to keep out of the Federal government's control? Not exactly. "Offshore" oil lands would have been a better term for what they were after, but that term never got into the public consciousness the way "tidelands" did. What was the difference? About ten miles in width and some billions of dollars in potential revenues. (No one has been sure just how many billions.)

The issue did not become an important one until the economic relationship between conventional dry-land prospecting and deep-water prospecting had changed, and that change took its time coming. But it came; and when it did, in 1947, what had been a small issue quickly grew into an enormous one.

It began in 1921, when California's State Legislature approved the issuance of leases to oil enterprisers on state lands. The legislature added to its definitions of such lands all "tidelands and parts of navigable lakes and rivers." Of course in 1921 no one was aware of the potential riches of underwater oilfields. Consequently California's definition may have had curiosity value, but it aroused no objections.

In 1933, when the Roosevelt Administration came to power, Secretary of the Interior Harold Ickes endorsed the view that such offshore lands belonged to the states. By 1937, however, he had changed his mind. Instead of rejecting several applications for Federal leases out of hand, he held them in abeyance until there could be a judicial determination of ownership. Ickes's action stirred the oil interests and their devoted allies, the partisans of states' rights, to cries of betrayal. Ickes was equal to the contest—which went on for the rest of his public career:

> I did not, when I assumed office a good many years ago, take an oath that I would always be right nor even that I would never change my mind. I did take an oath to do my duty, and I viewed my duty in this matter as plain, once I realized that the ownership of submerged coastal lands had not in fact been settled by the courts. Show me a man who takes stubborn pride in the fact that his mind, once made up, is unchangeable, and I will show you a man who is not fit to be a public servant.

There the matter rested until May, 1945. Why the issue should have remained muted for those eight years is not completely clear. No doubt one good explanation is that offshore oil production was faced with severe obstacles in those years quite aside from the high cost of underwater drilling. For one thing, the threat of submarine attack discouraged such ventures. For another, as Professor Robert Engler has written:

> During the New Deal [oilmen] made many cash contributions [to the Democratic Party]. In 1936, for example, H. L. Dougherty of the Cities Service Company reported giving $55,000. . . . Sid Richardson was friendly with Franklin D. Roosevelt, and his contributions helped maintain a Democratic congress in the 1942 election. In fact the Democrats received sizable sums as late as 1944. Postponements of antitrust action until after the 1940 election and of "tidelands" and further antitrust litigation until after the 1944 election were not unrelated to their desire to maintain such generosity.[9]

Oilman Edwin Pauley was credited by Ickes with having the impending California offshore oil case postponed. Pauley interceded with President Roosevelt, who, the story goes, was worried about holding California in the Democratic column. Ickes went on to say that Pauley pursued the same subject with the new President, Harry Truman, on the train that brought Truman back to Washington from the Roosevelt funeral at Hyde Park. Whatever the truth of the matter, it is interesting to note that scarcely six weeks after Roosevelt's death, and only three weeks after victory in Europe, the Truman Administration went ahead with its action against state ownership of the offshore oil lands. On May 29, 1945, apparently under the initiative of Ickes, Attorney General Biddle brought suit against the Pacific Western Oil Corporation, a lessee of California. Meanwhile, in the House of Representatives, legislation that hopefully would emasculate the Federal suit went into the hopper. H.J. Res. 225, as it was called, was a "quitclaim" bill by which the Federal government would simply renounce its claim to the offshore lands. Meanwhile, Ickes feared that the court action, filed in the Federal District Court rather than in the Supreme Court, might take fifteen years to get to the ultimate court of appeal. Therefore the papers were refiled in October before the Supreme Court itself, but not before the House had passed the quitclaim legislation. The Senate did not get around to hearings on the bill until the next January. Meanwhile, a curious thing had occurred. Forty-six of the forty-eight state attorney generals had endorsed the bill. The attorney general of California had prepared a brief in opposition to Federal control of the offshore lands and had circulated it to his colleagues around the nation. He followed up with telegraphic solicitation of signatures. No oil-company leaders seemed to have anything to do with that campaign, although, as Professor Lucius Barker has pointed out, both the brief and the pending legislation itself had been drafted by lawyers whose fees were being at least partially met by oil companies leasing offshore lands from California.

Oilman Pauley was playing a discreet role in guiding the legislation through the Congress, and Ickes was playing a prominent role in obstructing it. Ickes appeared in February, 1946, before the Senate hearings on the bill. He had scorn for the legal acumen of the state attorney generals. "I should think," he said, "that Congress, as well as the courts, would be suspicious of a legal argument conducted along the lines of a bathing-beauty contest." He furthermore insisted that the debate was not over states' rights or the "overruling of settled law," but that it was over oil, pure and simple. The Senate did not agree. It passed the bill 44–34. But President Truman vetoed it. An attempt to override the veto in the House failed on August 2, 1946, and the center of interest swung back to the Supreme Court, where the government's case had yet to be settled.

California's response to the government case was not exactly concise. Ickes claimed that the California brief that soon arrived in Washington weighed three pounds, nine ounces. It was 822 pages long, and required a 14-page table of contents. The Federal government found it uncommunicative: "[T]he answer leaves this case in such a state of obfuscation that it becomes virtually impossible to segregate the relevant from the great mass of the irrelevant. . . ." The government then retaliated with a 258-page brief of its own in support of the Federal case, and California came back with a two-volume 508-page brief. After that massive display of paperwork, the antagonists devoted four days to talk before the High Court. By a 5–4 decision, the Court ruled in favor of the United States. The Federal government, it said, has "paramount rights in and power over" the offshore lands to the three-mile limit. The Court did not say that the government owned the offshore territory, however. Nevertheless, in *United States* v. *California,* as the case was styled, the principal of Federal control of the offshore areas was clearly affirmed—for the time being, as it developed.

· 9 ·

At that chronological stage of the extended war, offshore oil production was just beginning to become commercially feasible. Despite the great difficulties, 1947 was the year of the first recorded offshore production. What had been for many years just a dream at last began to take on the appearance of a lucrative reality. (A few figures here will help explain the intense pressure brought on the Federal government by the oil interests. The same figures also foretell what finally happened in the long debate, and when. In 1954 there were 65 producing offshore wells. By 1958 the figure was almost 1,600.)

Rejected by the Supreme Court, the oil interests turned once again to their favored forum for government help, the Congress. A cascade of bills followed the *California* decision. Most of them had the clear goal of overturning the Court's decision. The year 1948, in fact, saw an unprecedented attack by the oil interests against the government's position both in the Congress and in the presidential election that came in November. Most of the spring of that year was devoted to exhaustive hearings in the Senate on the offshore-oil issue. The House, meanwhile, passed quitclaim legislation without more than token debate. Only twenty-nine congressmen voted against the bill. In May, the bill went on to the Senate, and in June the Judiciary Committee reported the bill favorably to the Senate. Adjournment came, however, before any action was taken. The impending election made the Senate even more deliberate than usual.

Offshore oil was fortunate in having states' rights as a slogan behind which to advance its cause. In 1948 most southern states bolted from the Democratic party to form their own party and their own presidential ticket. The Dixiecrats, as they were called, enjoyed important financial support from the oil interests. Some have argued that without such support their campaign would have been a financial impossibility. Oil provided not only money but also leadership in organizing the new party. As Professor Engler has noted, oil lawyers held positions of prominence in the Dixiecrat apparatus in Alabama, Mississippi, Texas, and Louisiana. A major plank of the Dixiecrat platform was state control of offshore oil. The regular Democrats were sufficiently disturbed by the issue to leave it entirely out of their platform. The Republicans, meanwhile, favored state control, although their candidate, Governor Thomas Dewey, was noncommittal on that issue and almost all others, as well. As the victor-presumptive, he did not think it wise or necessary to commit himself. Harry Truman won that election, in spite of the three candidates arrayed against him. (On the far left, he had the Wallace Progressives; on the far right, the Dixiecrats; and to the near right, the Republicans.)

Seven weeks after that victory, Truman's Attorney General Tom

Clark filed suits (similar to that which had been filed and won against California) against Louisiana and Texas. The Federal government asked the Court to enjoin both states from trespassing on submerged lands that were under the control of the United States. Shortly afterward, Texas came forward with an argument that it enjoyed a "special position" because of the events surrounding its entry into the Union. Texas claimed three "leagues" of offshore territory. The Texas claim amounted to something more than ten miles, an interesting claim in view of the fact that the United States as a nation claimed only three miles of offshore jurisdiction. Almost two years after the suit was filed, the Supreme Court spoke again, and again upheld the position of Federal primacy. The Court found no cause for special treatment of Texas, despite the treaty that had been tacitly accepted on its admission, or "annexation," as the legal niceties required. Texas, said the Court, came into the Union on "equal footing" with the other states.

The decision raised a huge outcry from legal experts. Almost to a man they objected loudly to what they thought were fundamental errors on the part of the Court. The *Baylor Law Review* came forth with a "symposium" on the case in which one article bore the title "Expropriation of the Texas Tidelands by Judicial Fiat." A Texas congressman named Gossett said "the Supreme Court has given the nation another long shove down the road to national socialism." Texas Attorney General Price Daniel lamented the loss of land that "belongs to the Texas public school fund." Governor Allan Shivers said, "I want everyone to know that Texas will fight to the last ditch. . . ." And the state land commissioner said he would go to jail before he turned over some $8 million claimed by the United States on the oil lands. Thus flourished violent opinion in the most notoriously violent of American states.

The oil interests retaliated in the best way they knew how. They got quitclaim legislation introduced once again in the House. The debate now rose to a higher key. Congressman Charles Halleck, of Indiana, found a sonorous note for his comments:

"Once again the Congress is called upon as a bulwark to resist the schemes of the planners who would chip away, piece by piece, the foundation of American freedom established by customs and the Constitution." Congressman Cleveland Bailey, of West Virginia, speaking with some thought of the moribund coal interests in his state, favored more ornate prose: "Though my voice may ring through these sacred Halls as the voice of one crying out in the wilderness, I make bold to denounce this rape of the judiciary." Bold as he wanted to make it, the votes were going Halleck's way. On July 30, 1951, the quitclaim legislation passed the lower house. It took almost a year to get through the Senate, but it did get through. President Truman vetoed the measure, at the end of May, 1952, saying he would preside over no "free gift" by all the people of the United States to those of a few states.

The second Truman veto stirred the oil interests to another tactic. They had failed with two-thirds of the Federal government, the judiciary and the executive. Only the legislative branch would listen to them. Therefore, they reasoned, they had better attend to changing the two-thirds that opposed them. Only the oil interests could hope to accomplish such a task, but they did what they intended. The man who made their long-nurtured dreams come true, General Eisenhower, knew nothing about the offshore oil issue when first sounded out. But by the time he was on the stump in the 1952 presidential campaign, he knew enough to make the issue one of the big talking points in his successful campaign for the White House.

· 10 ·

In rereading some of the rhetoric that this issue inspired, one has a hard time imagining how such emotion could have been generated by a sticky, smelly fluid laid down in the Tertiary Period of the Cenozoic Era. But of course that was not the issue at all. The issue was states' rights, or the sanctity of property, or Texas schoolchildren, or freedom, or seaweed. Yes, seaweed. As Candidate Eisenhower asked a Louisiana audience in 1952, "What of the kelp of Maine?" Eighteen miles offshore were rich beds of the weed, and if Maine, why not all coastal states? Why didn't every state have submerged lands? And why couldn't they enjoy them under their own control? "Powermongers" in Washington, Eisenhower explained. (He did not explain, however, just what stake Maine had in the issue: its revenue from kelp amounted to about $26 annually.[10])

"Yes," said a Virginia congressman, "more is at stake than land or oil or sands or oysters. The sanctity of private property and the lifeblood of our democracy is hanging in the balance." Yes, said Louisiana's Leander Perez, it was "a plot . . . to adopt the European or Russian ideology that the national government . . . is a government of unlimited powers. . . ." Yes, said Candidate Eisenhower, the Supreme Court had spoken, but it had left it to the Congress to decide matters of ownership and title. "Twice by substantial majorities, both Houses of Congress have voted to recognize the traditional concept of state ownership of these submerged areas. Twice these acts of Congress have been vetoed by the President. I would approve such Acts of Congress."

No, said the Democratic candidate Adlai Stevenson in Louisiana during the campaign. "I do not think it wise policy for the Congress to institute a practice of giving away such national assets to individual states. . . ."

The yeses carried the day. Harry Truman, however, was still President of the United States, and he was not going to leave office without doing what he could. He transferred the offshore lands to the naval reserve by executive order in the closing hours of his Administration. The new Administration transferred them right back again. As incoming Interior Secretary Douglas McKay described the new climate in the White House, the Eisenhower Administration intended no give-aways of natural resources. "All we are doing is giving it back to the people where it belongs." The people were overjoyed. At least the people who stood to gain the most. As Texaco said in its annual report that year, the 1952 elections "strongly indicated endorsement of a great deal of what the petroleum industry stands for and believes in."

The Eisenhower team's first major piece of legislation concerned offshore oil. "The Submerged Lands Act," as it was known, inspired that oddest of spectacles—a filibuster by the liberals. Senator Wayne Morse spoke for 22 hours and 26 minutes on April 23–24, 1953, in opposition to the bill. Before his stand, Senators Douglas, Kefauver, Fulbright, Humphrey, and Lehman had all voiced their objections. Senator Lister Hill advanced an amendment to the bill that would have applied all revenues from offshore oil to aid for education. It was defeated. Meanwhile, proponents of the bill began noting with dwindling amusement the wide range of subjects the opponents had introduced in their long debate: sliced bologna, Sunday-school hymns, country stores in Arkansas, the New Testament, and baseball among them. The bill passed on May 14th. It "returned" to the states control of offshore oil lands within "their historic boundaries," thus skirting the difficult question of whether that boundary was to be three miles or ten and a half miles—whether California's needs or the needs of Texas were to influence the wording of the bill. (The point was of great importance because of a trick nature had played. The continental shelf drops off abruptly after the three-mile limit in California, but in the Gulf of Mexico it extends out seventy to one hundred miles. In some measure that difference accounted for the divergent arguments of California and Texas-Louisiana before the Court and the Congress.)

When President Eisenhower signed the bill on May 22, 1953, he said: "I deplore and I will always resist Federal encroachment upon rights and affairs of the states. Recognizing the states' claim to these lands is in keeping with the basic principles of honesty and fair play." Republican National Chairman Leonard Hall was positively euphoric: "the first sharp turn from the drift toward the superstate in America," he said.

To avoid the stigma of being the authors of an immense giveaway program, the Eisenhower Administration had insisted on a related piece of legislation, which went through at about the same time. The Outer Continental Shelf Lands Act stipulated that the Federal government would control all the offshore areas from the outermost limit of the state boundaries to the edge of the continental shelf.

The battle was not yet over. Alabama and Rhode Island brought suit against Louisiana, Texas, Florida, and California by challenging the constitutionality of the Submerged Lands Act shortly after its passage. The next year, 1954, the Court held (in *Alabama v. Texas*, as the case came to be known) that the Act was valid. Thus the previous Court decisions were overridden and "states' rights" were reaffirmed, but not enough affirmation for the tastes of Louisiana. If Texas had three leagues, Louisiana ought to have the same. But Louisiana had suffered some difficulties in being readmitted to the Union (after the Civil War) in 1868; legal technicalities attending the readmission put a cloud over the state's claim to ten and a half miles of territorial waters. In deciding against Louisiana, the Court found that both Texas and Florida did indeed enjoy three-league territorial rights, but not Louisiana. (The Court handed down its decision on May 31, 1960.)

The Congress, shortly thereafter, began studying bills to grant Louisiana, Mississippi, and Alabama the same offshore boundaries. When those bills become law, as they probably will, the problem of parceling out the rich prizes will still not be resolved. From where does one measure to establish the border? High tide, low tide, or mean tide? And how does one mark the boundaries? What do you do with a wiggly coastline? Forget the deepest impressions and measure from the mean coastline? To these questions Federal government attorneys and state attorney generals will address themselves in future years. The Federal attorneys will be $8,000-a-year men backed by good but not spectacular talent. The state attorney generals will have friendly aid and advice from $80,000-a-year men from the best firms in the best cities. This latter group will be the brightest and most inventive team of attorneys that money can retain. The problems of the wiggly coastlines, given that probable array of legal talent, will no doubt be resolved to the enduring satisfaction of the oil interests. Enduring for a while, anyway. After all, the continental shelf is a broad and promising terrain, just awaiting the right argument to make it bloom with Texas towers under state, not Federal, control.

As Professor Barker has pointed out, when a diffused interest (in this instance advocates of national control) runs up against an intense, concentrated interest (state control), intensity prevails over diffusion. No interest seems as capable as the oil interests of mustering intensity of purpose. Their successes have been nothing short of spectacular.

Thus the city-slicker school of economic seduction enjoys a reputation that has been well earned. Even the frostiest and most remote of objects becomes for it a rather easy mark.

· 11 ·

In sum, then, the object of economic seduction breaks down into about a half-dozen major rights the interests intend to enjoy and a half-dozen responsibilities they intend to evade:

The rights they wish to enjoy are a high return on investment, loyalty from workers, stability in the "business climate," honor from neighbors and lookers-on, freedom from government interference, and power to define the public interest.

The responsibilities that they do what they can to evade are high wage payments, the costs of maintaining good work conditions, the costs of social-welfare payments, accountability to neighbors and the general public for their actions, deference to the public interest, and constraint from the government.

These general goals have shown themselves time and again in both major types of vested interests—the primitive and the sophisticated. They have recurred in the foundation of the first textile manufacturing, in the battle against child-labor restrictions, in the fights against unionism, in the euthanasia of free enterprise in the days of Rockefeller, in the quest for preferment by the oil interests in the 1920's, and in the defeat of the public interest in the thirty-year war for offshore oil. The pattern is well fixed and highly visible. That it is denied today with consummate skill by the vested interests must be charged to their skill at ventriloquism. The sounds they make usually come from some hired larynx of smooth and charming timbre.

FIVE

The Poor and the

Vested Interests

⌐⌐⌐⌐⌐⌐⌐

The poor feel the policies of the vested interests with particular force because they are in no position to escape the effects of these policies. Failure clings so close that the poor suffer what amounts to a paralysis of will. They are not very well organized. The mere idea of formal cooperation still remains somewhat alien to their spirit. Their impulsive cooperation is something else again, but it is not the sort of thing that counts for much in the marketplace. Disorganized generosity has never been much of a match for organized avarice.

In 1950–1960 there were about 40 million Americans who lived below the line that separates the affluent from the other America. What made the position of these poor especially notable was that their relative economic power was growing weaker, not stronger. The goal of progressive taxation, for one example, was more remote in 1960 than it had been in 1946. The tax burden falling on the family earning less than $2,000 a year in 1960 was 28.3 percent of its income, while the burden for the family earning $10,000 to $14,000 a year was closer to 24 percent of its income.

The poor threaten their financial superiors. The presence of a sizable group of substandard consumers in the economy represents a clear danger to the continued material welfare of the middle classes. The threat is not overt but indirect; not immediate, perhaps, but far-reaching nevertheless.

Because they are unable to carry their proportionate share of the consumptive burdens, these poor are causing the vested interests to do without a substantial part of their domestic markets; they are causing investment capital to suffer some of the early pangs of unrequited affection; they are undermining the traditional optimism that has always been a hallmark of their financial superiors. Their betters, in their turn, are turning to artificial stimulation of the optimism that used to come without being forced.

Although the poor are hardly doing these things deliberately, the mere idea that there is such a large group of Americans is unacceptable. They constitute a chorus of specters at the feast. Their sight is most unwelcome, and therefore their presence is being successfully ignored by a surprisingly large number of revelers. The poor can almost be explained away and out of sight.

· 1 ·

At this point a short description of the social hierarchy as it seems to be arrayed may help fix the relative position of these poor people with more precision than statistics alone can impart. In the first place, these other Americans are at the bottom of society. That much is plain enough. What may not be equally clear is the nature of those who rise above them. Directly overhead, ranging through the middle classes, are the employees and managers of the vested interests (who may be called collectively the Organization). Above the Organization—above it in some respects, anyway—is the Establishment. This last group is made up in important part of the leaders of the vested interests. It is also populated by certain statesmen, educators, clergymen, scientists, authors, and philanthropists. Without going into great detail, a few general comments may be made here on the relative positions of these three groups.

The Establishment is closely linked with passive wealth that no longer lusts after profit. In fact the Establishment tends to be associated with wealth intent on eradicating itself, the wealth of such great foundations as Ford and Rockefeller. The Organization is also linked with wealth, but with aggressive wealth stalking large-scale gains. The poor are of course without wealth; furthermore, their incomes are often scandalously low.

As a guess, but perhaps a fairly accurate one, the numeric relationship among these three is roughly 20:75:5. A large number at the bottom, the overwhelming majority in the middle, and a very few at the top. The relative influence of these groups, however, does not depend on numbers as much as it depends on how highly organized each group is and how clear its long-range goals are. Thus the influence ratio among these three is more on the order of 5:65:30. While these figures suggest that the vested interests are thus regulated to a disproportionate degree by the Establishment, it should be borne in mind that the Establishment is populated in part by the leaders of the vested interests.

It is no doubt true that when a corporate archon gains clear title to a place in the Establishment he becomes less economically parochial and more of a business statesman. But he probably influences as much as he is influenced. For that reason, there is some justification for regarding the Establishment and the leadership of the vested interests as interchangeable. They are not completely interchangeable because they do not always seem to agree; but they agree more than they disagree.

There is another distinction that should be made here. While the leadership of the vested interests is the ruling class, the Establishment is the reigning class. The former excels in power, the latter in dignity. Each, in some measure, is the client of the other. There is some higgling and bargaining between them, but the terms of trade seem to favor those who have the dearer commodity, dignity. (No doubt it is dearer because of a great expenditure of labor to attain it, an accumulation of generations of habit to wear it well, and consequent reluctance to part with it even for a good price.)

As dignity is the mark of the Establishment, it is the great desideratum of the Organization. It is furthermore a goal of the poor man's ambition; but for him, the terms of trade are far worse than for the Organization. It is a recorded trait of the vested interests (and of their constituency) that they levy a direct tax on the dignity of the poor as the price the poor must pay to survive: to collect unemployment checks, to enjoy aid-to-dependent-children benefits, or to get medical attention in a public clinic. ("Attention," in this connection, is used not because that is what it is so much as because that is what it is called.) The major reason for this attitude on the part of the vested interests is not a basic meanness but a common regard for cost accounting. To meet the social-welfare needs of the poor is to raise the costs of doing business and to permit more scope to government administration.

A last important distinction between Organization and Establishment is that the former is basically quite conservative, while the latter is more moderate in its views. That is not to say, as some do, that the Establishment is liberal. It is not. It is merely less conservative than the Organization. For an archon to win a secure place in the Establishment he must pay the soft coin of moderation that disappoints his former associates of the National Association of Manufacturers, the United States Chamber of Commerce, or the Foundation for Economic Education; but that hardly makes him an incandescent liberal.

Being more moderate and disinterested than the Organization, the Establishment is naturally more sensitive to the plight of the poor. The Establishment has had a fairly consistent record of support of social progress, particularly in civil-rights legislation. The Organization, on the other hand, as suggested above, snipes at the poor, often with small concession to subtlety. As the mass media, particularly the big magazines, are under the direct control of the vested interests, they provide cover for such sniping. (This process will be explored in fuller detail in Chapter 9.)

Even though the Organization prevails over, more than it defers to, the Establishment, the poor do have their occasional tribunes, although cautious ones at that. Whether they know it or not, the hopes of the poor for a better day rest very largely with the Establishment's success in restraining its truculent milch cow, the Organization.

· 2 ·

The poor, as Michael Harrington has pointed out, are politically invisible. "As a group, they are atomized. They have no face; they have no voice." [1] The gains of the 1930's, such as unemployment relief and social security, have passed the poor by, leaving the nation with the curious arrangement of "socialism for the rich and free enterprise for the poor." As Harrington observes, "We have given them bare survival, but not the means of living honorable and satisfactory lives as valued members of our society." [2]

It takes roughly $6,000 a year in 1960 dollars for an urban family of four to maintain a "modest but adequate" standard of living, according to the Bureau of Labor Statistics. This standard is somewhat below the average standard in America, nevertheless. Low though it is, about a fifth of the population falls below it. Of these 40 million poor, almost 11 million are children. About a fifth of the poor are Negro. (They are twice as likely to be poor as are white Americans.)

These poor live in crowded city apartments or in blighted farm shacks. They suffer bad education and frequent unemployment. They are menial or at best semiskilled workers. As a fair representation of these poor, consider the status of the Negro: *

In the field of housing, the Negro begins with a large handicap: he must pay more than whites for equivalent quarters, but his chances of getting a decent place to live are slim. One of six Negro dwelling places is dilapidated (only one of 32 white houses

* Figures cited herein are taken from "Economic and Social Status of the Negro in the United States," National Urban League (New York, 1961).

is similarly run down). About a fifth of the houses rated "sound" that are occupied by Negroes still lack some or all plumbing facilities. Not only are the houses shabby; they are also crowded: the nonwhite family is larger by one person than the white family.

In the structure of the family itself, there is a tendency to disintegration of the Negro family, beginning with the frequency of common-law marriage and continuing when, for example, an unemployed father leaves home so that the family may collect aid-to-dependent-children payments. Death comes earlier in the Negro community than in the white community. Maiming and loss of physical vigor also come more certainly and earlier. The rate of separation between husband and wife is six times greater for nonwhite than for white families. About one of four recipients of disability aid is Negro—a figure two-and-a-half times greater than an unskewed average would provide.

In employment, the Negro is more than twice as likely to be laid off or fired as is the white. When he does work, he does menial or semiskilled jobs that no one else much wants to do anyway, and he works fewer hours a week than his white counterpart. His earnings are about half that of the white.

Because his educational attainments are considerably lower than the white's—he had to leave school to help support his family in his time—he cannot apply for the best jobs, nor can he win the apprenticeship training that provides a way into many of the skilled crafts.

When it comes to collecting unemployment payments, the Negro is again at a disadvantage. Because he and his wife work disproportionately in agricultural and domestic fields—neither of which is covered by unemployment insurance in most states—he again comes out short.

The "culture of poverty" also makes its effects felt on the Negro young. They leave school earlier than their white counterparts, and in many instances they cannot find work. During the 1960 school year 344,000 children between the ages of 16 and 24 dropped out of school, more than a fifth of them nonwhite. Of the 1.7 million who graduated from high school that same year, only

7 percent were nonwhite. Of the 750,000 of these graduates who went on to college the next October, only 5 percent were non-white.

Even at the cradle, the threat of premature death hangs heaviest over the Negro. He cannot afford the medical care that reduces infant mortality as well as his white counterpart because of his low income. Therefore in 1958 the Negro infant mortality rate was 92 percent above the white rate. The maternal mortality rate during childbirth was four times higher for Negro than for white mothers during the same year. And of the 340,000 children served in the crippled children's program in 1959, almost a fifth were nonwhite.

The cumulative burden borne by these poor, then, is a mixed encumbrance: inferior employment opportunities, restricted educational chances, bad housing, early death, abnormal incidence of disease, volatile family relationships, and pervasive discrimination whenever the Negro leaves his rural shack or his urban ghetto.*

There is nothing new in the assignment of the lowest members on the social scale to the least esteemed work. It has been a re-

---

* Detailing such a story in aggregates and by citation of statistics leaves it at a comfortable level of abstraction, at which it may be more easily shunted out of mind, unless something may have happened to have dramatized the reality in an unusual way. For me, the sight of early and violent death provided an enduring reminder.

I have chanced to see 25 violent deaths in my life—not in all cases at the instant of death, but near enough to it (either before or just after) to know something of its presence. Of these 25, 24 involved Negroes, and 23 of those 24 were group deaths. The Negro who died alone went in a lethal gas chamber. Three small girls were burned to death one winter morning in a kerosene-stove explosion in their parents' shack on a tobacco farm. (The landlord chided the grieving mother for leaving them alone. But the mother had had to drive the father to search for work in the family jalopy, and in her brief absence death came.) Then there were the 20 migrant farm workers who went to their death on a North Carolina highway early one spring day as the old truck in which they were riding turned into the path of an oncoming tractor-trailer. It had been my task to get their names for a newspaper account of the accident. Some of them had no last names, as far as I could ever discover, and most of them had no addresses. They were born anonymous and rootless, and that is how they died.

current theme of American history that the immigrant has done the dirty work. As the Immigration Commission of the Sixty-first Congress noted in 1911, the pattern of undesirable jobs for recent immigrants was well established: "Southern and Eastern Europeans are confined to pick mining and the unskilled and common labor jobs. The same situation exists in iron and steel and glass (and textile) manufacturing, and in all divisions of manufacturing enterprise." The pattern has governed discrimination against Slavs, Italians, Irish, and, in more recent years, Puerto Ricans and Mexicans. Through it all, the Negro has enjoyed less improvement, relatively, than any other ethnic group. He began as a slave but he remains a peon, serving in economic bondage in a harsh and unyielding system.

· 3 ·

The barriers thus erected against the lower classes serve to block the full performance of their economic function as consumers. In their own time, the middle classes faced similar barriers with similar bad results to their performance as producers. An example cited by Professor Jacob Oser [3] will, perhaps, make the analogy clear: In 1685, a merchant transporting planks from Saxony to Hamburg down the river Elbe had to stop and pay tolls in kind at regular intervals. He left Saxony with sixty planks, but by the time he arrived downriver at Hamburg, he had just six planks left. Such internal barriers to trade channeled capital into the hands of the feudal lords who more often than not expended their wealth in sumptuary excess, in a day when more massive production, not consumption, was the urgent need.

Today, the Negro American, the most visible victim of poverty, suffers his poverty in large measure because of similar artificial barriers put in his way; by the entire apparatus of discrimination that seems to have for its goal the maintenance of this lowly reference group against which even the lowest white may imagine himself elevated and better. (At the risk of laboring the point, in common parlance, "better" means "richer"; the definitions of the positive and superlative forms of this adjective follow accordingly.)

In Birmingham, Alabama, the case of "Mr. B," a Negro contractor, as described by the Commission on Race and Housing, provides a twentieth century version of the seventeenth century plank merchant forced to contend with irksome restrictions.[4]

Mr. B studied at Hampton Institute in preparation for his intended career, and after an interruption in his schooling for army service (he served as a lieutenant), he went to Howard University and finally to the University of Michigan. With his architectural and engineering training, he went on home to Birmingham to begin work. He contented himself with small remodeling and minor alteration jobs for a time, but through the good offices of a white civil engineer, he gained introductions to a contractor and an architect, who agreed—after inspecting the jobs he had done—to recommend him for a state contracting license. He filed his application, and waited.

He got a notice some time thereafter to report for a contractor's examination at the capital. He made it a point to arrive early. The other hopeful contractors, all white, shortly began to assemble. A clerk began to call out names. Finally no one was left in the anteroom but Mr. B. He questioned the clerk, but learned that his name just wasn't on the list. He couldn't take the test at all, it appeared.

His sponsors intervened for him, and within a few months he was again summoned to the capital for a special test. He spent the morning on the written questions, and for two or three hours after lunch he faced the state board in an oral examination. After a brief recess, he was called back in, and was told that he had been licensed as a contractor. His examiners offered him their hands and their good wishes.

Mr. B's early years as a contractor were the hardest. He was limited to small remodeling, but gradually worked up to churches and some home construction, mostly on a very small scale with just a few workers to help him. At length, a white real-estate company contracted with him to build a house, but when he finished the $6,000 job he discovered that he had lost a great deal of money on the deal—so much that the company voluntarily paid Mr. B an extra $700. (The company turned around and sold the house for $10,000.) Then a lumber company asked him to build three houses, with its materials. Mr. B discovered that wood that had been quoted originally at $100 was billed to him at $200 by the company.

If he did not work with the real-estate or lumber companies, he was forced to take very small jobs. In an attempt to move up to bigger things on his own, he sought financing. His first try was among Negro businessmen, who did not have resources enough for his purposes. They suggested he try the banks. The banks said he would have to be bonded before they could lend him anything. Mr. B went to the bonding companies. They asked him what work he had in progress that might require bonding. He discovered that he would need about $10,000 to bid on the kinds of jobs that would meet with the bonding companies' requirements, which seemed to put him back where he started. Thus for want of money he had gone to friends who told him to go to the bank, who told him, in effect, that without money he could not borrow money.

Mr. B decided to use what funds he did have on deposit as leverage, and thereby he did get some financing, but, as he said, not on terms open to his white competitors. He would have to pay a little more.

Given a bit of room to maneuver, Mr. B began to win bigger jobs, and at one point he had forty men and a secretary working for him. But he had it brought home to him once again that he faced massive barriers. Most of his Negro workers simply were not skilled enough to do the work. Why not? For one thing, they were barred from apprentice positions by union restrictions in all but the carpenters', bricklayers', plasterers', and cement-finishers' unions. That meant inevitable bottlenecks in electrical, plumbing, painting, and bulldozing work. That meant that Mr. B was limited to a relatively small scale because he not only had difficulty finding skilled Negro manual help, he had also to get by with one-man management, because of the scarcity of trained Negro managers. The limitations of size that these circumstances put on him were illustrated by his discovery that he netted less in the year in which he grossed $500,000 than in the year in which he grossed but $80,000. Another barrier in Mr. B's way was that he was barred from access to professional groups, and thereby missed the news that other contractors trade among themselves. Such talk very often has high commercial value. For instance, Mr. B lost out on a library branch job in the Negro district to a white contractor who got the job as a result of a social relationship.

Thus Mr. B has had to settle for limited horizons. He must pay higher interest for the money he can borrow, and he must make do with a lack of information vital to his business, and with a Negro community under severe economic and social strain.

Mr. B can get neither the financing nor the labor and managerial help he needs at competitive cost, and as he assesses his career in Birmingham, he has to compute the probable long-range effects the increasing emigration of Negroes from the city is likely to have on his future. The day may come when he himself will have to go with his family from his native city, where, in spite of all, his prospects and hopes once seemed so high.

Mr. B may stand as a symbol of a man who has risen above the culture of poverty just as his shrinking horizons may stand as a symbol of the deteriorating position of the class from which he sprung. As has been indicated earlier, the basic changes taking place in industry are resulting in the expulsion of the unskilled and semiskilled worker from their jobs with gathering speed, thus aggravating the problems of the poor.

To restate the problem very briefly, the vested interests are bending every effort to reduce their labor costs by introducing automatic machinery into their plants. To pay for the new and improved machinery, they have been successful in obtaining tax concessions from the Federal government for "modernization" of their equipment so that they can "compete more successfully." Whatever the exact sequence of justifications for these tax concessions, the result has been to hasten the departure of the worker from the plant; the result has been to contribute materially to the excess of unemployment that has been visible for a decade in the United States. The result has been to create a condition in which industrial overcapacity is a normal way of life, and in which underconsumption is a concept apparently alien to all but a few labor leaders and academic economists; to create, in short, a condition in which the poor are losing their relative economic power.

The end result of these efforts by American industry is that something very close to an enclave economy is being created. Manufacturing industry has progressively been lowering its break-even point so that steel, to take one example, found itself able in the 1960's to turn a profit operating at somewhere between 40 and 50 percent of capacity, and furthermore to fix for itself the approximate cruising speed of 70 percent of capacity. Not content with that, it directly began campaigning for advantages that would let this sluggish performance produce profits equivalent to that won when, in a more robust day, the industry was running at 94 percent of capacity. The goal, in real measure, was to build an enclave predicated on high unemployment and widespread nonconsumption in the lower economic strata.

The notion of an enclave—of a high wall that keeps those inside safe and those outside outside—is one to which I shall have reason to return. For the present, it will be enough to note in some detail that this wall has not only its economic but also its political aspects. In certain of these political aspects, the poor have made token breaches, and those through the agency of the Supreme Court.

· 4 ·

It would be a mistake to imagine that the obvious clash between the goals of the vested interests and the goals of the poor is something new. It is not new at all. It has been a continuing drama in the United States for a century at least, and it has been played out to a large degree in the various branches of the Federal

government. To trace one phase of that history briefly, it should
first be reiterated that its present outlines derive in large measure
from the collapse of the agricultural interests as prime influences
after the Civil War and the rapid rise of the manufacturing-finance
interests at the same time. There was a brief period in which the
Congress was firmly aligned with the Negro poor through the
power of the Radical Republicans. The Civil Rights Act of 1875,
the last broad attempt to establish civil equality for the Negroes,
provided for "the full and equal enjoyment of the accommoda-
tions, advantages, facilities and privileges of inns, public convey-
ances on land or water, theatres and other places of public amusement. . . ." However, the arrangement whereby Rutherford B.
Hayes won several blocs of Southern electoral votes the next year
and thereby became President brought the era of Federal control
of the South to an effective end. At the same time, the Republican
party became less intent on prosecuting the collapse of the southern agricultural interests than on meeting the needs of the rising
manufacturing-finance interests of the Northeast.

Meanwhile, the Fourteenth and Fifteenth Amendments had
been passed, and both promised to serve the interests of the Negroes. That promise has never been fulfilled. The Supreme Court,
in 1876, in *United States* v. *Cruikshank*, found that the Fourteenth
Amendment in particular "adds nothing to the rights of one citizen against another." It simply prohibited states from encroaching
on the rights of its citizens. Seven years later, in the Civil Rights
Cases, the Court added that the 1875 Civil Rights Act was therefore unconstitutional. The Fourteenth Amendment, Justice Brad-
ley pointed out, was "prohibitory upon the States" but not on
single citizens. The same year, the Court found that the Fifteenth
Amendment was equally subject to lawful evasion, and the Enforcement Act of 1870 that had assured the vote to Negroes was
found unconstitutional. Thus the way was open for states to con-
coct tests that do not ostensibly leave any particular group of
voters off the rolls but that in fact bar the black man from the
vote. A few years later (1896), the Court promulgated its famous
"separate but equal" doctrine, which provided virtual *carte*

blanche for segregation. (The spirit of that doctrine was successfully evaded in the South until the May decisions of 1954, after
which "separate but equal" attained universal support, to the extent of inspiring the more moderate of those states to spend considerable sums on Negro schools, hospitals, and other public facilities.)

When the Fourteenth Amendment was applied positively by
the Court, in 1905, it turned out that it had unsuspected utility.
It provided the basis for striking down a New York State law
limiting the workday. No such law could prevail, the Court said,
because it violated the protection of personal liberty provided for
by the Fourteenth Amendment. Furthermore, it put freedom of
contract under unconscionable limitations.

The unorganized poor, as typified by the Negroes, found themselves overmatched on every front. In 1909, however, a group of
whites and Negroes introduced the idea of organization to Negro
affairs with the founding of an obscure association whose purpose was the advancement of these poor. It would not be in-
accurate to say that the Establishment has provided constant and
considerable support for the activities of that association, the National Association for the Advancement of Colored People, almost
from its inception. The Organization, on the other hand, perhaps
less by design than by circumstance, has found itself aligned with
the opponents of the NAACP, and therein has been one of the
enduring sources of friction between Establishment and Organization, one of the very few instances in which they are arrayed
on distinctly opposite sides.

The NAACP turned to the law to redress the wrongs its constituents had endured. Turning to the law meant that the Supreme
Court would be a principal object of the association's activities
and that legal argument would be the means. Neither was likely
to produce quick results, and neither did produce quick results.
Nevertheless, by slow stages, the association brought restrictive
laws and constitutional doctrine itself under attack. The association set for itself the task of persuading the Supreme Court that
the apparatus of the Constitution had long enough served property interests and should now begin to serve other interests.

At first, the way was slow and uncertain. The Court had other dispositions. An early campaign that took up much of the NAACP's resources brought these organized poor into direct conflict with the commercial interests generally and with the real-estate interests specifically. Racially restrictive clauses in property contracts had been enforced by the court system for years. Beginning in 1918, and continuing until victory in 1948 (*Shelley* v. *Kraemer*) and confirmation of victory in 1953 (*Barrows* v. *Jackson*), the NAACP accomplished fundamental change in constitutional doctrine. Its battle on the issue of restrictive covenants could be summed up as the battle to end the narrow interpretation of the Constitution that for so many years had served the vested interests. The goal was nothing less than the conversion of the nation's legal scholarship from the attitude of a Schoolman examining a single filament to that of a Humanist concerned with the entire social fabric. In the *Barrows* v. *Jackson* case of 1953, the allies that the NAACP had against the National Association of Real Estate Boards and various neighborhood property-protection groups were the Federal government itself, Congregationalists and Unitarians (who argued the brotherhood of man), the AFL-CIO (protesting that housing discrimination nullified Negro economic gains won by collective bargaining), the American Civil Liberties Union (concerned for constitutional rights of individuals), and the American Association for the United Nations (worried about foreign relations).

The May Decisions of 1954 climaxed the drive of the NAACP for a remedy to what many considered the root of poverty, inferior education. The Court held unanimously in the series of cases involving public school segregation that "in the field of public education the doctrine of 'separate but equal' has no place. Separate educational facilities are inherently unequal."

The influence of that series of decisions on the Negro poor has been so widely noted and so meticulously chronicled that it requires nothing more than to note that the principle of organization in the years since 1954 has gained widening application in the black man's quest for equality. At the same time it has raised what may be a more important question: Will equality be good enough? That is to say, will equality now make up for centuries of inequality, or will something more like privilege be necessary to accomplish a broad and bona-fide restitution?

· 5 ·

Supreme Court victories are victories in abstraction. They are essentially meaningless until enforcement takes place, susceptible to endless evasion, subject even to functional nullification. Therefore the successes of the organized poor in the High Court should not be taken as a fair indication of their improved circumstances. While such victories no doubt prepare the way for eventual improvement, to date there is little evidence to support an optimistic view. For one thing, to accord the poor a full measure of citizenship involves what seems to the vested interests intolerably high costs. (The interests do not in any sense regard such costs as investments in a more prosperous future. They do not readily concede that reduced police protection per city block, for example, justifies the outlay of funds that could make such municipal cost-reduction possible.)

The vested interests, as I said above, snipe at the poor. So do the servants of those interests, the middle classes. Their continual tongue-clucking, in fact, is one of their most highly audible sounds. The subject is a broad one, and it is worthy of a chapter all to itself. A short preview here is in order, however, as it may help to establish the style of such sniping and tongue-clucking. It also illuminates the particular burden put onto the poor by their superiors in solvency.

The daily press is one means by which these sounds are transmitted, and one instance of particular notoriety involved the so-called Lady in Mink in New York City. As A. J. Liebling has observed, that particular case illustrates the "negative larceny" of those who assail social welfare outlays because they themselves do not enjoy immediate and visible benefit from them. By such assaults, they hope to keep taxes down.

The Lady in Mink was discovered living on relief as a result of the enterprise of the Scripps-Howard press, whose *World-Telegram* stirred up an investigation in 1947. Even the *New York Times* joined in: [5]

WOMAN IN MINK WITH $60,000
LIVED ON RELIEF IN A HOTEL,
INQUIRY BY STATE DISCLOSES

Thus read the three-column, page-one headline in the *Times* of October 30, 1947. The subheads went on to describe forty-two cases under scrutiny, including one that was a "front for bookies." As Liebling pointed out, the $60,000 figure was an elusive one. The woman in question had won a divorce settlement seven years before of $40,000, some $3,400 of which was never paid. Two years later, she had sold $20,000 in stocks. $40,000 plus $20,000 is $60,000. Or is it $56,600? Or $36,600? Was, then, the $60,000 "with" her? "As a matter of fact, Benjamin Fielding, the newly appointed Welfare Commissioner, announced a couple of days later that he considered the woman, as she had reported herself to be, too poor to support her child." [6] And the mink coat? As it developed, it was a mangy thing that an appraiser said might be worth $300. It was six or eight years old and had a torn lining.

The New York press nevertheless had had a virtual field day. The *World-Telegram* noted with pride that its exposure of waste in the administration of the welfare program had been confirmed by the state investigation. The probe—as the paper said in its October 29th headline—"Shows Welfare Dept. Pampered Chiselers in Luxury Hotels."

That investigation finally involved 37 families, or a total of about 120 people at a time when the city rolls listed about 230,000 people. It petered out inconclusively. (But again, in the spring of 1962, a similar campaign was under way with the strong backing of the *World-Telegram*. It had devoted its winter efforts, in a series of indignant articles, to war on taxi drivers for being larcenous, surly, and unreliable.)

In 1949 the labor-liberal *New York Post* reported that a new system of welfare administration had bogged down seriously, with the result that many of the destitute had to wait weeks for relief assistance. Applicants were coming in at the rate of 3,000 a week, but the understaffed Welfare Department could handle the applications only after a three-week to one-month delay. The law required each new applicant to be interviewed within forty-eight hours. It was a problem of major proportions. To the poor. As the "CBS Views the Press" program noted, ". . . where two years ago the papers hardly let an edition go by after the first mention in the *Telegram* before they were howling in concert after the relief scandal, it was different this time. Not a single newspaper bothered to follow the lead of the *Post*." [7]

Lest one dismiss these events as a result of a transitory concern for costs in a time of inflation, the case of the city manager of Newburgh, New York, should have dispelled such a notion. He devised a simple program in 1961 that among other things would have restricted or refused food doles to unmarried mothers and their children. Though his program ran into immediate difficulties with the state welfare authorities, he nevertheless provided an inspiration to many. The *Herald Tribune,* the *World-Telegram,* and the *Daily News,* all New York newspapers, mentioned the city manager as a worthy candidate for Vice-President of the United States, on a ticket headed by Senator Barry Goldwater. What everybody knew but hardly anyone said of the Newburgh scheme was that it was directed almost entirely at the Negro, and was in fact very nearly an open declaration of class war.

· 6 ·

What, then, may be said of the relationship of the poor, the vested interests, and the Establishment? That the poor have a job to do, if they can be set free to do it. That the vested interests, for whatever reason, find themselves arrayed in opposition to such liberation. That the Establishment shows what concern it safely can for the poor, but not enough to cause doubts as to its essential soundness, which is probably as it must be. Doubts could dis-establish it.

It has been a recurring theme of American history that when the nation has needed a job done it has attracted doers by appealing to their self-interest in the most overt manner possible: it has granted licenses to steal. Such licenses, collectively, have come under the more modern heading "incentive."

Such licenses built the railroads. They financed the Civil War. They helped manufacturing industry develop its aggregate plant. They galvanized industry during two World Wars and during the Korea episode. In more recent times they assured the building and emplacement of defensive rocketry. (To be specific, the railroads won millions of acres of land grants and outright capital gifts. The Civil War financier Jay Cooke was given a monopoly in the sale of government bonds. From the early nineteenth century, the tariff aided manufacturing by protecting it against foreign competition on the one hand, and on the other, by allowing the manufacturer to sell his product dear to the farmer but to buy the farmer's product cheap in return. In wartime, industry has won special tax concessions—so-called certificates of necessity and rapid depreciation write-offs—that have had the effect of lowering taxes and of enhancing capital equity. Lastly, the modern defense contractors enjoy their license by means of "pyramiding" profits through the "tier" system of defense contracting.)

Given the demonstrable efficiency of such licensing in the past, to what good use could it be put today? What is the most pressing material need of this nation? An answer unexceptionable to almost any respondent would be "greater economic growth." Such growth, in turn, will most certainly be won by what the economists call high effective demand, that is, by hyperconsumption. Who, then, have the best credentials for this sort of activity? Those who, so far, have consumed least—the poor. And what means come most ready to hand to get these potential doers to do? The tried and effective means of providing privilege under government auspices. To provide the poor, in less elevated language, with their own overdue license for socially useful theft.

Vested Interests

and Government

⎍⎍⎍

It is not exaggeration to say that vested interests, and specifically the commercial, financial, and manufacturing interests, caused Federal government in this nation in the first place. Nor does it do any violence to truth to say that government has with some consistency answered the needs of these interests ever since, even to the detriment of other interests. But that is perhaps just another way of saying that the United States is an industrial nation.

At the outset, the Constitution itself was a creation of the city merchants, the early bankers, and the mechanical gentry. Circulating property, as opposed to fixed, landed property, was the common strand that united the advocates of a strong Federal government. The "personalty" (that is, liquid wealth) holders arrayed themselves against the "realty" (that is, illiquid wealth) holders, and carried the day for the Constitution.

It need hardly be said that it was a fortunate turn of events that brought the states together; but at the same time it should be said that their unity was cemented by an order of preferment that did not remain acceptable to all the states. The secession of the South in large measure was an agrarian revolt against the economic tyranny of the industrial interests—and from the stand-point of the South it was indeed tyranny. When Robert Toombs took the floor in the Georgia Legislature on November 13, 1860, to urge the South to act, he summed up this one important aspect of the South's position:

The instant the Government was organized, at the very first Congress, the Northern States evinced a general desire and purpose to use it for their own benefit, to pervert its powers for sectional advantage, and they have steadily pursued that policy to this day. They demanded a monopoly of the business of ship-building, and got a prohibition against the sale of foreign ships to citizens of the United States, which exists to this day.

They demanded a monopoly of the coasting trade, in order to get higher freights than they could get in open competition with the carriers of the world. Congress gave it to them, and they yet hold this monopoly. . . .

The North, at the very first Congress, demanded and received bounties under the name of protection, for every trade, craft, and calling which they pursue, and there is not an artisan in brass, or iron, or wood, or weaver, or spinner in wool or cotton, or a calico-maker, or iron-master, or a coal-owner, in all the Northern or Middle States, who has not received what he calls the protection of his government on his industry to the extent of from fifteen to two hundred percent from the year 1791 to this day. They will not strike a blow, or stretch a muscle, without bounties from the government. No wonder they cry aloud for the glorious Union. . . . By it they got their wealth; by it they levy tribute on honest labor. . . .[1]

The historian Charles A. Beard established in *An Economic Interpretation of the Constitution of the United States* that without a determined minority of creditors, entrepreneurs, merchants, and financiers, ratification would have been doubtful if not impossible, and that opponents of ratification were basically the smallholding agrarian elements. At the outset, then, in some degree the towns prevailed over the farms, the tidewater over the uplands, the middle and northern states over the South, manufacturing-finance over agriculture.

No less an observer than the fourth Chief Justice, John Marshall, in his *Life of Washington,* described this enduring conflict; he not only described it, he clothed the industrial interests with the cloak of moral refulgence that has proved such a durable and effective raiment ever since. On the one side of the ratification debate, Marshall noted, were those who "struggled with unabated zeal for the exact observance of public and private engagements" —that is, for the prompt and full payment of debts. "By those belonging [to that side], the faith of a nation or of a private man was deemed a sacred pledge, the violation of which was equally forbidden by the principles of moral justice and sound policy." These Federalists, as Marshall said, saw the remedy for individual distress "only [in] . . . industry and frugality, not by a relaxation of the laws or by a sacrifice of the rights of others. They were consequently the uniform friends of a regular administration of justice, and of a vigorous course of taxation which would enable the state to comply with its engagements."

"The other party," Marshall noted, set "a more indulgent course. Viewing with extreme tenderness the case of the debtor, their efforts were unceasingly directed to his relief. To exact a faithful compliance with contracts was, in their opinion, a harsh measure which the people would not bear. They were uniformly in favor of relaxing the administration of justice, of affording facilities for the payment of debts, or of suspending their collection, and of remitting taxes." [2]

These vignettes of opposed points of view might stand with fair accuracy for the interests, respectively, of what we now call producers and consumers, creditors and debtors, investors and workers, or even Republicans and Democrats.

From the beginning, then, the idea of industrial preferment has been an important element of the national consensus; but always it has been at least partially balanced and challenged by the anti-industrial view. This last has rarely been respectable, and has enjoyed widespread support only during the Progressive Era and the New Deal within the past hundred years.

The nation has had its balance to strike between the ideal and the expedient, between democratic freedom and economic freedom. The tension between these opposed views shows no sign of abating, but rather of increasing.

To recapitulate, to build a nation of first importance meant to build a commercial nation and to convert it to a manufacturing nation. Destiny lay clearly with circulating, not stationary, property. Government solicitude, therefore, necessarily tended toward the essential instrument of circulating property, money.

These material mandates were answered at a cost—the cost of what may be loosely termed economic injustice. But, as Lord Russell has written, "To some extent, civilization is furthered by social injustice. This fact is the basis of what is most respectable in conservatism." [3]

It may be observed that economic justice has hitherto been a luxury more costly than whatever material returns it might make. There are those to argue that it is no longer a luxury but is more like a necessity.

· 1 ·

How has the balance between contending interests been struck? How was the economic pecking order fixed? To sum up briefly, a short catalog of certain economic legislation is in order here.

The first great piece of economic legislation, as the above passages indicate, was the Constitution itself, and the First Article specifically (particularly Sections 8, 9, and 10.)

The next major legislation favoring the emergent manufacturing interests was the Tariff of 1789, which was followed by other tariff legislation in 1816, 1824, 1828, 1832, 1842, 1861, and 1894. Up and up was the direction of the protective wall that insulated manufacturing interests from overseas competition and conferred particular advantages on manufacturing-finance in general, while causing agricultural interests extreme discomfort. The American System, as its advocates called it, aimed to create a self-sufficient industrial nation by means of a "territorial division of labor." The South and the West were to be the growers of food, the choppers of wood, the diggers of ore for the East; the East was to be the banker and manufacturer, the clerk and distributor, the ultimate organizer and master. It was not exactly a program to inspire mutual trust.

The first protective tariff of modern times, the Act of March 2, 1861, provided a base on which, by amendment, the average rate of duty on listed commodities grew to more than 45 percent by 1864. The figure had fallen somewhat by the end of the century, only to be raised again, by the Payne-Aldrich Tariff of 1909, to more than 40 percent. Under Woodrow Wilson, the Underwood Tariff of 1913 reduced the general average by more than 10 percent. But in 1930, up it went again, under the provisions of the Smoot-Hawley Act, called by its critics, "a virtual declaration of economic war by the United States on the rest of the world."

In more recent years the tariff has fallen considerably, and it again became a key issue in 1962, as President Kennedy sought and won greater power to negotiate reductions with foreign powers.

The general effect of the tariff throughout its history has been to permit American manufacturing industry to prosper by insulation from foreign competition. The tariff secured to domestic industry the largest of markets, the market of the United States itself. It has been in a real sense a tax on the South and the West and a subsidy for the East. It kept the price of manufactured goods high, while the price of farm goods remained low; it has caused unfavorable terms of trade for the farmers—they sold cheap but bought dear. It was what rankled Mr. Toombs in the Georgia Legislature in 1860, and it was what showed in clearer measure than almost anything else the uniform deference of Federal government for the prime vested interests.

As Woodrow Wilson told the Congress in his Tariff Reform Message of April 8, 1913:

For a long time—a time so long that the men now active in public policy hardly remember the conditions that preceded it—we have sought in our tariff schedules to give each group of manufacturers or producers what they themselves thought that they needed in order to maintain a practically exclusive market as against the rest of the world. Consciously or unconsciously, we have built up a set of privileges and exemptions from competition behind which it was easy by any, even the crudest, forms of combination to organize monopoly; until at last nothing is normal, nothing is obliged to stand the tests of efficiency and economy, in our world of big business, but everything thrives by concerted arrangement. Only new principles of action will save us from a final hard crystallization of monopoly and a complete loss of the influences that quicken enterprise and keep independent energy alive. . . .[4]

In so-called internal improvements, the Federal government was somewhat laggard, leaving the states for the most part to look to their own turnpike and canal development in the early nineteenth century. Those improvements enhanced land values immediately, and thus no doubt they proved of secondary allurement to the manufacturing-finance interests. But with the 1862 Pacific Railway Act, the Federal government set a pattern of subsidy that has since reached immense proportions. Over 180 million acres of land and more than $60 million in loans at favorable terms went to railroad entrepreneurs between 1862 and 1873 alone. It has been estimated that a total of over $1.2 billion went to the railroads to promote construction. (I shall return presently to the subject of subsidies.)

In 1864 the Contract Labor Law came into being. It didn't exactly reestablish the slavery that had been abolished only the year before, but it did provide manufacturing industry with hundreds of thousands of immigrant workers at low enough cost to keep wage rates depressed. The law permitted industrial agents to bring in groups of laborers under contract, one standard provision of which was that wages could not rise above the contracted figure for at least a year.

The influence of the industrial interests was not merely affirmative. In fact, these interests quite often preferred to exert negative influence in securing the suppression of laws they disliked. The Interstate Commerce Act of 1887 provides an example of this negative influence exerted through the judiciary. The Act sought to end the abuses whereby railroads kicked back to favored industrial customers a part of their freight fares. (There was apparently something of a ping-pong effect in these clandestine transactions. That is to say, a kickback got a re-kickback, and perhaps a re-re-kickback between particularly secretive officers of the lines and corporations themselves.) The courts quickly weakened the law by establishing crippling exceptions, and it took three more tries by legislation—1906, 1910, and 1913—to accomplish the modest goal of minimum government control over rates and kickback practices.

The Sherman Antitrust Act of 1890 also proved a toothless instrument under the courts' interpretation. In fact, the Sherman Act had greater utility against labor unionism than it ever had against concentrated manufacturing power. A long list of successor legislation was required to effect the goal of real restriction on concentrated industry and parallel establishment of the rights of labor in bargaining with management. The Clayton Act of 1914 made the first step, but the additional sanctions of the Norris–La Guardia Act and the Wagner Act, both New Deal laws, were needed to accomplish what the Sherman Act started out forty-five years earlier to do.

Not until the Progressive Era did government become less passive before the concerted demands of the industrial interests. Although much has been made of the apparent indifference of Congress to the famous memorandum "On Manufactures," set forth by Alexander Hamilton in 1791, Hamilton set the domestic policy for the next hundred years. Hamilton's program was to promote the division of labor, extend the use of machinery, expand employment among those who had not hitherto labored, promote immigration, promote "greater scope for the diversity of talents and dispositions," open new fields for industrial enterprise, create "in some instances" and secure "in all" a "more certain and steady demand for the surplus produce of the soil." What means to those ends? High tariffs and high bounties. Subsidies followed by more subsidies, to put the matter in plainer language. And the agricultural response? Civil War at one stage; domestic agitation at other stages; frustration at almost all stages: the Populists urged farmers to "raise less wheat and more hell."

As for the more recent history of this continuing struggle for comparative advantage, it can best be pursued under the heading of taxation, and specifically of income taxation. Before turning to an examination of the *indirect* government subsidies at work in income taxation, however, this is the place for the modern history of *direct* government subsidies to the various interests.

· 2 ·

The Federal government's direct subsidy payments to American business and agriculture amounted to $7.5 billion in 1960. Subsidy payments took about 10 percent of the Federal budget in that year and have done so in succeeding years, also. In the 1950–1961 period, almost $60 billion was paid to various groups and corporations. In that same period, according to a special study undertaken by the Joint Economic Committee of the Congress,[5] the annual rate of payment rose from $1.9 billion to $7.5 billion, or about 400 percent.

Coupling these direct subsidies with the indirect subsidies * compels some qualification to the definition of "free enterprise." Not only are these benefits pervasive now; they always have been. They have been operative in greater or lesser degree to protect the industrial interests from the unsettling effects of bona fide economic freedom, while securing to these same interests the good effects of such freedom. "The subsidy," as the House Committee on Agriculture has observed, "is the oldest economic principle written into the laws of the United States."

In direct subsidization, agriculture benefits most. It is the recipient of a kind of massive consolation prize. Having long since

* Protective tariffs, accelerated tax write-offs, special depreciation tax rules, depletion allowances, non-interest-bearing government deposits in private banks, and the myriad tax loopholes by which corporations and the affluent benefit.

faded to tertiary importance, this erstwhile prime vested interest received $3.5 billion in 1960. Over the eleven-year period covered by the congressional study, agriculture received a total of $22.4 billion, or nearly 40 percent of the total of direct subsidy. Other beneficiaries were business (about $12 billion—21 percent of the total) and labor ($3.7 billion—6 percent); the remaining 33 percent proved difficult to allocate precisely. It went to "national defense" purposes such as food and metals stockpiling, hospital construction grants-in-aid, and merchant-shipping subsidies.

It has been estimated that 25 percent of the recipients of agricultural subsidies receive about 75 percent of the total. Herein lies an ironic truth: this 25 percent, these large-scale farms, are not manned by farmers in the traditional mold, but are instead large corporations running what have been called "factories in the field." In this sense, to identify these subsidy payments in a category distinct from the "business" classification is misleading. Those who least need agricultural subsidies get the most, and they are not farmers; they are agricultural corporations.

The Post Office deficit is concentrated in second-class mail. Thus it represents a sizable subsidy for magazines and newspapers; the bigger the circulation, the bigger the subsidy. Third-class mail rates provide a subsidy to book publishers directly and to authors indirectly. (By keeping the cost of book postage low, this subsidy helps keep prices down, and thereby increases sales and royalties.) Fourth-class mail confers benefits on junk-mail disseminators, who are usually large-scale advertisers and manufacturers. First-class mail pays its way. Business mail does not. In the eleven-year period, $6.5 billion in such subsidies went mostly to business and to producers, not to consumers.

Shipbuilders have enjoyed large-scale subsidies, as have ship operators, the justification being national defense. Airlines have also enjoyed huge subsidies and so have the railroads. Truckers, too, enjoy a quiet subsidy through Federal support of the highway program—again sanctioned by national defense.

Business aids and special services—statistics gathering, economic forecasting, census marketing reports, and the like—represent another important subsidy of great long-range value to industry.

The stockpiling of strategic materials by various government agencies through long-term purchase contracts at favorable terms to producers has provided another subsidy, particularly to the nonferrous metals companies and in lesser degree to most metal manufacturers. The opium, duck-feathers, and castor-oil interests also have benefited under this particular subsidy.

Agricultural subsidies, in conclusion, have received particular notoriety because, unlike most straight business subsidies, they represent funds flowing out of the Federal fisc, whereas the other subsidies more typically represent money not paid to government. To the degree that such subsidies enhance productive capacity without compensatory concern for expanding consumptive abilities, they merely aggravate the widening gap between our powers to produce and our powers to consume. Thereby they create the need for still more subsidies, especially for those who have to do their jobs better, the consumers.

· 3 ·

Consider the enormous importance of the income tax to the economic pecking order. Here is the battlefield of the rich and the poor. Here is the focal point of the constant struggles for material supremacy among various factions.

The Internal Revenue Code is a complicated document. It is gray, hefty, and virtually unreadable. It is 1,148 pages long. I open it, at random, to page 341, on the bottom half of which this passage appears (under the heading, "Sec. 871, Tax on Nonresident Alien Individuals"):

(b) NO UNITED STATES BUSINESS AND GROSS INCOME OF MORE THAN $15,400.—A nonresident alien individual not engaged in trade or business within the United States shall be taxable without regard to subsection (a) if during the taxable year the sum of the aggregate amount received from the sources specified in subsection (a) (1), plus the amount by which gains from sales or exchanges of capital assets exceed losses from such sales or exchanges (determined in accordance with subsection (*a*) (2)) is more than $15,400, except that—

(1) the gross income shall include only income from sources specified in subsection (*a*) (1) plus any gain (to the extent provided in subchapter P; sec. 1201 and following, related to capital gains and losses) from a sale or exchange of a capital asset if such gain would be taken into account were the tax being determined under subsection (*a*) (2);

(2) the deductions (other than the deduction for charitable contributions and gifts provided in section 873 (*c*)) shall be allowed only if and to the extent that they are properly allocable to the gross income from the sources specified in subsection (*a*), except that any loss from the sale or exchange of a capital asset shall be allowed (to the extent provided in subchapter P without the benefit of the capital loss carryover provided in section 1212) if such loss would be taken into account were the tax being determined under subsection (*a*) (2).

If (without regard to this sentence) the amount of the taxes imposed in the case of such an individual under section 1 or under section 1201 (*b*), minus the sum of the credits under sections 34 and 35, is an amount less than 30 percent of the sum of—(A) the aggregate amount received from the source specified in subsection (*a*) (1), plus

Here, at last, the page comes to an end. The fusillade of exceptions, emendations, qualifications, and cross-references keeps the nonexpert from poaching on the expert's preserve. It also does a great deal more than that.

The language of "aggregate," "subsection," "in accordance," "relating to," "being determined under," "properly allocable," and "sources specified," is not the language of directness. Each sentence seems to have many escape hatches built into it. A boat of similar construction would no doubt sink directly on hitting the water, which is pretty much what has happened to the progressive income tax.

· 4 ·

The first American income tax was imposed under Civil War pressure in 1861. It was mildly progressive, not widely applicable, and short-lived. It lapsed in 1872, and for more than twenty years it seemed to be dead. It didn't come back until 1894, and then its reappearance was quite brief. The Supreme Court found it unconstitutional. The Court had guidance from the Honorable Joseph A. Choate, attorney for John D. Rockefeller. It was Choate who pointed out to the justices what a veritable fount of iniquity the law was.

Choate's language and that of his associates is worthy of note for what it conveys of the horror that the idea of progressive taxation aroused in many of the best circles.* Mr. Choate, in his 1895 argument before the High Court, was worried about communism. "Communistic in its purpose and tendencies," he said of the tax law. "There is protection [against such encroachments on property rights] now or never." Once the principle is accepted "it will be impossible to take any backward step." Mr. Choate proved an unreliable prophet.

Mr. W. D. Guthrie, who was the attorney for the principal,† took a more analytical tack: "It is the fundamental rule of all taxation that there shall be equality of burden among those of the same class," he said. "We are here to conclude that Congress cannot sacrifice one—the lowliest or the richest—for the benefit of others."

A third member of the team opposing the tax in this case was a former Senator from Vermont, George Edmunds. Said he:

This [tax law] would be followed by further invasions of private and property rights, as one vice follows another, and very soon we should

* It may not dissipate the suspense too much to inject here a sample of the contemporary horrification felt by income-tax opponents. Mr. Edward V. Rickenbacker, of Eastern Airlines, busied himself in the early 1960's urging repeal of "the cancerous Sixteenth Amendment," that is, the amendment to the Constitution by which the American people in 1913 signaled their approval of the principle of a progressive tax. Mr. Rickenbacker's views on an alternate source of Eastern Airline's large government subsidy were not fully developed, nor were his ideas on the alternate source of Federal-aid funds for airport development. But at bottom he no doubt saw these as mere matters of accounting, not political philosophy.

† The case bore the formal title *Pollock* v. *Farmers' Loan and Trust Company.* Farmers' Loan, the "defendant," took a discreet dive, and Pollock (Pollock in body, Rockefeller in spirit) emerged the victor.

have, possibly, only one per cent of the people paying the taxes, and finally a provision that only the twenty people who have the greatest estate should bear the whole taxation, and after that communism, anarchy, and then, the ever following despotism.

Yes, said Justice Field in his opinion concurring with the majority, "The present assault upon capital is but the beginning. It will be but the stepping stone to others, larger and more sweeping, till our political contests will become a war of the poor against the rich; a war constantly growing in intensity and bitterness."

The agricultural interests were not disposed to take the decision equably, nor was labor. William Jennings Bryan and the Populists began in earnest preaching for an income tax, for relief from the overwhelming privileges enjoyed by industrial wealth. The Progressive wing of the Republican party, also urged on by agricultural voters, began pressing for the same thing.

In 1907—these things take time—Theodore Roosevelt told Congress that such a tax was desirable to help bridge the growing chasm between rich and poor. William Howard Taft, the 1908 Republican candidate, found the force of public opinion on the issue so pronounced that he, too, advocated such a tax, and thereby neutralized one of his opponent's major issues. After those elections, Congress passed an income-tax bill that went out to the states for ratification as a constitutional amendment. Five years later, 1913, it became the Sixteenth Amendment—the belated response to the 1895 victory by tax opponents before the Supreme Court. The new amendment provided a base from which the returning Democrats under Woodrow Wilson went on to institute wide fiscal reforms.

The tax was a part of the Constitution. From then on, if you earned more, you paid more absolutely *and* relatively. Or did you? For a time, it looked as if you did.

· 5 ·

With the coming of the First World War, the need for additional revenue drove the income-tax rates upward. By 1918 the top brackets were paying up to 65 percent of their incomes in taxes. Later loopholes would do much to lighten the burden, but they hadn't been invented. That, too, would take time.

Normalcy. "Get government out of business." "Give enterprise its head." "Loosen the shackles on initiative." "Restore incentives." "Lift the crushing load of taxation." Those were the slogans of the age. Words of self-evident common sense to their authors, of oink-and-grunt to their critics. For observers of the ensuing enshrinement of business in Washington, all slogans seemed to reduce themselves to unity: "Get business into Government."

The new President, Warren Harding, asked Congress to reduce taxes, particularly in the upper brackets. Congress proved uncooperative. The Internal Revenue Code as amended in 1921 retained a 50 percent rate on the highest brackets; but even that was something. The top rate had been 77 percent. At this point, special treatment of capital gains first became legitimate.

Secretary of the Treasury Andrew Mellon was particularly unhappy with congressional obtuseness. In fact, so acute was his sense of injustice that he felt a book growing within him. It emerged in 1924 under the title: *Taxation: The People's Business.* Its message was simply that "the prosperity of the middle and lower classes depend[s] upon the good fortunes and the light taxes of the rich." By that beacon Mr. Mellon navigated, and in its steadfast pursuit came October 29, 1929; but that gets ahead of the story.

The early 1920's saw the initial plans laid for massive administrative tax reductions for upper-bracket earners. The unhappy Harding, dead in 1923, was succeeded by the purse-mouthed Calvin Coolidge, who paid out his words as if each were a debit on funded capital. Said Coolidge, "This is a business country . . . and it wants a business government." Mellon added his refinement: "The Government is just a business and can and should be run on business principles." Let there be government economy and efficiency. Let us balance the budget and pay off the national debt. But first, a thought for our sponsors. A thought for tax reform.

Mellon gazed anew on the tax rates and found them bad. It was an intolerable practice to force a man making $1 million a year to pay almost $300,000 in income tax. No, Mellon reflected, it wasn't fair. No one should have to pay more than 25 percent. Payments higher than that strained business confidence, drained incentive, chained creative forces. Said Mellon: "Any one at all in touch with affairs knows of his own knowledge of buildings which have not been built, of businesses which have not been started, and of new projects which have been abandoned, all for one reason—high surtaxes. . . . The spirit of initiative may still be there, but the present high surtaxes are driving it into idleness. America will become a nation of followers, not leaders." [6]

Under Mellon's pleading, and impelled by the spirit of the times, the tax rates dropped bit by bit. Congress slowed the trend somewhat; but for those tactics Mellon had countertactics. During his first eight years in office, the Treasury refunded $3.5 billion, in cash and credits, to wealthy taxpayers generally and also to big contributors to the Republican party. (Each of the seventeen men who gave more than $10,000 to the 1930 party campaign chest received adjustments in his taxes under Mellon's soothing program.) [7]

As Louis Eisenstein has written:

After a few frustrating experiences Mellon finally had his way with the income tax. He was not entirely successful with the estate tax, but in the end he did fairly well. . . . Between 1925 and 1932 the highest rate of income tax was 25 per cent. It did not apply until income exceeded $100,000. In the same period the highest rate of estate tax was 20 per cent. It did not apply until an estate exceeded $10 million. At no time since have the income and estate taxes been so pleasantly low as in the Mellon era.[8]

Mellon was looking out for his own interests, as well. The Mellon family companies enjoyed tax credits of several million dollars, Congressman John Nance Garner, of Texas, discovered. And somewhat later the *New Republic* revealed that at the same time, Mellon was doing what he could to reduce still further his personal taxes. The Commissioner of Revenue wrote to the Secretary: "Pursuant to your request for a memorandum setting forth various ways by which an individual may legally avoid tax, I am pleased to submit the following." Of the ten methods suggested, Mellon used five, including the sale of good securities under unfavorable terms to other family members, thus creating a "loss" for tax purposes.

It was a raucous feast—for some. Between 1919 and 1929 each worker in manufacturing industry increased his output 43 percent, without any comparable rise in wages. Costs of manufacture consequently went down; profits went up. Taxes were going down, too, as indicated above. Thus a great amount of money under the control of a very few went looking for something to do. Investment soared. Production of capital goods—that is, machinery, plant buildings, and the like—rose more than 6 percent a year. But purchases of the products of those machines and those factories by consumers rose at less than 3 percent a year. Thus what seemed to be general prosperity was in large measure an uneven prosperity in which there was an excess of liquid funds in the hands of the very rich at the same time that the consuming potential of the poor was enjoying no compensating growth. Investors consequently verged into an orgy of speculation of such proportions and audibility that hundreds of thousands of plain Americans joined in the fun. Sooner or later it would be apparent that an excess of investment money without consumption money to keep it honestly engaged will get itself into mischief.

When, as happened in the Mellon Era, an excess of capital rapidly comes into being, it apparently loses the esteem accorded to that which is scarce. Let the money come too easily, and the precaution motive, the evidence suggests, weakens and atrophies. For want of an object worthy of reverence, precaution becomes speculation in which essentially unreal values take on the importance of real values. In six months paper profits in the stock market soared by $20 billion. In three months they dropped $74 billion. Speculation went back to precaution, jaunty optimism to pervasive, impenetrable pessimism. And so in October, 1929, the stock market crashed.

Thus the golden age of tax reduction came to a sour halt. It would be nearly twenty years before oink-and-grunt would again be a respectable sound to the ears of a nation and its Congress.

· 6 ·

In the interval, fundamental changes took place in the means by which the economy creates and distributes its wealth. Under President Franklin D. Roosevelt, the investment tasks became more and more a matter of Federal responsibility. That is not to say that all investment became government investment, but rather that the Federal government assumed suzerainty over private investment—haltingly at first, and with bad economic effects. Unequivocally at last, and with excellent economic effects. As the economic historian Ross Robertson has written:

The return of something like genuine prosperity in 1940 led a majority of the electorate to give the New Deal credit for escape from mass unemployment and faltering production. There is no question that a program of positive action—any action—was sufficient to bring about an upturn in 1933 and 1934. From 1935 on, however, it became pretty clear that output and incomes were rising because of net income injections by the government. Had these income-increasing injections been made more vigorously, in spite of fears of a rising national debt shared by most conservatives, the American economy would doubtless have bounded ahead much sooner.[9]

It is a melancholy truth that the public consensus or the residual conservatism of the New Deal itself required a better justification for government investment than mere recovery. It needed war to make recovery possible.

However that may be, the subject of most immediate interest remains the income tax, and to that subject I return. In 1932, after enough time had elapsed to prove that the Depression would not cure itself, the Congress raised income taxes, lowered exemptions, and thereby restored some progressive features to the tax. It fell somewhat more heavily on the rich than on the poor—or would have, if evasion hadn't become so widespread in the upper brackets.

In 1934 revenues were falling drastically. To counteract the dwindling collections, the top surtax rate was raised from 55 percent to 59 percent. At about the same time, the Congress gave some attention to to corporate income taxes, also. In 1935 surtaxes on profits were increased. Meanwhile, the manufacturing interests began to withhold a sizable portion of dividends in hopes of thereby helping large stockholders avoid taxation of these undistributed profits (at least until such time as a more sympathetic Congress might come along to lighten the burdens on the rich). But the President and the Congress had other ideas.

Taxes were still not hitting where the new Administration wanted them to hit. Despite the increased rates, the general counsel of the Internal Revenue Bureau told the Senate Finance Committee in the late summer of 1935 that there had been a "steady drift toward a heavier burden upon the consumer and a lighter burden upon those classes which we rate as being able to pay." Figures from 1933, the counsel said, showed that almost 60 percent of Federal revenues came from taxes based on consumption, only about 40 percent from taxes based on production—income, estate, excess-profit, and capital-stock taxes, specifically. Even then, at the pit of the Depression, the doctrine of "ability to pay" suffered virtual neglect, while the "trickle-down" doctrine maintained its primacy.*

The heated public debate over these opposed doctrines brought forth a luxuriance of phrasing that would have made Joseph Choate feel vindicated. The "ability to pay" doctrine, William Randolph Hearst said, "is essentially communism." It was, as many other highly educated men said, a penalty on success; it

* "Ability to pay" is the doctrine that if you make more you ought to pay more in taxes, proportionately and absolutely. "Trickle-down" is the opposed doctrine so clearly expressed by Secretary Mellon: Take care of the rich and everything else will be all right; or, to put it in its more sophisticated modern guise: Make America safer for investment capital.

was even expropriation of private property without just compensation. Taxes should produce revenue first and only, said the "trickle-down" school; taxes should not seek to change social and economic realities.

To these charges there would be good enough answers, including an answer from the architect of the New Era himself, Herbert Hoover. "To those who believe taxes should not be designed to promote economic or social objectives," said Hoover, "I would remark that this Republic has been doing it ever since the first tax bill was signed by George Washington." [10]

But 1935, as events proved, was not to be the year in which the doctrine of "ability to pay" would result in legislation with teeth. The House was willing but the Senate was not. And thus, what began as an attempt to redistribute income became instead a measure to raise revenue—two objectives that are often incompatible, the evidence suggests. "What was significant," Arthur M. Schlesinger, Jr., has observed, "was not the [1935 tax] bill but the philosophy behind it." [11]

The year 1936 was an election year—not one in which to risk the extreme bitterness of higher surtaxes on upper-bracket incomes, the Administration decided. Instead, the problem of undistributed corporation profits loomed large. This huge pool of corporate savings was acting the part of a depressant on the economy. It was estimated that as much as $4.5 billion of such business income had been withheld in 1936, at a loss of revenue to the Federal government of $1.3 billion. The government response was an increase in the tax rate to as much as 75 percent on such undistributed profits. President Roosevelt went on to win the election that November with an unprecedented surplus of popular votes.

The manufacturing interests were not at all happy with the 1936 tax law, or with the 1936 election, or with their prospects. They were particularly distraught over the undistributed profits levies. Meanwhile, the liberalized Supreme Court made 1937 a year of terrors for business, and on top of that, the Administration cut back its spending. "Business confidence," the elusive essence of prosperity, seeped away. Capital investment slumped, in sympathy it seemed. In 1937–1938, business slowed perceptibly. Unemployment increased. A depression within a depression was getting under way. No word seemed right for such a phenomenon until "recession" was born to the unwilling parents, government and industry.

Congress got the message. The next year, 1939, it obliged by bringing the undistributed-profits tax to an end effective with the 1940 tax year.

The war came then, and with it a series of huge national deficits and Federal investments—in 1941–1942, $19 billion; 1942–1943, $54 billion; 1943–1944, $46 billion; 1944–1945, $45 billion. In those four years, Gross National Product doubled and unemployment dropped to the vanishing point. Meanwhile, income tax rates rose and deductions fell. The surcharge reached 94 percent, its highest point in history. Pay-as-you-go withholding came in during 1943. Excess-profits taxes increased. Progression in the rates never seemed more pronounced. I say *seemed* because there were loopholes of great magnitude. For one example, "certificates of necessity" were pieces of paper authorizing factories to write off quickly the cost of facilities expanded or modernized for war production. Thus there was a huge accumulation of capital that built up rapidly but that went untaxed, because by such certificates, and apparently only by such certificates, industry could expand quickly enough to meet a nation's need under favorable-enough conditions of taxation to meet its own peculiar needs.

· 7 ·

It was time for a change in the first postwar election, and change is what the United States got. It got its first Republican Congress in nearly twenty years. The Eightieth Congress was not a "do-nothing" Congress as President Truman charged. That Congress did do a great deal for upper-bracket income earners. A crowning innovation of that Congress was authorization by law (in 1948) of a device called "income splitting" by which a husband and wife are permitted to pay taxes as if each earned half of the total income. Like most artifices by which tax relief is granted to the wealthy, this one takes place with no outward disturbance of the surtax figures that stand there each April 15th to remind us one and all how demanding is the income tax on those in the upper brackets. Anyone can see for himself that 91 percent figure and can shudder in sympathetic appreciation of the burdens falling on the poor rich.

This innovation, despite its bland exterior, was a new way to reduce the levy on high-income earners. The Treasury has pointed out that 97 percent of the benefits of this new device have applied to just 5 percent of the beneficiaries. As one tax attorney has written:

. . . income splitting evinces no interest whatever in the household expenses of married couples with incomes of $2,000 or less, after exemptions. They are taxed at the same rate as single people. Over 50 percent of the married couples filing taxable joint returns fall within this lowly category. The substantial beneficiaries in income splitting are concentrated at the upper levels. At the same time the over-all revenue loss is now [1961] about $4 billion a year.[12]

The identity of interests between high-income earners and the corporations has been more firmly cemented than ever, since the Eightieth Congress set the tone for postwar rewriting of the income-tax laws. The technical details of this new development are necessarily dull, because these loopholes stand a greater chance of surviving unnoticed if they are couched in confusing, sleep-inducing prose. I shall attempt an exploration of these details below. Just now, to conclude this historical narrative, it will suffice to say that Korea brought higher surtaxes; but it also brought administrative tax relief for the rich by means of certificates of necessity for industrial modernization and expansion, to the enormous benefit of common-stock values, and therefore to the benefit of the rich by the capital gains thus accruing to them.

After Korea, the Eisenhower Administration urged, and Congress passed, a new tax law that once again conferred large advantages on the corporations and therefore on the high-bracket taxpayers. In place of the no-longer tenable certificates of necessity (the war was over), more liberal depreciation regulations were instituted. Again, the rich reaped large rewards through the rapid growth of corporate capital reflected in rising stock prices.

· 8 ·

In the course of gathering the materials for this chapter, I made an informal poll among my acquaintances in the higher income brackets. None of them is in the uncomfortable position of depending solely on an employer for income. Dividends, interest, rent, and entrepreneurial income help them make ends meet. Of the score of people I questioned, only one could make a fair estimate of the average amount of income tax, in percentage, paid by a couple filing as such and enjoying an annual income of $1 million. One of my friends, who enjoys a substantial annual income from tax-free municipal bond interest, estimated 90 percent. Another, somewhat less solvent, estimated 45 percent. Other estimates ranged from 65 to 75 percent, with one exception. The exceptional estimate was 30 percent, and it came from a young entrepreneur with substantial capital. This last estimate was the most nearly correct one. The answer is about 24 percent, according to Treasury figures. In fact, that has been the average effective rate of payment, which means half of the million-dollar-a-year couples pay less than that. Yet so strong is the common impression of extremely high tax rates for high-income earners, that even those who know very well that they pay little consider themselves exceptionally fortunate in having good tax advisers. They apparently don't believe that most of their solvent friends are equally successful in avoiding high tax payments. Or if they do believe, they are accomplished Pharisees, and say they don't.

The common definition of "income" is perhaps one source of confusion. "Income," quite naturally, is the money you get, your receipts, your inflow of cash, your revenue. But that definition does not apply to the wealthy. Their income, so far as the tax law is concerned, is not the same thing as their revenue. They are allowed to call their receipts by other names, and thus evade the high surtax rates that would otherwise apply to them.

"Income," therefore, is in large degree a meaningless word. "A nuisance," as Texas oilmen say. A thing to be avoided the richer you become. You want, instead, receipts that carry other labels: capital gains, municipal bond interest, depletion allowances, and the like. You want income all right, but you want it in such form that it can be called something else. Of course you don't want to evade taxes; that would be illegal. You merely want to avoid taxes, a highly legal pastime.

What effect has this virtual nullification of the progressive features of the income tax had? It has made the gap between the rich and the poor more pronounced in the United States, for one thing.

Professor Robert Lampman's statistical survey * for the National Bureau of Economic Research has established that since 1949 the proportion of wealth held by the top 1 percent of United States residents increased markedly and was still rising in 1962. From 1922 to 1949, as Lampman's figures show, the share of wealth held by these richest Americans fell from 31.6 percent to 20.8 percent. But by 1956 it was back up to 26 percent again, and was still going up. The effects of the post-Korean tax programs are particularly evident: In 1953 there were 27,000 millionaires in America. By 1962 the figure was 100,000. In 1953 there were 2,113 people whose wealth exceeded $5 million. In 1962 the number stood at 10,000. In 1929 the top 1 percent held 65.6 percent of common stock. By 1962 the top 1 percent held nearly 80 percent. Those were some of the effects of the changes in the progressive income tax.

· 9 ·

As I said above, the income-tax code is written in such a way that it tends to keep poachers out of the experts' preserve. I venture into that enclosure using the map of an expert. His name is

* Robert Lampman, *The Share of Top Wealth-Holders in National Wealth* (Princeton, N.J.: Princeton University Press, 1961).

Louis Eisenstein, his method, sustained critical analysis of the income tax as it had evolved up till 1961. His lively book, *The Ideologies of Taxation,* illuminates the continuous tug of war between "ability to pay" and "trickle-down." (For this last term he uses "barriers and deterrents.")

Trickle-down enjoys effective advantages: (1) capital gains, (2) state and local bonds, (3) depletion allowances, (4) income splitting, (5) trusts, (6) stock options, and (7) self-incorporation.

Capital gains Instituted in 1921, this device distinguishes between short- and long-term increases in the value of property, usually in the form of common stock. Six months is the dividing time. Hold an equity less than that and you are a speculator and pay at normal income rates for what gains you may make. Bear it out for six months before reselling and your status changes to investor, and you pay far less for your gains. As Eisenstein says, "No matter how much income the taxpayer may have, the top rate on long-term gains is 25 per cent. . . . In effect, the special rate for capital gains is a progressive tax reduction."

State and local bonds Generically known as "municipals," these bonds are favored devices of tax avoidance by the big rich. The interest from them is wholly tax free. This loophole has been in place ever since 1913 and is somehow connected with states' rights and local initiative. By such justifications, a man can avoid huge amounts of taxation.

Depletion allowances Perhaps the most notorious of all tax loopholes, percentage depletion is the natural offspring of the oil interests and Andrew Mellon, who at the time of its passage (1926) was the major stockholder in Gulf Oil as well as being Secretary of the Treasury. As Eisenstein notes, this concession is a special deduction for imaginary costs. A boon and little more. "Dean Griswold, of the Harvard Law School, has suggested that the risks of the large oil companies are akin to the risks assumed by the New York Life Insurance Company." [13] "The amount of the [percentage depletion] deduction is not in the least related to the cost of the property," Eisenstein adds.[14] "[T]he special taxpayers involved may deduct not only their imaginary costs, but also their actual costs of developing their wells." Given such a remarkable method of tax avoidance, it is not surprising that upper-bracket earners go into oil investment almost as a matter of course, and once there, come to regard Percentage Depletion alongside Magna Charta and Constitution as one of the foundations of Western Civilization.

Income splitting Described above, this device is helpful to the little rich, an advantage to the $50,000-a-year man. As Eisenstein has noted, "As a result of income splitting, husbands with incomes between $10,000 and $50,000 are now [1961] paying less than they paid in 1941." [15]

Trusts Another useful way to avoid taxation, the trust enjoys a personality of its own in the eyes of the law. Each trust is treated as a separate taxpaying entity under the tax code. Income from a trust is taxable neither to the giver nor to the receiver, but to the trust itself. Thus by scattering his largesse in numerous bundles, a man can effectively escape the effects of progression.

Stock options This and related means of executive compensation (deferred salary payments and the like) are of special importance to the little and middle rich. Stock options are granted to archons and their immediate subordinates by many large corporations. The option is to buy stock at bargain prices, to hold the securities at least six months (to qualify for long-term capital-gains treatment), then to sell. Profits from such sales are taxed at no more than 25 percent. As one disgruntled stockholder has said, the stock option is like "being granted the privilege to buy tickets on the winning horse after the race."

Self-incorporation Let a man get himself a charter of incorporation (total cost: about $200) and he may reduce his taxes to the corporate, not personal, rates. The top corporation income-tax rate is 52 percent. His earnings may be withdrawn by means of capital gains. Although there have been restrictions on this kind of avoidance, with minimum pretense it is possible to get around the law. All that seems necessary is for the corporation to give the appearance of being more than one person and to involve itself in a convincing variety of activities—all of which is harder work than most loopholes require, but still attractive to show-business people in particular.

Whether or not a taxpayer resorts to any of these stratagems, he will still have opportunities for tax evasion in proportion as he enjoys property, not labor, income. Surveys made independently by the National Bureau of Economic Research and the Joint Economic Committee of the Congress suggest that 95 percent of wage and salary income is reported but that only about 80 percent of dividends, 78 percent of entrepreneurial income, and somewhat less than 50 percent of rental income is reported. With the installation of electronic data-processing equipment by the income-tax authorities in the 1960's, the practice of evasion promised to become less widespread.

· 10 ·

The discussion of taxation and its avoidance above has had one glaring omission—the rhetoric that supports or assails the income tax and its provisions. A short glossary of phrases used by the vested interests in support of their helpmeets will convey, perhaps, some small part of the emotion that income taxation is capable of arousing. The listing will also suggest the breadth of appeal in the various imperatives and pleas loosed by the vested interests. Despite the apparent variety of such pleas, from the first invocation of "initiative," through the concerned citations of the little men, widows, and orphans, the basic appeal directed to Federal government by the interests reduces itself to a plea for greater concessions to those already enjoying large concessions.

"Provide initiative" is a favored sentiment in support of lower surtaxes in the upper brackets. "Restore incentive" (which always seems to be in danger of dying out) is a near relative of "Provide initiative," but should in no case be confused with "Call forth new effort," or "Promote risk-taking," which are distinct appeals suggesting a new age of adventure ready to dawn if given the right encouragement.

"Attract new investment" is a somewhat more moderate version of "Promote risk-taking," and is closely related to "Maintain investor confidence," "Encourage saving," and "Protect our gold balance," which are all essentially defensive mandates.

"Remove the shackles" and "Increase production" are variants of "Permit plant modernization" and "Fight back foreign competition," and are invoked in times of overcapacity with imprecise diligence. (Too much capacity? No matter. Remove the shackles and permit plant modernization to fight back overseas competition.)

Four terms suggesting paranoia came into public use in just the same period in which the burdens on the rich were lightening considerably. Nevertheless they have been taken up in the more aggressive circles and they promise to become standard adjuncts to the antitax breviary. "Lessen the burden on the productive" and "Don't penalize success" are the two most mild of the paranoid variety. "End punitive taxation" is more in the mainstream. And "Repeal the cancerous Sixteenth Amendment" is surely the prototype for a new series of admonitions, perhaps elaborating somewhat on the death associations and the overtones of degenerative disease of the original. Death, maiming, and disfigurement are recurrent themes in the glossary. "Crushing taxation" is a well-thought-of phrase that enjoys wide use, particularly in the Midwest. "Confiscatory taxation," on the other hand, seems to be more in favor in the Northeast and in the upper South. The Richmond, Virginia, *News-Leader* and the Scripps-Howard press, for example, have done bold editorial work with "confiscatory." Its variants, "ruinous," "back-breaking," and "murderous," have enjoyed wide use in newspapers everywhere.

Favored rhetorical devices in addition to those listed above are the "grass roots" (from which antitax sentiments always seem to come) and "freedom" (the standard to which antitax people are forever repairing). A third device enjoying wide use is "the goose that lays the golden egg." The goose, it need hardly be said, is constantly in danger of having its neck wrung.

The little man and the widow-orphan element are also subtle instruments in the hands of tax opponents, as was demonstrated during the 1962 debate over withholding of dividend and interest taxes.

Opponents predicted an administrative nightmare if government began withholding taxes on dividends and interest at their sources. It would be a pitiless burden to the "small saver" and to the "modest investor" who depended on their pittance from dividend and interest payments for survival. People's Capitalism would surely suffer a damaging blow were any such program put into effect. The fact that 80 percent of dividend income went to less than 7 percent of the taxpayers (as was pointed out by President Kennedy during the debate over withholding) never seemed to be a particularly telling argument to the friends of the little man.

In the Kennedy Administration's attempt to tighten up on expense-account abuses, the little man was again on hand. Opponents wanted to know what would become of the little restaurant owner—the man who laboriously saved to set himself up in business. What, furthermore, would become of small fishing-camp proprietors to whom tired executives (in company of other tired executives) take their expense-account monies and seek some intercorporate goodwill? What would happen to modest marina owners (at whose establishment modest expense-account yachts modestly rest between cruises)? To hunting-lodge owners, night-club comics, hatcheck girls, country-club busboys? All those little people would be needlessly hurt by arbitrary restrictions on expense-account regulations. The proposed new rules were slackened considerably.

Big people also mattered, if you got right down to it. The contributions they had to make were many and vital. They were the sources of risk capital for industry. They were the investors who provided jobs for millions of little men. They were the Americans whose confidence had to be maintained. Big people, however, pursue big affairs in a complicated way. Therefore they need particular care.

· 11 ·

The du Ponts provide an instructive example of such a group of big people whose interests came up against Federal government in a lengthy contest for comparative advantage. The du Pont affair of 1949–1962 is significant not only for what it may reveal about the art of tax avoidance but for what it demonstrates about the power of industrial interests when their wishes conflict directly with the desires of Federal government.

A word of background on the du Ponts will be useful. The family, as most everyone knows, is a sizable clan surrounded by holding companies, latifundia, and horses. It probably got its start back in the Middle Ages but came to prominence somewhat later. The earliest eminent du Pont was the eighteenth century French scholar who gave the term "physiocrat" to the French school of economics that popularized the ideal of laissez-faire. The school influenced Adam Smith greatly, and through him, most of the rest of the world in one degree or another. A son of the physiocratic du Pont emigrated to the United States in the eighteenth century, where, with Alexander Hamilton's encouragement, he set up a gunpowder factory in Delaware. The scholarly du Pont also came to America, but he did not get involved in the family business. He seems to have inspired one wing of the family, at least.

One hundred and eighty years later, the family had prospered to an extraordinary degree. Its gifts were particularly suited to wealth-gathering.

The du Pont interests had earned themselves great sums of money by their gunpowder dealings in World War I. Always somewhat bothered by the problem of excess cash after that time, the du Ponts bought into a then-obscure automobile company, General Motors Corporation, soon after their first big sale to the World War I belligerents. (An indication of the size of the du Pont munitions revenue during the war: total sales, 1915–1918, $1.25 billion. During that period the company paid dividends of 458 percent on the par value of its stock. In 1915, in addition to the regular $1.50 dividend, the company paid an extra dividend of $28.50; in 1916, a regular dividend of $6, an extra of $94; in 1917, $18 and $33; and in 1918, $18 and $3.) [16]

The du Ponts' early purchase of General Motors Corporation stock, in 1915, amount to a mere 3,000 of a total of 160,000 outstanding GM shares. An ensuing power struggle between the erratic founder of GM, William C. Durant, and a pair of investment banking houses (Lee, Higginson of Boston and J. & W. Seligman of New York) came to a standoff in which the du Ponts held the deciding vote. They cast it for themselves. Pierre S. du Pont moved into the chairmanship. Durant went out and bought Chevrolet Motor Company, built it up until it was a commanding entity, and with it he bought General Motors back again and thence returned as chairman.

Meanwhile, in Delaware, gunpowder was making money for the du Ponts with almost vulgar ease. Profits kept pouring in during 1916–1918, and something had to be done with them. Investment opportunities were somewhat restricted at the time. In 1918 and 1919, almost $50 million of du Pont money flowed into GM stock. In 1920 the du Ponts bought out Durant's interests for an estimated $30 million, bringing the total du Pont investment close to $100 million. Again Pierre S. du Pont moved into the chairman's position for a time.

The motor business was by no means the sole interest of the du Ponts. Their own plants promised rich rewards. They switched over from munitions to paints, cellophane, and dyestuffs. Of aid to them in their transition was the seizure by the United States Government in 1917 of German patents in dyestuffs. As the 1920's progressed, du Pont sold increasing amounts of paints, fibers, and chemicals to General Motors. In the process, both companies grew rapidly.

Chevrolet was the big reason for General Motors' rise to dominance over the Ford interests. And color was a big reason for Chevrolet's rise. Old Henry Ford had said, "They can have any color they want so long as it's black." GM retaliated with Ducopainted cars in a great profusion of color. Du Pont, as the name suggests, made the Duco.

By the time the Securities and Exchange Commission looked in on the du Pont–General Motors alliance in 1936, E. I. du Pont de Nemours & Company, by various indirect and direct means, owned nearly 10 million shares of GM stock (then worth $690 million), while four du Ponts sat on the GM board and personally owned another 220,000-odd shares, worth another $15 million.

In the succeeding twenty-five years, the du Pont holdings quintupled. By 1962 they held 63 million shares worth $3.5 *billion*. Their holdings gave them effective control of GM and, in the view of the Supreme Court, constituted a violation of the anti-trust laws.

The government suit had been filed in 1949. It was settled in 1962. Du Pont was ordered to get rid of its GM holdings. But simple divestiture was not what had the du Ponts worried. There would be other opportunities to invest their fortunes. What did have them riled up was the fear that they might have to pay income tax, of all things, on the income from the sale of their GM stock. Capital-gains treatment seemed to them the only fair way to handle such a regrettable appreciation of their stock values. The difference, as pointed out above, would be considerable. Capital-gains treatment could take no more than 25 percent, while income tax without embellishment could theoretically take as much as 91 percent.

The case attracted a great amount of legal talent, needless to say. It also aroused compassion for the little people who held du Pont stock, who would get an unexpected but highly taxable windfall from the divestiture proceedings. One survey showed that the average du Pont stockholder would have to pay a 50 percent tax on the General Motors stock he got from the du Pont family as a result of the divestiture.

The Congress came to the rescue. It passed special legislation permitting special treatment of the windfall. Instead of getting $1 billion in revenue, the Treasury had to be content with a mere

$470 million. The essential distinction was that instead of the windfall being in fact a dividend—which is income for income-tax purposes—it would be capital gains, which is not income for income-tax purposes.

The State of Delaware, meanwhile, was concerned about its biggest employer, landowner, and taxpayer, the du Pont company. Consequently, the legislature took steps to ease the burden on the 18,000 du Pont stockholders in the state by declaring that divestiture proceeds would be treated as capital gains, not dividends, for state tax purposes. The law went into effect a few months after the similar Federal law was signed by President Kennedy in February, 1962. Delaware, however, was somewhat more far-sighted than the Congress had been. Some of its legislative leaders began making plans to alter the state tax laws so that any future securities sales under similar circumstances might enjoy similar treatment.

· 12 ·

If the foregoing passages should somehow convey the impression that the attempts to reduce taxes are haphazard, the idea should be dismissed. There is nothing haphazard about tax-reduction campaigns at all. They go forward under the most carefully coordinated planning. They proliferate under industrious organization. They call forth the highest talents in speech writing, article planting, and advertising. They go on and on.

The prime interests in America, as pointed out in Chapter 3, are the manufacturing interests. As such, they have particular wishes to reduce taxes. Their standing antitax mechanism and their public-relations ornament is the National Association of Manufacturers (NAM). What stirs up the NAM, given its constituency, is the problem of ruinously high taxation in the upper brackets. In 1959, after a decade of successive relaxations of upper-bracket taxation, the NAM set out to reduce upper-bracket taxation. Its favored vehicle to this end was a piece of legislation called the Herlong-Baker bill, written in bipartisan amity by a conservative Democrat and a conservative Republican in the House of Representatives.

The bill would have halved the surtaxes in upper brackets while cutting the rates in the lowest brackets by just a quarter. Everyone would have paid less, but the high-income earners would have enjoyed by far the largest reductions, proportionately and absolutely. Meanwhile, corporate profit surtaxes would have fallen from a top rate of 52 percent to 47 percent. Also in the package was a sweeping liberalization of estate taxes, depreciation regulations, gift taxes, and capital-transfer regulations.

To advance the cause of such a bill takes a coordinated effort. Coordinated effort, in turn, requires some kind of philosophical impulse. A confidential memo circulated in 1960 by the NAM helped spell out the organization's philosophy. If the prose was a bit spongy, the point of view was clear enough:

The "philosophic" thrust of the opposing forces is set forth in writings of the Galbraith's, [sic] Schlesinger's, [sic] etc. On the side of freedom, there are not many writings. . . .

On that sobering note, the memo began enumerating the woes of the friends of freedom:

The failure to place tax action in pre-eminent position perhaps reflects what might be called the "great American illusion" that capital is what we always have plenty of. . . . [E]ven among freedom groups there has seemed to be a tendency to take capital for granted. . . .

The tax loophole calling technique is essentially a diversion, or red herring, formented [sic] by the same forces which drive for new ideological-spending programs and complete centralization of government power in Washington. . . .

To win on tax rate reform would be a hard and perhaps fatal blow to the centralists.[17]

As the campaign got under way, it attracted important support from groups that don't endorse just any old bill. The United States Chamber of Commerce came in, as did the United States Junior Chamber of Commerce. The American Cotton Manufacturers As-

sociation also stood up to be counted, and so did other less influential groups.

From 2 East Forty-eighth Street in Manhattan, NAM headquarters, a flood of literature began coursing outward to the
heartland. Down in Tulsa, the Jaycees were also preparing themselves for action. There would be special speeches, press releases,
women's features, booklets, broadsides, canned radio talks, special slogans, and speakers' kits.

NAM's Women's Editor sent out a cluster of pastel-shaded
documents to feminine campaigners:

DEAR PROGRAM CHAIRMAN:
   This program is a serious one. It presents—in *primer* form—the
story of taxes, their growth to the present strangulation point in this
country, the reasons *why* we must all *"bother"* about taxes, and what
we can *do* toward tax reform, NOW . . .

Enclosed in the packet were form publicity releases ("Be sure
that your releases are *double-spaced* when typed for the newspapers. . . ."):

   The nation's present federal tax policy is a "virtual graveyard for
personal ambition and incentives," the _____ Club was told (today
or yesterday) at a special program on "Why Bother About Taxes?"
   With four members taking part as speakers, the program emphasized
that the income tax system is denying the American people the just
rewards for dedicated effort and hard work; that exhorbitant [*sic*]
taxes are siphoning off money that should be going into savings and
investment; that, as a result, there is a shortage of capital needed for
creating new jobs and providing for economic growth.
   The club speakers described tax rate reform proposals now pending
in Congress—the Herlong-Baker bills. . . .
   Mrs. _____, program chairman, who urged the women of (city)
to get behind the tax rate reform movement, introduced as speakers:
_____ . . .

Speakers One, Two, Three, and Four were supplied, in the
same bundle of documents, with speeches:

SPEAKER ONE: "As a matter of fact, WHY BOTHER ABOUT TAXES? Which one of us hasn't said it at one time or another? In the first place . . .

SPEAKER TWO: "A somewhat technical definition of a tax is . . ."

SPEAKER THREE: "The existence of taxes can be traced into dim antiquity. Some idea of the age of the tax problem can be obtained from LUKE II–1 . . ."

SPEAKER FOUR: "In order to 'right' any 'wrong,' we must have a clear picture of what the present 'wrongs' *are*. . . ."

CONCLUSION FOR PROGRAM CHAIRMAN: "(Note: You may wish to have a slight pause before rising to give your conclusion so that the audience will have the chance to applaud the preceding speakers.) This is the *end* of today's program on tax rate reform. . . .

We have a number of posters and booklets here which explain in some detail the provisions of the Herlong-Baker bill. We also have a listing of the proper address forms to use when writing to our representatives. I'm sure that a great many of us will want to do just that, for government leaders recognize that women's clubs have things to say which represent mature judgment. . . ."

The posters were catchy, too. "Incentive-Killing Graduation Is the JOKER in Our Income Tax System!" said one. "Will There Be a Job Waiting for Them?" asked another. The answer was a qualified "Yes." *If* the Herlong-Baker bill became law. A third admonished: "Wishing Won't Help! ACTION is Needed for TAX RATE REFORM!" The body type urged: "Don't stop with a letter (or a dozen) to your Congressman; buttonhole your friends, your neighbors, your family. . . ."

The men's posters were tougher, and appealed more directly to the male love of slaughter. "How to Deal with WOLVES and BIG SPENDERS!" was a pink-tinted broadside that told the story of how Eskimos killed wolves by implanting blood-drenched knives in the ice. The wolves lick the knives, taste blood, keep on licking, drop dead. It was an agile transition from the wolves back to the men. "In a less grisly way American taxpayers are being forced into a wolf-pack trap of monied-bloodletting by big and unprincipled federal spenders. . . ." There was a poster for sports, also: "The Rate of Economic Growth Is *Not* a Political Football!" Sportive to the end, it concluded, "Faster economic growth should be a full-time goal. . . ."

The Jaycees, meanwhile, were not sitting on their hands. "NAM field program men," as an NAM policy memo said, "should ask members to give encouragement or aid to Jaycees who are employed by their companies, or with whom they are acquainted in their communities, in developing full scale local chapter projects in support of the Herlong-Baker legislation. . . ."

The Jaycees rustled up a special Tax Rate Reform Resolution at their national convention in 1960. It took them nine *Whereases* to get down to business: "Now Therefore Be It Resolved that the Board of Directors of the Junior Chamber of Commerce strongly endorses the principles, procedures and rate reform objectives of the Herlong-Baker bills, and to urge the prompt passage by the Congress . . ."

"Speakers!" the wallet-sized special speakers' kits said inside, "Be Enthusiastic. . . . Stress the Positive. . . . Be Prepared to Answer Questions." The little kits provided answers to almost any question except why, really, any such law was necessary in view of the many escape hatches already in place and in good working order.

Despite all the coordinated effort in their behalf, the Herlong-Baker bills never got the support they needed, no doubt because such support and the following passage of the bills would have violated an important rule of American politics—"Change anything but appearances."

Grant that rule validity, and a good deal becomes clear. As long as the tax tables continue to show steep progressive rates, that long, no doubt, will the escape hatches stay safely in place. In return for symbolic "ability-to-pay," the tax code confers real, not symbolic, "trickle-down" loopholes. Balancing the simple outward appearance so comforting to most Americans is the complicated inner reality so welcome to a few Americans.

As Louis Eisenstein remarks:

All in all, the alleged pain on the upper levels of income is far less acute than it is supposed to be. The rates bark more than they bite. Married couples with incomes over $100,000 pay, as a group, an average effective rate of only 28 per cent. The arithmetical results are even more impressive if we compare married couples at different levels. The average effective rate rises from 23 per cent on incomes between $25,000 and $50,000, to 30 per cent on incomes between $150,000 and $200,000. It then declines until it reaches 24 per cent on incomes over $1 million. Or, to take another look at our alleged progression, the average effective rate of $1 million is only about twice as much as at $10,000, though one income is 100 times as large as the other. According to the table of progressive rates, the effective rate should be 26 per cent at $10,000; 40 per cent at $25,000; 78 per cent at $200,000; and 88 per cent at $1 million. Of course, an average effective rate for a particular bracket presupposes that a number of those within the bracket are paying more. But it also indicates that others are paying even less.[18]

· 13 ·

A parting, necessarily complicated, glance at the notion of trickle-down is in order here. The notion is simply based. It has for its root premise the conviction that private savers are the people who provide the seed money; that privately generated capital plays an indispensable role in promoting the economic welfare of everyone else; that people who can produce this kind of money deserve privileged treatment.

The question then becomes, Are these people really as important as all that? Figures advanced by Adolf A. Berle, Jr., in his book *Power Without Property*,[19] suggest that the answer is "No." Berle estimates that the American economy generated $770 billion in capital between 1919 and 1947. The best that can be said for the private saver-investor is that he accounted for just $15 billion of that total, which is only 2 percent. During 1947–1957, as in the earlier period Berle studied, business savings played the big role in capital formation. Other important investors were the United States Government ("particularly in respect of research, experimental, and development work in connection with armaments"); [20] "an extremely limited number of foundations, as, for instance, the Mellon Institute of Technology, the Armour Institute . . ."; and some few universities who "have played a little with the idea of risk capital." Berle estimates that four-fifths of industrial capital in the 1947–1957 decade came from industry itself and from bank credit, the rest from the "capital market," in which the individual investor plays a minor role, so far as any creative contributions are concerned.

The Federal government is of course aware that the industrial corporations are of prime importance in providing capital; it turned time and again in the 1950–1963 period to relaxation of the depreciation regulations affecting industry. Government thereby enhanced the abilities of these corporations to finance themselves. The corporations, in turn, got their monies from consumers in the form of payments for the products that are manufactured. In this sense the consumer plays the key role in investment because it is his decision to purchase, and his payment in response to his decision, that provides corporate revenues, from which come the reserves that accumulate as capital and that inspire new increments of growth.

Corporations, however, are devoted to their prime beneficiaries, the very rich. Therefore they complain about their shrinking profit margins, saying that a better tax break for big private investors is necessary to promote "investor confidence," which alone can improve those profit margins (by permitting these large private investors to provide modernization funds, which will lower unit costs and raise profits). What makes the argument particularly baffling to the onlooker is that it is carried on in the language of accounting, which is far from being a dialect of hard, objective truth. It is instead honeycombed with soft, subjective inclinations. Liberalized depreciation regulations established by Federal government permit corporations to call part of their income "depreciation reserves" instead of "profit." Because there are more dollars in "depreciation reserves," there are less in "profits." Because there are less in "profits," the archon can then say that his company's profit margin is shrinking dangerously and that the only way to ensure industrial survival is to make conditions more attractive for large private investors so that they will provide funds to modernize equipment, to lower unit costs, and thereby to increase profits.*

In the sense that consumers provide corporate revenues, it is they who are ultimately the real investors. To the degree that Federal government assumes control over investment—a very large degree, considering national defense outlays—the taxpayer assumes the role of prime investor. The real taxpayer is the little man.

Only about 30 percent of income-tax revenues came from brackets in excess of $2,000 in 1961. Only 15 percent came from brackets in excess of $4,000. As investment counselor Peter L. Bernstein has said: "This is a highly inflammatory statistic. It means that 85 percent of total federal income-tax revenues is earned on taxable incomes of under $4,000, although substantial amounts of personal income are received at higher levels than that." (Bernstein cautions that these figures do not mean that people earning $4,000 or less therefore bear 85 percent of the burden, but that the first $4,000—of the man of modest means or of the millionaire's income—is the revenue-producing bracket.) [21]

· 14 ·

The vested interests are highly vocal in their advocacy of less Federal government activity—a commonplace that hardly needs

---

* Among themselves, archons and investors stay closer to reality. The large investment-advisory firm, Lionel D. Edie & Company, advised its clients in October, 1960: ". . . the Internal Revenue Code of 1954 introduced certain basic changes in accounting procedures for tax purposes that have the effect of lowering the reported profit figures on a historical basis. The figures prior to 1954 are no longer comparable to the figures after 1954. . . ." That same month, the *Survey of Current Business* of the Department of Commerce said the same thing: "The profit . . . figures for recent years, reflecting the wider applicability of the new accounting methods, are not precisely comparable with the past figures which were based . . . on . . . traditional calculation. . . . The shift to the new method tends to influence the downward tendencies of profit ratios." (Quoted in my *Men Who Make Us Rich*, p. 133.)

documentation. One particular line of attack is directed on the public debt, which archons and fiscal conservatives alike say that they abhor.

Not in great detail, but just enough to suggest the cul-de-sac to which that particular line of debate leads, a word on the public debt may be useful here. In the first place, of the $285 billion of Federal debt in 1959, the public held $204 billion of it. Few investments proved more attractive to the millionaire than a good, sound United States Government bond. Take a man worth $10 million or more, for example. Professor Lampman's statistics indicate that only corporate stock and tax-free municipal bonds are more welcome guests in such a crowded portfolio.[22] A poorer millionaire, on the other hand (a $5-to-$10-million man), prefers other government paper—cash—to U.S. bonds, but not by a very wide margin. The $500,000-to-$1-million man is more addicted (as far as aggregate investment is concerned) than any other rich American to United States bonds. Only stock, miscellaneous property, and real estate command more of his affection. Among all Americans worth more than $60,000, in fact, United States bonds stand quite high. First come corporate stocks, next real estate, then miscellaneous property, then cash, and then United States bonds. These bonds stand higher than municipal bonds, higher than plain old corporate bonds, and higher than mortgages and life insurance.

Imagine an Administration that set out to reduce the public debt one day, in a businesslike manner, according to the lights of a Senator Harry Flood Byrd. It certainly could be done. The Federal government does have vendible assets. The White House and its eighteen acres of land, for example, is carried on the government books at just $1,000, while the Hope Diamond in the Smithsonian Institution is carried at nothing. The other assets are also listed at less than market value, but they still come very close to balancing the national debt. They totaled about $285 billion, as of 1961, reassurance somehow against the cries of impending national bankruptcy.

Debt reduction (to draw back a bit from the patently absurd

notion that either public debt or public assets belong to a count-inghouse milieu) could have serious adverse effects. It could, for one thing, upset the national bank credit apparatus now regu-lated by the Federal Reserve System. It could furthermore impair the scope of the government trust funds such as unemployment, disability insurance, and old-age and survivors insurance funds. It could inhibit the stabilizing effects of the long-term portions of the public debt, which are somewhat illiquid assets. It would cer-tainly upset interest rates, and it would probably take much of the joy out of the weekly Treasury bill auctions. Finally, it would give financial officers of large corporations, commercial banks, in-surance companies, and state and local governments a great deal of inconvenience, not to say alarm, to find other equally riskless investments.

A public debt may not be an unalloyed public blessing, but it nevertheless presents attractive investment opportunities for highly solvent folk with an eye for security. Whatever the large-scale investor may say out loud, inside he knows a good thing when he sees it, and his purchases of government bonds in such large quantities make far more persuasive testimony than any merely symbolic outburst, such as antidebt talk.

· 15 ·

As the vested interests are vocally opposed to greater domestic government activity (on grounds, largely, that the national debt will thereby increase), so are they opposed to greater foreign gov-ernment activity if it in any way impairs or conflicts with the normal foreign policies of large industrial corporations.

What, one may ask, are those policies? To take one example, in the 1920's Mexico was one of the most promising oil areas in the world, and was then producing about 25 percent of total world output. That natural-resource wealth attracted American oil com-panies who invested about $300 million in Mexican oil. Through one circumstance or another, the oil companies and the Mexican government came to view each other with suspicion. In the period of the Good Neighbor Policy, there was a direct clash of wills between the private government of oil and the United States Government. The proximate cause was the expropriation of Standard Oil of New Jersey and Shell Oil properties by the Mexican government. The seizures took place in 1938, and the companies were unwilling to accept what seemed to Mexico a fair market valuation for their seized assets.

The companies did settle for what they could get. But not before an attempt to win, in addition to compensation for their outright investments, payment for oil still in the Mexican ground (which the American companies listed as part of their corporate assets). That attempt failed. So did the oil companies' hopes of a counterrevolution in Mexico. As Robert Engler has described the attempts of the oil interests to even the score with Mexico, the first step was a boycott by the big companies of tetraethyl sales to the nationalized Mexican industry. The big tank fleets shunned Mexican ports. United States equipment suppliers refused shipments into Mexico. As Engler says: "The [oil] interests sought to get the United States Government to adjust its import quotas to discriminate against Mexico. . . . A proposal to cut off United States Government purchases of Mexican silver was weighed. . . . They also pressured the United States Government to turn down requests from Mexico for capital loans, hoping that public development of oil would be discredited and that the Mexicans would be forced to seek the return of foreign private capital and management." [23] Elsewhere, corporate foreign policy continues to exert strong if not determining influence.

The large industrial interests have supported governments that promise the safety of their capital investments. That has meant, more often than not, the support of reactionary or dictatorial governments that maintain conditions of safety for foreign industrial capital at high cost to the welfare of the native populations. Franco, Batista, and Jiménez have all, in their times, enjoyed firm support from American oil companies because of their concern for preserving investment values. In the Arabian-American Oil Company's domain, a touring British peer in 1960 discovered that in full sight, and apparently without complaint from the Americans, "human credit cards" were enjoying a vogue. Slave-owning pilgrims would make the journey to Mecca with a slave or two in tow and sell them on arrival to provide funds for the visit. Conditions not quite so prefeudal but nevertheless inhumane by modern standards recur in nation after nation in which large capital investment from American interests goes, particularly if that investment is directed to extraction of raw material. American copper interests in Peru and Chile, American iron-ore interests in Brazil, and American oil interests in Venezuela represent enclave economies in which the massive capital investments by American corporations seem far more effective as a means of focusing discontent among the native populations than of raising the living standards of any but a few privileged nationals. A further manifestation of the foreign policies of American vested interests, the ultimate device by which these commercial colonies are maintained, is the tariff.

As Professor Jacob Oser has noted,[24] the net impact of American commercial policies seems to be to restrict manufacturing development in underdeveloped nations by putting high barriers in the way of such development through tariffs. For example, in 1953 crude bauxite "not refined or otherwise advanced in condition in any manner" paid an import duty of only 50 cents a ton; refined bauxite, $5 a ton; crude aluminum metal itself, $30 a ton; aluminum utensils, $85 a ton plus an additional 20 percent of their value. Iron ore came in duty free, in like measure, but pig iron paid a levy of 60 cents a ton; metal ball-bearings paid $80 a ton plus 17½ percent of the value. The pattern has applied to almost every raw material. It has been in many respects a virtual program for keeping the poor countries the choppers of wood, the diggers of ore, the drillers of oil while the American interests perform the tasks of bankers and managers, clerks and distributors, organizers and masters. Hardly a means of promoting friendship, any more than was the nineteenth century "American System."

On the election of President Kennedy, a British observer noted that the greatest problem facing the new President would be the contest between the foreign policy that he would like to have America pursue and the competing policies that private American corporations would be pursuing for their own peculiar reasons. While that view sounds strange to many American ears, to some, the negative role of the prime vested interests seems neither novel nor surprising.

As the enclave-building propensities of the prime interests were becoming visible enough in the United States during the 1960's, so the American prime interests were building similar enclaves in foreign lands. While in the United States the depreciation reserve acted as the catalyst to such developments, in foreign lands the tariff seemed to provide similar catalytic service.

Whether or not the United States Government can soften and mute the more noxious effects of such enclave building remains an unanswered question. Whether or not the government will be successful in making the world over which it has influence—within and outside its own borders—safer for consumption also remains an unanswered question.

· 16 ·

Of the vested interests and Federal government, then, it may fairly be said that the spiritual forefathers of the contemporary interests got the United States under way; that their successors established the order of preferment that confers particular distinctions and privileges on industrial corporations and on the well-to-do.

The ideal of an industrial civilization in which highly active pursuit of personal gain is accepted as a form of moral excellence has swept everything before it. It has created habits of mind and patterns of deference that have never been reversed, merely slowed or slightly altered from time to time. One may cite the Progressive Era and the New Deal as perhaps the only extended periods in which the "outside" America, the America that remains excluded from the industrial enclave, has enjoyed any real prospects for relative betterment. Absolute betterment, of course, is another question, and hardly an open one. With the possible exception of the rural Negro, no group of Americans seems to have suffered an absolute reverse.

In sum, the national tradition of exaggerated respect for production and producers (and the equivalent neglect of consumption and consumers) has been marked ever since the Republic was founded. The order of preferment has all but enshrined production and producers, and has permitted these groups and their basic motive to attain enormous scope.

The range of economic motives could be represented on a continuum from "transaction" through "precaution," to "speculation." * The one extreme, transaction, is the most common of motives. It is the poor man's whole reason for being. The other extreme, speculation, is the mark of the affluent. The first motive provides consumption, the last, production.

To this last has Federal government made the most grand and constant concessions. From this last have we all gained national might, material splendor, and a kind of contentment. From it we have suffered continual recessions, domestic unrest, and bombast —always bombast. Of these elements are our prime vested interests constituted.

* The originator of this series of terms, Lord Keynes, added a fourth term in response to criticism. He called Number Four the "finance" motive. This additional label seems to serve no vital purpose, as it falls between "precaution" and "speculation" on the continuum. No doubt it was offered to provide a more honorific aura to the large investor: it makes him seem less a crapshooter and more a presbyter.

SEVEN

The Rise of Administered

Optimism

ЛЛЛЛЛЛЛ

Modern vested interests have to have a climate of optimism in which to operate. Optimism, however, tends to be a mark of the well-to-do or of those who are upwardly mobile. A reservoir of poverty in a society tends to generate large amounts of pessimism.

Faced with that unwelcome minority response, the contemporary prime interests have two opportunities: they can aid in the eradication of the disease, poverty, or instead they can try to relieve the symptom, pessimism. The interests seem to direct their efforts primarily to the treatment of the symptom. To accomplish this therapy, the prime interests go to great lengths to buoy public spirits by organizing the output of good news and by suppressing bad news. The prime vested interests, in fact, are busy purveyors of what may be called administered optimism. The exact techniques will be explored in a moment. First, an examination of unorganized optimism may be instructive.

· 1 ·

Optimism has always flourished by feeding on good news. In turn, specific good news followed by more of the same has been a powerful influence in the attainment of industrialization. For instance, in a real sense, Great Britain was provided with the financial basis for its Industrial Revolution by the impact of one electrifying bit of good news in the seventeenth century.

The classic example involved the adventurer William Phipps, who got a joint-stock venture started for the purpose of recovering sunken treasure. Good as a pastime, said some, but hardly a sound investment. Nevertheless, a few foolhardy investors came into the Phipps venture. Thus financed, Phipps went off to the Island of Hispaniola, where a Spanish bullion ship was supposedly lying in a few fathoms of water. After a time, Phipps got to the alleged spot and his divers found the hulk, and in the hulk, gold. Great, incredible quantities of gold. The expedition pulled up ingots, bar, and coin worth between £250,000 and £300,000. Phipps returned to London in 1688 to the frenzied delight of his shareholders, each of whom received dividends of 10,000 percent. Not even Sir Francis Drake on his best day had paid more than 4,700 percent. As Lord Keynes noted, "The excitement and stimulus occasioned by this event was the proximate cause of the remarkable Stock Exchange boom which reached its climax in 1692–95 and ended with the foundation of the Bank of England. . . ." [1]

In the South Sea Bubble, which followed a few decades later, the specific good news of huge paper profits was as effective a promoter of optimism as had been the specific good news of Phipps's bullion discovery. So widespread and indiscriminate grew the speculative fever that even this prospectus attracted investors: "Subscription of 2 million pounds to a promising scheme the details of which will later be made public." [2]

The Dutch Tulip Craze and the French Mississippi Company bubble likewise provided evidence that extreme and widespread optimism can extract a great deal of coin from many small purses and can concentrate it in a few large strongboxes. Those booms also helped define the extent to which optimism can substitute for calm analysis—a great extent, the evidence suggests, if there is no untimely resurgence of pessimism. Furthermore, they demonstrated that wild optimism has been limited to no single nation, nor has it reigned uninterrupted, once abroad. Inevitable disillusionment sets in. On a wave of pessimism the bubbles burst and a chastened populace sets about the time-consuming task of forgetting its folly so that a new bubble may be blown. From the crashes arise the banality, "You can't get something for nothing," and that patent untruth inhibits another speculative orgy—until people forget. Of course you can indeed get something for nothing, but not everybody, and not all at once. As soon as a few rediscover that enticing truth, the foundation of a new boom is laid.

Something for nothing seems to provide at least a partial definition of profit. The promise of profit, in turn, is the spark of life to industrial enterprise. "Thrift," wrote Keynes, "may be the handmaid and nurse of Enterprise. But equally she may not. And, perhaps, even usually she is not. For enterprise is connected with thrift not directly but at one remove; and the link which should join them is frequently missing. For the engine which drives Enterprise is not Thrift, but Profit." [3]

The material progress inspired by paper profits of the stock exchanges has been no less real for being based on ethereal values. As long as optimism holds, that long is almost anything in the way of material progress possible. Purely psychological wealth can apparently last indefinitely, or for as long as good news—even highly abstracted and indefinite good news—continues to circulate. Unreal values can enhance real values,* can result in large profits, can attract more and more plain folk to the public lottery, can inspire invention and industrial growth.

Pessimism always seems to make a comeback, however, and paper valuations on future profits fall. With the fall of the symbolic representation, the real thing itself is also likely to fall in value. The tide-like motion of optimism and pessimism catches investors in its undertow, and these investors do as their fellows do.

---

* As Keynes put it, "A country is no richer when, for purposes of swopping titles to prospective gain between one of its citizens and another, people choose to value the prospects at twenty years' purchase, than when these are valued at ten years' purchase; but the citizens, beyond question, *feel* richer" (*Treatise on Money,* II, 197).

· 2 ·

The progress from William Phipps to the South Sea Bubble and to the modern-day stock-exchange excitements has been representative of the progress from a natural economy (which is essentially barter—that is, distribution in kind) to a money economy (characterized by manufactured-goods distribution) to a credit economy (in which paper values assume first importance). The progress since the early speculative frenzies has been to an economy in which, as Veblen said, the market becomes "a vent for accumulated money values and a source of supply of capital." [4] By way of further distinction between the money and the credit economy, Veblen added, "The commodities bought and sold in the goods market are the outcome of a process of production and are useful for a material purpose; those bought and sold in the capital market are the outcome of a process of valuation and are useful for purposes of pecuniary gain." [5] That "process of valuation" is where optimism plays its supreme role as arbiter of fungibility.

To the extent that plain folk are involved in the credit system, they too are carried along and caught up in its enthusiasms. Optimism becomes truly worthwhile under those conditions because optimism helps sustain values created by belief in future gains. These hopes of future gain, in fact, often assume as much importance psychologically as do real values founded on present reality. As the economist Joseph Schumpeter observed, "While I cannot ride on a claim to a horse, I can, under certain conditions, do exactly the same with claims to money as with money itself, namely buy." [6]

· 3 ·

A short digression here may help fix the utility of administered optimism with somewhat more precision, and may furthermore suggest how such boosterism helps maintain paper profits. The place to start such an examination is with the corporate mode of doing business—the separation of ownership from control.

Because the corporate form permits great amounts of capital to be assembled with minimum risk to investors, that institutional system provides a perfect vehicle for the creation of ethereal values. Although the physical assets of a corporation may be, say, $100 million and no more, the company may in fact issue stock backed by intangible assets, as well. "Good will," "know-how" and prospective gains of one sort or another, including those gains made possible by the extension of loan credit, are capitalized right along with tangible assets. The aggregate stock that is backed by these assets and by the presumptive earning power of these assets may have a market value far in excess of the "book value" of the assets themselves. And the "book value," in turn, may be far in excess—probably is far in excess—of real value for the assets were they to be sold off, machine by machine. As Veblen said, this total capital is no fixed amount. It "fluctuates from day to day. . . . The precise pecuniary magnitude of the business community's invested wealth . . . depends from hour to hour on the quotations of the stock exchange. . . . Both capital and credit, therefore, vary from hour to hour and, within narrow limits, from place to place." [7]

These fluctuations in value confer gains on some, but can act as taxes levied by private enterprise on others. These ups and downs tend to make an "owner" of a corporation no sedentary adviser and creditor but an eternal transient. The investor is forever churning his portfolio—buying new stock for some small advantage, real or putative; selling old stock to avoid some small disadvantage, concrete or probable. "It is," as Keynes said, "as though a farmer, having tapped his barometer after breakfast, could decide to remove his capital from the farming business between 10 and 11 in the morning and reconsider whether he should return to it later in the week."

Such fluctuations in ethereal values make the investor a pecuniary vagrant. His major concern becomes capital appreciation —that is, a rise in the value of the stock he holds. He does not buy to have; he buys to sell. Under the tax law as it has evolved since 1921, long-term capital gains enjoy preferential tax treatment. Thereby the Federal government is in the curious position of discouraging dividend payments because such distribution of profits falls under the regular tax provisions for income. Thus corporate investors naturally become more interested in rises in value of the stock itself than in the dividends it pays. They therefore approve plowback of profits, rather than payout in the form of dividends, because plowback promises to enhance market values of stock and thereby a new capital gain may be assured (which will be taxable at far lower rates than dividend payments). Therefore the precaution motive is under constant temptation to verge into the speculation motive.

While the corporate method of organizing capital produces these effects on stocks, it occasions other innovations no less significant. Great financial power typical of the American manufacturing corporation combines with government solicitude for the wishes of these prime interests to free these giant organisms from any real dependence on the stock exchanges as sources of capital. Internally generated funds that come from mass purchases by masses of consumers permit the typical large manufacturing corporation to provide itself with upward of 75 percent of its own investment capital—not from the sale of new stock issues but from depreciation reserves and other retained earnings. (Again, under tax law, corporations are permitted to set aside part of the revenues as depreciation reserves against the day when machinery and plant buildings must be replaced. These funds are not taxable, yet they are nevertheless able to perform the precise function—namely, buying new machines—that the stock-market sale of new issues of securities is supposed to accomplish.)

The stock market is then in many instances a mere alternate source of capital. It is an arena for manipulation of ethereal values for reasons that often have nothing to do with production. The stock market then may be seen as a sort of gigantic lottery that provides useful diversion for the solvent, and as such it may be regarded as a branch of the entertainment industry. Nevertheless, some corporations do indeed go to the stock market for capital. Public utilities under government regulation and non-manufacturing corporations that may not have the financial power of the giants provide two examples of the kinds of companies that expect to get capital largely from Wall Street, not from consumers or depreciation reserves. Nor does the marginal nature of the stock market mean that corporations shun new stock issues. They of course do undertake new issues, and there again optimism plays a crucial role. If a large corporation needs an extra few million dollars for expansion, for example, it has a variety of choices. It may issue new stock and get the capital that way or it may instead go to loan-credit from its bank to accomplish the same end. It probably goes to the market without fail if it can do so without thereby depressing the price of its already outstanding stock. If such depression in price seems likely, it will instead go to its bank, assuming all the while that it cannot assemble the funds from its own depreciation reserves.

The corporate archons are of course greatly interested in maintaining the ethereal value of their corporations' stock because they themselves, through stock-option schemes, are significant players of the stock market. Therefore they will not willingly get new capital from the stock market if the result of the new issue of stock is to cause an oversupply of their own corporation stock and consequently force down the per-share price. Again, optimism plays a key role in maintaining the value of the archons' stock-option emoluments. If public confidence is so elevated that no price seems too high for a blue-chip stock, no spread between book value and market value, between earnings and price, too incredible, they can dribble out considerable amounts of new stock, thus diluting the equity of present stockholders (but assuring themselves against criticism so long as optimism keeps carrying the stock prices upward).

Without further detail, it can be said in conclusion that optimism is no longer a spontaneous matter. It is no longer haphazardly organized. Historically, optimism has been hit or miss so long as a significant proportion of the populace has had an out. So long as the American could dig a turnip for himself, could survive on his own food, for that long could optimism remain unorganized and free from manipulation. But let a time come when an entire populace depends for its welfare on the credit system and concentrated industry, and optimism can no longer remain a laughing matter. Given a time, like the present epoch, in which a great overhead of paper valuation has to be maintained for the general continuity of economic welfare, optimism can no longer be left to come as it will. Then it becomes a deadly serious affair, and pessimism, proportionately, a mortal enemy of the general welfare.

A crisis in optimism results in less euphoric estimates of future gains. Therefore such a crisis results in the escape of the gas that keeps ethereal values inflated. Then follows lessened business confidence, lowered investment, excess saving, lowered consumption, lost jobs, and lowered production, in a sadly familiar cycle.

· 4 ·

The ebb and flow of optimism in American economic history began to leave indelible traces when the credit superstructure started to rise, which was in the second decade of the nineteenth century.

After the War of 1812, refinements in the young nation's monetary system began to be made. Along with increased sophistication in the money system came repeated panics, recurring whenever optimism faltered. The faltering came not as a result of any diminution of the promise of the vast continent, but because of erratic behavior in the money capitals. Eastern panic could destroy paper values, but it could not really destroy the ultimate opportunities. A man ruined in the East could always go West to seek another kind of fortune founded on the realities of agriculture. The open frontier was there as a constant source of spontaneous optimism, a land that could make anyone secure against the tyranny of paper-manipulating city creditors. It was the haven for the victims of eastern panics and depressions (which began to occur with regularity in 1819).

The year 1815 had seen American commercial agriculture flourishing. A hungry Europe was still reeling from the Napoleonic Wars, and remained a good customer for American farm crops. British looms badly needed American cotton. Therefore land values soared, and the need for farm credit to help farmers take advantage of their new marketing opportunities brought a national bank back into existence. In 1816 the Second Bank of the United States was given an exclusive twenty-year charter by Congress; the bank gathered $35 million in capital and opened 25 branch offices. State banks, encouraged by the Second Bank itself, extended credit with expansive nonchalance. As the *Niles' Weekly Register* reported, farmers found the lures of speculation irresistible:

. . . the farmer is courteously invited to borrow money, whether he wants it or not. There is no difficulty in his getting loans to the amount of nearly the value of his farm. Nay, it appears by a report of a committee of the assembly of the state of New York, that he is actually *coaxed*, seduced, into borrowing, by the cunning jackalls of the country banks. . . .

All suffer more or less by this substitution of ideal, for real wealth. . . .[8]

The Richmond *Enquirer*, at about the same time, was noting,

The iron business languishes; the waggon shops are shut up; taxes cannot be paid in the required money; the flinty creditor asks Virginia paper, or gold and silver, for his debt: the debtor, unable to raise either, gives up his land, and, ruined and undone, seeks a home for himself and his family in the western wilderness.[9]

Illinois, meanwhile, typified a natural economy that was becoming a money economy and, even more quickly, a credit economy. "Before the war [of 1812]," one historian observed, "such a thing as money was scarcely ever seen in the country, the skins of deer and racoon supplying the place of a circulating medium. The money which was now brought in, and which had been paid by the United States to the militia during the war, turned the heads of all the people and gave them new ideas and aspirations; so that by 1819 the whole country was in a rage for speculating in lands and town lots." [10]

Throughout the nineteenth century crises of optimism recurred. They inflicted progressively greater misery after the close of the frontier about 1870. Until then, there had been enough good news from the West to make any panic a transitory bother. The gold rush, for one thing, was a great creator of spontaneous optimism. The specific good news of gold apparently became generalized into a universal sense of expansiveness. As the gleam slowly left the California placer streams, the news from elsewhere in the West more than compensated. The Comstock Lode in Nevada was enough to inspire great ebullience. (It made several foreign nations stop using silver for currency; and it caused doubts as to silver's continued status as a precious metal, so common did the blue ore seem to be in the veins under Virginia City.)

Panics coming in 1873 and 1893, then, struck with far more virulence than had those of 1837 and 1857, if for no other reason than that more people were by that time committed to the credit economy. These later panics caused extreme distress in the cities as well as in the countryside, feeding the Populist party's political discontent all the while. More restricted panics—largely limited to money itself and not seriously restricting production—came in 1907 and 1913, but various monetary reforms and growing economic resilience did much to soften the effects.

The crises that gave administered optimism its mandate came in the second and third decades of the twentieth century. Between 1919 and 1929, the collapses of ethereal values and the paroxysms that followed caused sharp and extended woe, largely because a man could no longer retire from the credit economy. There just wasn't any way to soften the pain without radical changes in the credit superstructure itself.

· 5 ·

These latter-day crises deserve fairly close scrutiny, for in their development one may detect the psychological climate that has helped produce massive modern paper valuations. This climate has also created a selective ideology that characterizes the prime vested interests and their beneficiaries.

The 1919 crisis may be quickly passed over once its bare details have been noted. World War I was over, peacetime conversion was under way, and farm prices were weakening as European farms came back into production. Domestic industry, meanwhile, was uneasily hoping for a return to normal peacetime business conditions. For these and other reasons, the stock market became a focus for vague pessimism. Paper values dropped sharply, by more than 40 percent. It took five years for these values to surpass their 1919 highs. Unemployment, by 1921, rose to 12 percent. "Normalcy" and Coolidge prosperity, with their policies of constant preferential treatment for the ranking interests and large investors, restored stock values and ameliorated unemployment (although they accomplished almost nothing in the way of broad prosperity: wages lagged well behind productivity gains, and profits accordingly soared, far outstripping costs of production). A brief interruption of the long bull market came in 1926, when more than 20 percent of paper values quickly disappeared. In less than a year's time, however, the stock market was again suffused with optimism, and the prices moved upward once more. Nothing seemed capable of clouding the cheery outlook of American investors, so uniform was the good news of paper profits and so friendly to speculation was the Federal government. To be sure, Teapot Dome caused some consternation during these years, and so for that matter did Florida, but neither was taken as a real sign of danger.

The Florida Bubble is worth a glance. It was significant because of the advances in the arts of administered optimism that made it possible. Florida in this respect typified the 1920's, a decade in which new refinements in ritual confidence were made. Nowhere in that decade were the new methods used with greater effectiveness than in Florida.

Public relations was what made the Florida land boom of 1924–1926 the great success that it was. Not public relations by itself, but that in concert with the general optimism of the age, with Florida's superlative climate, and with the diffusion of automotive transport. Spontaneous optimism, by way of comparison, might have said of Florida, "It's a hell of a state—warm all year round!" Administered optimism rendered the feeling more memorable:

> Go to Florida—
> Where enterprise is enthroned—
> Where you sit and watch at twilight the fronds of the graceful palm, latticed against the fading gold of the sun-kissed sky . . .
> Where the whispering breeze springs fresh from the lap of the Caribbean and woos with elusive cadence like unto a mother's lullaby. . . . [11]

By 1924 wooden stakes were sinking into the Florida loam from Palm Beach to Miami. A fifty-foot lot became as negotiable as a sound common stock. As Frederick Lewis Allen noted, "By 1925 [the public was] buying anything, anywhere, so long as it was in Florida. . . . 'Manhattan Estates' was advertised as being 'not more than three-fourths of a mile from the prosperous and fast-growing city of Nettie'; there was no such city as Nettie, the name being that of an abandoned turpentine camp, yet people bought." [12]

A 10 percent down payment would hold a lot long enough for a man to turn around and sell his newly bought land for a handsome gain. But at last it became apparent that values were grossly inflated. The boom collapsed. As Allen noted, two hurricanes, the last of which smacked into Miami, blew away most of the hot air that had supported the bubble.

The brief 1926 sell-off in the stock market (mentioned above) was as much of a sympathetic reaction as Florida's punctured pretensions could evoke. Onward and upward went the Dow-Jones averages.

· 6 ·

The forces that fed the great Harding-Coolidge-Hoover bull
market were set loose by systematic reductions of taxation in
upper-income brackets. As pointed out in Chapter 6, these reductions took various forms. In 1921 preferential tax treatment of
long-term capital gains was instituted. In 1926 preferential tax
treatment of oil income (by means of percentage depletion allowances) was established. Meanwhile, the Treasury was adminis-
tratively forgiving $3.5 billion in taxes and the Congress was cut-
ting surtax rates on high incomes and on large estates with particular zeal. The result was the creation of an immense reservoir
of liquid funds under the control of the rich.

The delicate balance of investment opportunity and consumption ability thus suffered a deep maladjustment. National Bureau
of Economic Research figures suggest just how deep the disloca-
tion was: In the 1923–1929 period, the productivity of the economy rose 32 percent, yet wage earners won only an 8 percent
increase in wages during this same period. The transaction motive consequently suffered relative restriction, but the speculation
motive enjoyed broad enhancement in scope.

Without solid purchasing power that could provide the rock-
bottom good news of consumer purchases, paper valuations simply
could not maintain their elevation. Because the interests of the
poor man were not attended to, the quest of the rich man for
paper profits ended in frustration. That was the lesson waiting
to be enunciated. October 24, 1929, framed the first draft of that
message. Stocks slid steeply on a huge volume of trading. The
market rallied weakly and fluttered to no effect the next day and
the Saturday following. Then, on Monday the 28th, the stage was
set for the ultimate debacle, which came on Tuesday the 29th.
Almost 16,500,000 shares changed hands, and the stock average
dropped 43 points on the *Times'* industrial average. The work of
those two October days—and the succeeding drear weeks—wiped

out more than $70 billion of paper values. Not until 1955 were 1929 highs eclipsed.

It was during the horrifying weeks of October and November, 1929, when most of the paper wealth of American industry was evaporating, that the ritual of reflex optimism became more highly formalized:

Charles M. Schwab said that steel as an industry was in a "fundamentally sound condition."

The chairman of the Baldwin Locomotive Works let it be known that "fundamentals are sound."

President Herbert Hoover noted that "the fundamental business of the country, that is production and distribution of commodities, is on a sound and prosperous basis."

The President's Assistant Secretary of Commerce said in a radio address, "The main point which I want to emphasize is the fundamental soundness of . . . economic activities."

John D. Rockefeller made an unusual public statement from his Pocantico Hills seclusion: "Believing that fundamental conditions of the country are sound . . . my son and I have for some days been purchasing sound common stocks."

Alfred P. Sloan, Jr., president of General Motors, assured his fellow citizens: "Business is sound."

A bank took a half-page ad in the *Times* to advertise its belief "that the general industrial and business condition of the country is fundamentally sound and is essentially unimpaired."

"That day," Professor Galbraith has noted, "the market started on another ghastly slump." [13]

A month after the crash, President Hoover convened what Galbraith has called a "no business" meeting—a purely ceremonial conference that is occasioned by the need for ritualized cheer. The November 21, 1929, meeting drew Henry Ford, Owen Young, Alfred Sloan, Pierre du Pont, and Andrew Mellon, among others. "The expressions of confidence were so robust that Julius Rosenwald, who also attended, said he feared there might soon be a bad labor shortage." (There was indeed a labor shortage. It came in 1944, at the height of World War II production.)

· 7 ·

Before these humbling events cast the American businessman into the unaccustomed role of public villain, administered optimism had been measurably furthered by the thousands of chapters of various civic clubs, chambers of commerce, and business associations that had grown to positions of vast influence during the 1920's.

Boosterism became a practical personal creed, for by such means could paper valuations and the promise of future gains retain a sound semblance. Rotarians, Kiwanians, and Optimists alike talked up the promises of the future with loud and continuous affirmations. "The Optimist Creed," for example, provided a canon of conduct for the commercially pious:

Promise yourself—
To be so strong that nothing can disturb your peace of mind.
To talk health, happiness, and prosperity to everyone you meet.
To make all your friends feel that there is something in them.
To look at the sunny side of everything and make your optimism come true.
To think only of the best, to work only for the best, and to expect only the best.
To be just as enthusiastic about the success of others as you are about your own.
To forget the mistake of the past and press on to the greater achievements of the future.
To wear a cheerful countenance at all times and give every living creature you meet a smile.
To give so much time to the improvement of yourself that you have no time to criticize others.
To be too large for worry, too noble for anger, too strong for fear, and too happy to permit the presence of trouble.[14]

Elks, Moose, Eagles, Odd Fellows, and Lions likewise contributed to boosterism during the golden decade of the bull market.

Literature followed life. The unforgettable fictional booster,

George F. Babbitt, full of pep and zip, whooped up "rational prosperity." Babbitt was a caricature, to be sure, but not much of one. His tireless enthusiasm for commercial gain epitomized a wide segment of the business community. The more paper valuation such men had to protect, the more vigorous and pervasive became their affirmations:

> Good old Zenith,
> Our kin and kith,
> Wherever we may be,
> Hats in the ring,
> We blithely sing
> Of thy Prosperity.[15]

After the Great Crash, these devices were not so well received, and in fact the pure repetition of cheery outlook—the attempt to weld ought to is—became less straightforward. Boosterism as it evolved in the succeeding years became more self-conscious, more subtle, and less pointedly affirmative.

One particular thread of boosterism will be pursued in a separate chapter, so to do more than indicate that thread now would be premature. Suffice it to say that popular religion has proved a valuable support and ally of paper valuation and of ritual optimism in general. In the 1920's Bruce Barton, an advertising man, provided much of the religious exegesis in a brilliantly clear little book called *The Man Nobody Knows*. The object of his scholarship was to establish that Jesus Christ was the first Rotarian, the eternal booster, and the consummate business organizer. The fact that the book ranged high on the best-seller lists both in 1924 and 1925 tells a good bit about the *Zeitgeist* during the great bull market of 1921–1929. A distinct parallel in religious interpretation came just as the Eisenhower bull market was getting under way some thirty years later. Norman Vincent Peale's *The Power of Positive Thinking* was not the only uplifting best-seller of the times. Catherine Marshall's *A Man Called Peter* and Bishop Sheehan's *Peace of Soul* were also prominent on the lists.

On the evidence adduced in a *Reporter* magazine analysis, one can see the dimensions of ritual cheer with fair precision.* What seems to have happened since the Great Crash is that boosterism no longer poses as a narrow diction of commerce but is instead more closely equated with national morality. Furthermore, national morality seems to have grown into an essence that follows (or maybe leads) common-stock valuations in Wall Street.

National self-chastisement, research indicates, came in cycles in the 1950–1960 decade. In the 1951–1953 period, the "U.S.: Moral conditions" heading in the *Reader's Guide to Periodical Literature* listed no fewer than 54 entries. In 1953–1955, however, the total had fallen to just five. In 1955–1957, there was just one entry. Thereafter, the total began to build up again, until in 1960 —after the bloom had begun to fade from the Eisenhower bull market—there were, in the *Reporter's* words, "more articles . . . for three months ('Age of Payola,' 'Aimless Affluence,' 'Our Rigged Morality') than there had been in the entire four-year period of grace [1953–1957]." Although no attempt was made by the *Reporter* to lay the Dow-Jones Averages alongside these findings, an opportunity seems to have been missed. Taking the year-end quarterly figures, the Dow-Jones Industrial Average stood at 269 (rounded to nearest whole number) in 1951, 281 in 1953, 488 in 1955, and at 436 in 1957. Stocks climbed rapidly in 1958 to 584, and in 1959 to 679. The 1960 average dropped off at year end to 616.

The Eisenhower Era began, of course, on the note of a great moral crusade. The Secretary of State was a pillar of morality and a firm advocate of a "moral foreign policy," pursued if possible without limitations from "immoral" neutral nations. In view of the internationalist flavors of national morality, the *Reporter* found nothing untoward in the discovery that "as we get better, foreigners get worse, and vice versa. . . ." There is sound scholarship to be done in comparing the balance of morality with the balance of payments. No doubt morality would prove to have a direct relationship to the gold position of the United States. On

* See Meg Greenfield, "The Great American Morality Play," *The Reporter*, June 8, 1961.

a brief examination of the figures, the relationship does appear to hold. As national morality flows out and accrues to Europe, so does monetary gold—at least in the 1958–1961 period.* That period saw the television scandals, payola, cheating in schools, and agonized questings for Answers. (*Newsweek* magazine asked in 1959, "How can the church remain enmeshed in a culture that is going rancid?") † Therefore the outflow of gold from the United States viewed from this perspective did not seem entirely undeserved. After 1958 the claims by foreign nations on American gold reserves soared. By 1959 these claims reached to $3.5 billion for the year; they went to $3.4 billion for 1960, and to $2.5 billion for 1961. This apparent relationship between national morality and the outflow of gold, tautology though it may be, suggests what rigorous optimism may be worth. Without such an outlook, not only common stock but the Dollar itself comes under pressures from alien forces.

· 8 ·

The next chapter will return to these matters of popular religion. Just now it is necessary to go back to the beginning of the Eisenhower bull market, which began in 1953 and lasted—with its afterglow—until the end of 1961.

The Eisenhower bull market was of course fed by high expectations of future gains. What gave those expectations sub-

---

* There is something of a tautology here that should not pass unremarked. "Morality," to many, is merely another aspect of solvency; that is to say, there is a functional identity between the terms. The Calvinist heresy that makes such an equation possible will be examined in the next chapter. Here it is enough to say that the events of 1958–1961 may simply provide additional proof not only of the equation of riches and moral excellence, but of the related equation of the expectation of future riches and the assessment of present morality.

† A nuance there was the obvious interest of the magazine world to make the most of the TV quiz scandals, as television was a competing medium for advertising revenue. Therefore the quaking indignation of many magazines over the alleged moral crisis may have been at bottom an oblique pitch for advertising dollars.

stance was the new set of tax concessions to upper-income earners as one of the first steps taken by the new Administration. In fact, the Eisenhower Era was bracketed by two actions that summed up the whole period. The first major piece of legislation was the law giving the states control of offshore oil (out to three miles or ten and a half miles, depending on which state was involved). One of the last things the Eisenhower Administration did was to lay out some $300,000 for a study of unemployment figures to see if there was "any deception" in them; to see if they were giving an unnecessarily gloomy picture of the extent of idleness in the workforce. At the outset came concrete good news for private business interests; at the close came a last attempt to reduce an indicator of possible pessimism. For those with an eye for symmetry, there was much in those events to admire.

The Congress finished its revisions of the Internal Revenue Code in 1954. The new concession took the form of greatly liberalized depreciation allowances for industrial corporations, which inspired a great deal of investor activity. New rules had the effect of hastening automation while building up common stock value. As common stock rose in price, the itch to merge grew all but irresistible to industrial corporations. A huge wave of mergers and acquisitions followed the new tax relaxations, and once again there was solid cause for joy in investment circles. A corporation could buy a competitor by issuing its own money. That is to say, it could acquire a smaller or financially weaker company by paying for the company it was buying with its own common stock. In such circumstances, almost everything depended on a healthy stock-market valuation of the paper assets of the buying corporation. The rich basked in the warm glow of easy gain as these consolidations went into effect. Capital gains, tax-loss carry-forwards, and other arcane tax maneuvering filled many days with new zest and gusto.

The stock-market indexes rose very steeply in that favorable climate. The Dow-Jones Industrial Average more than doubled between 1953 and 1961. That was the ethereal valuation. The real evaluation of the capacity reflected in those corporate shares was Gross National Product, which grew by less than half the rate of the paper values. Thus, on a glance, one might say that optimism improved by a factor of 2 during those years. That estimate seems about right when viewed from another angle, the relationship of per-share earnings to the price of common stock. This ratio is computed by dividing the selling price of a stock by its earnings record. Thus if IBM, for instance, is earning at an annual rate of $8 per share but is priced at $400 per share, its price-earnings ratio is said to be 50. At the beginning of the Eisenhower Era, the price-earnings ratio for all stocks stood at 11. At the end of that era, 1961, it had risen to 23.

Things didn't grow *that* much better all by themselves. Administered optimism during those years made significant new breakthroughs in technique. One innovation was essentially negative in nature, and was called into being by the disconcerting recurrence of recessions during that period. The balmy years of easy winnings were punctuated by sharp downward turns in the business cycle in 1954, 1958, and 1960. Unemployment rose swiftly in each downturn, and when "recovery" was achieved, the residue of unemployment was higher than at the last "recovery."

One of the standing policies of the Eisenhower Administration was a restriction on the use of the word "recession." As a historical allusion, it was permissible. As a descriptive term for the present or future, it was strictly banned. Therefore various substitutes appeared. "Rolling readjustment" was one of the more memorable euphemisms.

With or without euphemisms, unemployment would not go away. It remained there as a potential source of widening pessimism and ill-cheer. Political rules-of-thumb in the early 1950's had made a 3 percent unemployment figure acceptable; in the mid-1950's the figure was 4 percent; in the early 1960's, it became 5 percent. As the actual figure climbed near 7 percent in 1960–1961, a new tactic seemed to be in order. Euphemism alone was not doing the job that had to be done.

Something must be wrong with the figures. That quickly became the consensus among some of the nation's soundest thinkers. Sure enough, on closer examination, something *was* wrong. The wrongness began with the method of gathering information. Census Bureau enumerators were going to each of 35,000 households scattered in 641 counties and cities. They were asking who was at work, who was out of work, who was seeking work. The sample return was then blown up to yield a national unemployment figure. The system had been instituted in 1940 and had, for more than twenty years, given fair service. But then, in 1960, it began producing uncomfortably large figures. Clearly, something had to be done.

Critics thought they had found part of the trouble. It was the enumerators' zeal for their work. For instance, if an enumerator called on a family in which the mother had recently watched the last child get married and start out on his own, the result might be this:

CENSUS ENUMERATOR: Mrs. Jones? Did you work at a job last week?
MRS. JONES: No, but—
ENUMERATOR: Did you look for work?
MRS. JONES: Well, I did go by the placement bureau. They didn't have anything for me, but I filled out an application anyway.

That month, Mrs. Jones was added to the unemployed. Furthermore, recently graduated college students who had not yet found jobs were also added to the rolls.

The McGraw-Hill Publishing Company took space in metropolitan newspapers and in its own trade journals to explain a few of the noxious effects of such overzealous statistics-gathering. "We're Giving the United States a Black Eye That Is Not Deserved," the advertisement's headline said. "The broad concept of unemployment we use exaggerates the amount of unemployment in the United States as compared to most other countries. Our reporting system also falls short of presenting a balanced picture by concentrating on people who are idle, while neglecting jobs that are idle because people cannot be found to fill them." [16]

The defective figures were damping a lot of cheer, the advertisement added. "It used to be that graduation from college was regarded as a day for great celebration and rejoicing. But, because of the way the Labor Department does its counting of unemployment, it is now a day of sorrow."

Reader's Digest joined the campaign. "Let's Look at Those 'Alarming' Unemployment Figures," a September, 1961, article advised. The major point the article made was that the figures were grossly misleading because a "bureaucratic compulsion" in the Bureau of Labor Statistics was forcing overstated estimates. Just why should anyone want to exaggerate the bad news? "[T]o push Uncle Sam into new federal spending programs and new controls over the economy," the magazine explained.

The Bureau of Labor Statistics responded to this attack by writing to the *Digest* chief editors and citing twelve major errors of fact or interpretation in the article. No retraction appeared.

U.S. News & World Report magazine carried a copyrighted article the next month in which the Commissioner of Labor Statistics indicated that "hard core" unemployment was really a minor worry. Of the total unemployed, he said, 10 to 12 percent were "looking only for part-time jobs." The *New York Times* columnist Arthur Krock applauded the Commissioner's "honest and valuable effort to clarify the statistics, and put them in the true perspective, which is obstructed by politics as usual." [17]

President Kennedy, in response to these pressures, appointed a six-man committee of economic experts to examine the validity of the unemployment figures.

Meanwhile, the other side of the controversy found itself nearly jammed out for a time. As the AFL-CIO pointed out, the figures did not show all those who were working less than a full forty-hour week—those who kept their positions by accepting a reduction in hours (and pay) to twenty-four hours a week, for instance. Furthermore, if a man had not looked for a job, because he knew it was no use, he was reclassified. "Not in labor force," was his new designation. Therefore he was no longer among the unemployed as far as the statistics indicated.

"Squeezing the unemployment statistics to make a very unsatisfactory performance seem somewhat less so seems to be a waste of talent," wrote former presidential economic adviser Leon Keyserling to the *New York Times*.[18]

Indeed, I suggest that the new commission, appointed to re-examine methods of counting unemployment, look to the fact that unemployment is very much higher than the official figures disclose.

These official figures do not take account of the gross under-utilization of employed manpower due to chronic economic slack, which explains why our economy is now running 10 to 15 per cent below maximum production. . . .

Nor do the official figures take account of the fact that fewer people are being drawn into the labor force than would be drawn in if the economy were performing more satisfactorily.

Nor do the official figures even include the full-time equivalent of part-time unemployment. Taking into account this last factor alone, the true level of unemployment was close to 9 per cent of the civilian force in January [1961], and not much different in October [1960].

As the *Economist* of London concluded, "It will be surprising if [the new presidential commission] gives much support to the critics." [19] The "critics" the *Economist* had in mind were not those who thought the figures understated unemployment. That case had no status to speak of in Washington.

Thus the essentially negative attempt to brighten up the unemployment statistics sputtered out. But elsewhere, administered optimism was busily at work during that era with other negative schemes. The automotive industry provided one example and the steel industry a second.

The auto complaint was that the Commerce Department was making unfavorable forecasts of future auto sales at a time when there was already enough uncertainty without help from government agencies. The departmental forecast in December, 1960, said auto sales during 1961 would be 14 percent below the 1960 level. The auto industry protested. The Commerce Department was taking auto production figures, not sales figures, to predict how sales would go. Not fair, said the auto men. Furthermore, it might spread unwarranted gloom. The Commerce Department agreed. Thereafter, officials said, they would take steps to make the forecasts "less precise."

The steel industry efforts concerned the public announcements of operating rates made by the American Iron and Steel Institute. As long as this figure remained high, no one seemed to object much to its use. But when the operating rate got embarrassingly low, the steel industry found many reasons why such figures were defective. It was difficult to measure total industry capacity, in the first place, because of rapid technological advances. Who was to say whether the American steel companies could turn out 150 million or 195 million tons a year? The announcement of the withdrawn figures came after Christmas, 1960. It was a week in which the operating rate, couched in those defective figures, was 38.7 percent of capacity, lowest in twenty-two years.

Into darkness went the percentage index. In its place came a weekly production figure expressed in tons. But when the level of output climbed steeply a year later, the vanishing figure became visible again. "Production last week was equal to about 83.5 per cent of capacity, up from 82 per cent for the preceding week," the *New York Times* of February 6, 1962, reported. Somehow, there just wasn't any way to suppress good news.

Negative steps like those described above remained largely curiosity pieces, not at all in the mainstream of administered optimism. That mainstream was still marked by uplifting discourse. The Advertising Council, in March, 1961, for example, announced that it was planning "psychological warfare" against recession. The campaign was modeled on the "You Auto Buy Now" campaign of 1958 and was called "Operation Optimism."

At about the same time, the National Retail Merchants Association urged its members to express their

confidence in the basic soundness of the free American economy and its prospects for continuing growth. Merchants, as representatives of the consumer, should take the lead in stimulating the new and healthy economic growth that lies ahead.

There are many ways a merchant can express his confidence in the economy and instill the same confidence in the customer. For example, these are the things you can and should do now: (1) Demonstrate your confidence by going ahead with your plans for expansion and modernization; (2) Instill this same confidence in your customers . . . ; (3) Work with moulders of public opinion in your community . . . to spotlight the positive elements in the economy and the steps that you and others are taking to strengthen the economic conditions in the community. . . .

Shortly after these plans had been made, large advertisements began appearing in the mass media. The most striking of them was the Advertising Federation of America's "Miracle at the spot marked X" ad. A large photograph showed a blackboard on which was a break-even point made by an ascending arrow marked "volume" and a descending arrow marked "unit cost." Pointing to it was a young man sparse of hair but ample of tooth. He was leering or chortling (it was hard to say which), but it was optimism; that much was clear.

United States Steel, meanwhile, was running full-page ads in metropolitan newspapers that showed Lowell Thomas, a radio-television commentator, "Watching America Grow." Thomas was shown in such places as Levittown, Pennsylvania, and Circleville, Ohio, overseeing various manifestations of booming conditions. Vacuum towers, food mixers, public buildings, assembly lines, and cornfields all appeared in photographs. The religious and cultural "booms" were also carefully chronicled. (The campaign was ungraciously cited by one advertising trade magazine as one of the worst of the year. "Corny," the magazine suggested.)

American Telephone and Telegraph Company, at the same time, was announcing "New Horizons in Communications" in double-page advertisements in national magazines. A more tangible showing of confidence could not have been made than to announce an investment program of $2.5 billion in "new equipment, new services and new ideas." The ad ended with a small commercial-within-a-commercial in behalf of the beleaguered

American investor. "Investors will continue to put up the billions only if they expect to be reasonably well paid for the use of their money." That, of course, would be impossible without "continued adequate earnings." Those worries were peripheral, however. The here-and-now message was that "Our job is BIG—and growing at a fantastic rate."

The same period saw General Motors announcing that it planned an investment of $1.25 billion for the year. *Business Week* noted that it was "another move to bolster business confidence."

The confluence of all that good news no doubt did soften the 1960–1961 recession, but it did very little, if anything, to reduce unemployment. The figures seemed stuck near 7 percent, and no treatment of symptoms appeared able to remove the disease itself.

As that year progressed, there was a severe strain on optimism occasioned by the pressures over Berlin. As July came, the warlike atmosphere deepened, and it became worse month by month. There was talk of "tough-mindedness" in the air, while generalized optimism faded somewhat. The crisis passed, by the end of the harvest. In October, an indicator of some small importance for the domestic economy showed up. It was the publication of Norman Vincent Peale's first important new book since the great best seller *The Power of Positive Thinking*. As described by his publisher, the book was

> A new, dynamic approach!
> NORMAN VINCENT PEALE
> reveals how to become
> The Tough-Minded
> —practical and realistic—
> Optimist
> —minimizes adversities, anticipates the best

Dr. Peale adds a new dimension to positive thinking, the quality of toughmindedness. He speaks straightforwardly to millions of Americans who want to meet life's problems, and, through real faith in the outcome, turn these problems into the building blocks for successful tomorrows.

Unlike its predecessor, which sold some two million copies and signaled (and perhaps helped to cause) the great bull market of 1953–1961, the new Peale book never showed up on the best-seller lists. Shortly thereafter, for reasons harder to assign, the Dow-Jones Industrial Average began slipping downward from the high at year-end of 731. Within five months in 1962, in fact, the average had dropped more than 100 points, and marked the onset of a new bear market, "The Kennedy Bear Market," as it was called by those who do not feel wholly at ease until they are given a slogan that seems to reflect some sort of thought process.

For those with an eye on the balance of morality, there had been warning signals. A skillful demonologist might have followed a trail something like this: An obviously immoral dance had been trying without success to catch on in an obscure West Side Manhattan bar for months. One day, a Hearst gossip columnist mentioned that certain socialites had gone to the little bistro and were dancing the "twist," as it was called. Uptown, at Time-Life Plaza, the fad-watchers got wind of the dance, and before anyone knew what had happened, a national craze for the ludicrous dance swept from coast to coast and carried as far west as Japan and as far east as Poland.

Dwight Eisenhower made the vague misgivings of many of his fellow Americans concrete in informal remarks he made on May Day, 1962, at the dedication of the Eisenhower Library in Abilene, Kansas. "What has happened to our concept of beauty and decency and morality?" the former President asked. "I wonder," he said, "if some of those people [the pioneers] could come back today and see us doing the twist instead of the minuet—whether they would be particularly struck by the beauty of that dance.

"Now, I have no objection to the twist, as such," he added, "but it does represent some kind of change in our standards." He went on to remark on the "vulgarity, sensuality, indeed, downright filth" in movies, plays, books, and magazines.

That was May 1st, a day that saw a modest gain in the Dow-Jones Industrial Average, to 671. Within days of this authoritative warning about moral decline, stock values resumed their decline.

A week later, the Average had dropped to 664. Two weeks later, to 655. Then, from 90 miles up the Hudson, came a confirming signal that might have proved useful, had there been such a thing as a Dow-Jones Morality Theorist available to interpret it. Vassar College president Sarah Gibson Blanding told a convocation of her students that their own moral conduct was something of a disgrace. Standards of maidenly virtue, she suggested, were sinking precipitously.* The Dow-Jones Average continued down. By May 22nd it was down to 636. And finally, on a single day, the Average dropped a sickening 35 points. That was May 28th, the worst day in Wall Street since Tuesday, October 29, 1929. Over $20 billion in paper valuation disappeared.

· 9 ·

The Kennedy bear market had started, as it appeared in retrospect, back on December 13, 1961, when the Average stood at an all-time-high figure of 734. Paper valuations started on an irregular decline thereafter, but to many, that did not seem significant. First-of-year tax selling had long been a Wall Street convention. The figure was briefly down to 690 in January, and hovered near that plateau until mid-April. Optimism, by then, had paled noticeably. Price-earning ratios fell back from 23 to 21. The promised Federal government liberalization of depreciation regulations did seem to stir faint investor euphoria, but it wasn't to be that simple. The Kennedy Administration had caused a few scares. It had talked about tightening up on expense accounts and withholding dividend and interest taxes. The atmosphere was not wholly clear from the standpoint of corporate America.

Then came the Steel Pricing Affair. At first, there had been general agreement that United States Steel had handled itself with inspired gaucherie. It became known, however, that the President had called businessmen sons of bitches, that the Justice Depart-

---

* Although Miss Blanding had delivered her speech in early April, it remained in obscurity for more than a month until, on May 8, 1962, the *New York Herald Tribune* published its version of the talk.

ment had threatened to speed up pending antitrust prosecutions, and that F.B.I. men had made nocturnal calls on newspaper reporters in quest of damning evidence against steel leaders. Under those circumstances, investors could hardly be expected to feel stout of heart.

What caused the May, 1962, panic? The investment community blamed the President. Had that community been equipped with less rigid instruments of analysis, perhaps it could have cited Chubby Checker, William Randolph Hearst, Jr., Henry Luce, Dwight Eisenhower, John Hay Whitney, or even the student body of Vassar College as at least subsidiary causes for the collapse in ethereal valuations. But it did not. The President was really responsible, they said.

After the new deluge, the ritual optimists, as is their custom, became ritually lachrymose. They had held on as long as they could, however. In fact, *Time* magazine made an interesting discovery. The American press had missed "by a country mile . . . the biggest financial story of the year," the magazine noted in its June 4th issue. "All during the wild skid that led to last week's 'Black Monday' [May 28th], the U.S. press maintained what amounted to an unintentional conspiracy of silence [about the falling stock market]." Suddenly, a "feast" of coverage. It was "perplexing," *Time* said. Was it all that perplexing? Just two wire services supplied most of the nation's newspapers with what market news came from Manhattan, and neither had won a reputation for cold-blooded analytics where the American economy was concerned. Was it, then, an unintentional conspiracy? The canons of administered optimism seemed to suggest otherwise.

The stock market went into a series of wild gyrations that Memorial Day week. Down more than 35 points on Monday, up 29 on Tuesday, holiday Wednesday. Thursday saw a further increase of 9 points, and Friday a gentle sagging of 2 points. For the week, the average was off less than a point. Volume of trading, however, had averaged 10 million shares a day. Succeeding weeks saw another series of slides—of 17 points in one instance—and weak rallies. The market valuations progressively worked down-

ward toward the middle 500 range, 30 percent below their previous high level. Needless to say, the erstwhile optimists had not
entirely fled the arena. Nor had they uniformly lapsed into their
alternate incarnation of lachrymose paranoia. There was some
paranoia, however.

It began in a systematic way shortly after the Steel Pricing
Affair in April. Presidential initiative became a presidential
"power play," and ultimately became, in the horrified eyes of
some, as reported by the New York *Daily News,* "a savage,
Gestapo-like attack." Steel men showed up at a two-day general
meeting of the American Iron and Steel Institute in New York on
May 24–25 emitting dense clouds of provisional gloom. Their rate
of operations was down to 57 percent, for one thing. For another,
they still labored under the psychic levy of April 13th. A sprin-
kling of orange buttons appeared on steel executives' lapels. "SOB
Club," they said. The chairman of Jones & Laughlin seemed to
speak for his fellows—and simultaneously to explain why the
gloom was not unalloyed. He said, "If the Kennedy Administration really wanted to assure us that this is a pro-business administration, the most electrifying statement he could make would be
that he would work to give our country the best depreciation
policy in the world instead of the worst." A more formalized complaint was delivered in an address to a plenary session of steel
executives in the Grand Ballroom of the Waldorf-Astoria. An
attentive audience of more than a thousand industry leaders heard
the president of Pittsburgh Steel Company lambaste the administration for its "effrontery." "The obvious direction of all of its
policies is toward a form of socialism," the executive said. He
added that "a tiny handful of Government officials" was seizing
"monopoly power over business and industry. . . ." The address
drew a standing ovation.

Elsewhere there were signs of real, not provisional, gloom. The
agreeable Kingdom of Monaco sadly reported during the same
week that the season at Monte Carlo threatened to be lusterless.
Worry hung over the Riviera because of the downward drift in
stock prices in the United States. "Cancellations have already

been received," the *New York Times* reported, "and one long-time hotel man said he longed for the days his father knew when the rich were not so dependent on such erratic things as stock markets."

Back in America, that week also saw the New York Stock Exchange president, Keith Funston, telling Securities and Exchange Commission investigators that charges of serious laxness in market practices might have the effect "of highlighting a few drops of rain . . . [and making] people think there is a thunderstorm." As Funston was making his defense of market practices, exchange officials quietly announced that minimum training time for limited registered representatives would be increased to three months from the customary one-month minimum.

The same day, Henry Ford II let it be known at his company's annual meeting that "something important [is] missing from the current scene—confidence on the part of business in the basic attitude of the Government toward a free market economy." Mr. Ford added, "I fear that the enormous power that can be mustered by a determined and resourceful President might be used increasingly to impose . . . direct controls on the legitimate actions of business and, possibly, of labor."

The following Monday—"Blue Monday"—opinions began to harden. Investor confidence, it then could be told, was badly shaken. At 3:30 P.M. that day the Associated Press sent out a bulletin that must have shocked many with its unexpected message: "The stock market closed drastically lower today in one of the worst crashes in the history of Wall Street."

The day after, the *Wall Street Journal* said in its lead editorial, ". . . recognizing the connection between the President's display of anger [at the steel leaders] and the beginning of the market decline is not the same thing as blaming that incident for the fall itself." The *Herald Tribune* was less circumspect. On its front page it editorialized: "Yesterday's shock in Wall Street calls for more than a formal word from the White House. It calls for a convincing—and immediate—demonstration that investment, i.e., business itself, has in Mr. Kennedy the friend he claims to be."

The *Times*, the same day, noted equably that in spite of the panic, the year promised to be quite prosperous. If things really should turn steeply downward, the *Times* suggested, there was the Keynesian apparatus, specifically the Employment Act of 1946, to serve as a guide to government policy.

In the succeeding days, there was talk of a tax reduction to spur investor confidence. There was also talk of the impending depreciation liberalization. And there was a great deal of assurance that the American economy was in a fundamentally sound position.

Former President Eisenhower showed up in Washington shortly thereafter. In response to reporters' questions about the market panic, he said, "When something like that happens, I don't allow any newspapers in my office." [20] On further reflection, Mr. Eisenhower said that "reckless spending programs" of the Kennedy Administration were at least partially responsible for the panic. On earlier occasions Mr. Eisenhower had let it be known that such spending programs contributed to budget deficits, which he considered "immoral." Henry Ford II, meanwhile, had had second thoughts about his earlier saturnine observations. The market panic, he said, had been caused basically by foreign investor panic. Aliens, he suggested, had taken their short-term money out of the stock market in America. As for the auto industry, he said the year looked promising indeed. In general it was a "bright business picture."

Others, however, were rapidly becoming inconsolable. A Scripps-Howard columnist, Henry J. Taylor, wrote on June 4th: "One after another of our basic (job-giving) industries is in deep, deep trouble. These include the entire vast railroad industry, steel, copper, aluminum, every metal mining company, the domestic petroleum producers, the airlines, textiles, glass, farm implements, shipbuilding, cement, aircraft and missiles . . . , electronics, and coal." Why? The profit-squeeze, for one thing. For another, presidential economic advisers who know as much about business "as the tropical fish of the Emperor of Japan." These advisers were "a crowd debauching their prejudices with vindictive and specious logic." What hope? None, really, unless the President discovered that "it is grass-roots self-reliance, planning, thrift, indi-

vidual effort and risk-taking . . . that makes America tick." [21]
Unless, one might say, there were some kind of return to basic
American morality.

The *Herald Tribune*'s financial editor took a somewhat more
irenic line. Still, he made it clear that bad administration tax policy was causing a great deal of trouble. He held out hope for historic greatness for the government, however. "The Administration has an opportunity to make a great record on taxes. It
could produce a tax reform that would cause it to live in history."
The editor's suggested legislation was the Herlong-Baker bill that
had for years been stirring great enthusiasm at the National Association of Manufacturers headquarters (where, some said, it
had been drafted). Roger Blough of United States Steel was also
in a peacemaking mood. He told a meeting of the large utilities
in Atlantic City that business-government relations had to be improved. "Confidence," he said, "needs support on both sides." He
added that "restoration of confidence would get a major boost if
something was done basically to improve the depreciation situation."

For those intrigued with paradoxes, the Kennedy bear market
had great charm. The vigorously advanced views of the vested
interests before the onset of that new market underwent an instantaneous modification by emphasis after the downturn. The
interests had been opposed to inflation, Federal deficits, foreign
competition, the gold outflow, rising costs, falling profits, and in-
adequate depreciation regulations. Gold seemed to embody most
of their sentiments.

Because that metal serves to settle international accounts, its
movements are taken as an index of the relative economic strength
of various Western nations.*

---

* In the 1950's and 1960's, when there was talk of a gold "outflow," it
didn't mean the gold was really leaving the country—except, perhaps, in the
sense that some of it left Kentucky for Manhattan. In Manhattan, it shuffled
between various subterranean cages in the Federal Reserve Bank's sub-
basement, or it occasionally moved from the United States Mint in lower
Manhattan to the Reserve Bank, a few blocks away. New York bedrock, investors almost everywhere agreed, was a safer place for the gold than under
an Arles haystack, in a Geneva strongbox, or in a West End wall safe.

In October, 1960, there had been great excitement in London bullion markets as the price of gold rose steeply. The price rise was a sign of diminishing confidence in the dollar. There was worldwide frenzy as the speculation against the dollar increased. At one stage, so great grew the excitement, brokers on the floor of the Johannesburg, South Africa, gold exchange tore each other's ties off, in their anxiety to make deals. In Hong Kong, Toronto, and Zurich there was a fleeting conviction that the dollar might have to be devalued (and if so, a well timed gold purchase might double a man's money overnight). Soundest opinion in world financial centers at the time appeared to be that the dollar was weakening because candidate Kennedy was the likely victor in the coming American presidential election. Mr. Kennedy was thought to have an inflationary package of legislation to advance once he was installed in office. The world had heard candidate Nixon's charges and had noted them. Nixon said time and again that were Kennedy elected, the price of everything the American housewife bought would soar 25 percent. The gold rush was over within a few weeks, however, because of close cooperation between various foreign central banks and the Federal Reserve.

As it developed, the Kennedy Administration soon made it quite clear that reasonable price stability would be preferable to full employment. Although it is something of a simplification to say the choice was either/or, those were the basic alternatives. Because of growing foreign competition, however, and because of the continuing expense of maintaining overseas military bases and personnel, the United States found itself faced with a large imbalance in international payments. That condition threatened to get worse if American prices were to rise more than prices in other Western nations. If that happened, the gold outflow would worsen, as gold is one medium used to balance international transactions. If gold flowed out at a still faster rate, the dollar would lose value relative to other Western currencies. Thereby a whole new set of problems would rise to confound the Administration. For example, the military balance within the Western alliance might well change, and therefore the power of the West could conceivably decline. American unemployment with price stability thus was a means of paying for continued military preeminence, and it was also a means of avoiding risky adjustments in the Western alliance.

The Kennedy Administration therefore made continual efforts to keep inflationary pressures under control. The Steel Pricing Affair was just such an effort.

The prime interests at that juncture regrouped. Neither an end to the gold outflow nor reasonable price stability seemed a wholly worthy goal any longer. Not, at any rate, if those goals had to be pursued by means of price controls. American industry could not tolerate interference in the free market economy. Principle clearly came first, and the cardinal principle was the preservation of "liberty." The government's policies were thus most unwelcome, once it became clear that they would be pursued at the cost of "liberty." The Federal government thereby lost the confidence of America's investors, said some of America's biggest investors. When that confidence was lost, the optimism of happier days quickly dissipated. Stock prices declined—gently at first, then steeply. And thus for pursuing noninflationary policies, the Administration had caused a grave loss of buoyancy.

The investors' response was to begin buying gold shares, on the theory that as the dollar could not stand inflationary policies from Federal government, neither could it stand the sustained funk of investors.

The only news that seemed to soothe the jangled nerves of America's prime interests was the presidential assurance, the Secretary of the Treasury's assurance, and the Secretary of Commerce's assurance that taxes would come down soon. Further balm was forthcoming in the form of liberalized depreciation regulations. It would have been untrue to say that the government engineered a handout to America's investors to buy back their confidence, for clearly the government was not paying out anything. It was merely making arrangements not to collect as much as it had planned to do in a day of greater optimism. In any case, that confidence was restored by the end of 1962, as were 90 percent and more of the lost paper values of Blue Monday.

· 10 ·

In conclusion, it may be said that the psychological climate in which America's vested interests operate most efficiently is that of sustained and widespread optimism. Because of the huge super-structure of ethereal valuations, which is an important adjunct of continued material growth and progress, the prime interests go to some lengths to maintain a mood of cheer and confidence throughout the populace.

A grave threat to the sustained optimism of the population is the large and growing numbers of poor who have no real reason to feel cheery about their future, so bleak is their present. The vested interests, therefore, find themselves in the position of having to increase the output of affirmations by means of advertising and public-relations techniques. They occasionally find themselves suppressing bad news, and they constantly find themselves exag-gerating good news—unless Federal government actions provide a means by which administered pessimism may produce impor-tant tax concessions. That last behavior pattern was highly visible during the 1962 stock-market panic. There, a short campaign of organized pessimism produced concessions of magnitude great enough to inspire a new increment of optimism in the upper-income brackets.

· 11 ·

An instrument of great utility in maintaining the proper psycho-logical climate has been popular religion. On the one hand, popu-lar religion has done much to create an ideology of achievement well suited to industrial conditions. On the other hand, popu-lar religion of a more specialized sort has also done much to soften the effects of pessimism among the poor. The fundamentalist sects that attract wide support from the poor arm those folk for a long-range optimism by concentrating on the rewards to be won in the next life. Therefore, rewards not won in this life become unimportant. A large part of the population in that way shuns the hierarchy of values held by the middle and upper classes.

It is to an examination of the religious doctrines that have helped create and now help sustain the favorable climate of achievement in the middle and upper classes that I now turn.

EIGHT

Vested Interests and Religion

ЛЛЛЛЛЛЛ

Vested interests, as one might suspect, have had noticeable influence on religious thought; at the same time, religious doctrines have had great impact on the development of modern industry: The influences have flowed both ways.

There is a great deal of evidence that the Protestant varieties of religious belief very nearly created the cultural climate in which industrialism could progress to its present eminence. (Calvinist innovations growing out of the Reformation seem to have been of key importance.) On the other hand, there are those who argue that the rising commercial spirit of the late Middle Ages virtually called the new Protestant doctrines into being; that industry flourished best where heresy had raged most virulently in medieval days. (The examples of Switzerland, Languedoc, Catalonia, northern Italy, and Bohemia all seem to provide at least partial support for such an argument.)

To the question of who is influencing whom in twentieth century America, the modern popular religious literature seems to yield an answer. In addition, for those interested in the possible equation of heresy (in its traditional sense) and business dominance, this body of literature provides a gamy hunting ground. As Bruce Barton said in *What Can a Man Believe?*

What sort of questions would Jesus be likely to ask of candidates if He were examining them in a church convocation?

Speaking very reverently, it seems as if He might be interested in points like these:

"Could you conduct a successful carpenter shop or fishing business? Have you demonstrated that you can make a success of business?"

These are sensible questions. They reach down toward the sources of Jesus' own power and success.[1]

Or as Norman Vincent Peale asked twenty-five years later in *The Power of Positive Thinking:*

Where is the old-fashioned businessman who says that religion is theoretical and has no place in business? Today any successful and competent businessman will employ the latest and best-tested methods in production, distribution, and administration, and many are discovering that one of the greatest of all efficiency methods is prayer power.[2]

The point of view suggested by those passages of course does not reflect the only stance taken by modern Protestantism. But if popularity is a reliable index of which branch of Protestantism commands the greatest residual support, there seems to be little question that Calvinist mutations such as those of Barton and Peale rank very high if they do not predominate.

There are three business themes in modern Protestantism that the popular literature emphasizes time and again: work is worship, wealth is goodness, and positive thinking is a rewarding frame of mind.

· 1 ·

Calvin Coolidge in 1921 described the ideal of work-is-worship when he said, "The man who builds a factory builds a temple, the man who works there worships there, and to each is due not scorn and blame, but reverence and praise. . . ."[3] During the same year industrial publisher James A. McGraw told the annual meeting of the Associated Business Papers, Inc., that what was needed to spur industrial revival was a resurgence of "the gospel of intelligent work." "The first nation that gets hold of the idea that the only salvation comes from work will come out on top and really win the peace," McGraw added.

In the 1930's and 1940's the shock of Depression muted the equation of worship and production, but in the 1950's and 1960's it had come back in slightly changed fashion. In the 1960's popular religion became more of an ideological tool. Of these matters, something will be said in a while. Just now, a further word on the development of this "neo-Calvinism" is in order.

The entire body of modern American inspirational literature was subjected to an exacting analysis by two scholars in the 1950's. Professors Louis Schneider and Sanford M. Dornbusch took the fifty-odd best-selling books with religious themes that had appeared between 1875 and 1955 and coded each paragraph in each book on the basis of its content. Many paragraphs, of course, were neutral and therefore were not included in the final analysis. The others, however, were filed according to what views they advanced on such things as the function of religious faith; the relationships of God, man, and nature; change in oneself and in the world; and the rationale, attitudes, and techniques of salvation. Their conclusion appeared in *Popular Religion: Inspirational Books in America*.[4]

Schneider and Dornbusch found "the elements of what we may call a special kind of 'neo-Calvinist' doctrine." The basic thrust of the new doctrine was that a man's worldly condition tells him something about "whether he is saved or not." In the Schneider-Dornbusch analysis there appears a clue as to the philosophical roots of ritual optimism as well as illumination of much else peculiar to American Protestantism. In the lexicon of neo-Calvinism:

(1) . . . Terms like "good" and "bad" and "sinful" and "wicked" refer to psychic processes or states. States of anxiety, fear, hostility, and the like are simply instances of wrong or bad thinking. (2) Closely associated with this is the stress which plainly implies that the "good" man is the positive thinker, the "bad" man the negative thinker. In principle, "good" or "bad" thinking is the only kind of good or evil there is. All moral or ethical references in any traditional sense have thus been lost. (3) Otherworldly references have also been dropped

out. . . . (4) . . . Not only does prosperity argue that positive thought is taking place (as it once argued that a man had God's approval of his work and himself), but so also do good health, happiness, and, on a grander scale, peace among nations or good business conditions or any other desired set of circumstances. (5) Finally, if we may employ a phrase of Kipling's, "the law runneth forward and back." . . . Positive thinking leads to good things. The presence of good things *also* means that positive thinking occurs. Negative thinking leads to disaster, and disaster argues negative thinking. . . .[5]

Schneider and Dornbusch also detected a pervasive loosening up of the old Talmudic God of Judgment. They observed that Hollywood actress Jane Russell let it be known that while once God was a stranger to her, she got to know him and he was revealed as a "livin' doll."

The theme of judgment was not prominent in the inspirational best sellers. God instead seems to be ready to shower riches on those who worship by the right methods, which turn out more often than not to be business methods.

> You should be a righteous man; if you were, you would be rich.
> I say then that you ought to be rich.
> No man has a moral right to transact business unless he makes something out of it.
> The foundation principles of business success and the foundation principles of Christianity itself are both the same. . . . He who can do the most to help fellow men is entitled to the greatest reward himself. Not only so saith God's holy book, but also saith every man's business common sense.
> It is cruel to slander the rich because they have been successful.
> . . . . They are not scoundrels because they have gotten money. They have blessed the world. . . . Go through this city and your very best people are among your richest people.

Thus ran the peroration of the enormously popular "Acres of Diamonds" lecture delivered by Russell Conwell all over America at the turn of the century to packed lecture halls.[6]

A further strong theme of this body of literature is the essential political and economic conservatism of the popular religionists. Reform, they seem to say with nearly one voice, should be carried out on an individual basis. Social institutions are not considered nearly so important as individual predilections. Earthly evils, therefore, are the aggregate of human evils and should be mitigated—if they can be at all—by individual reform. Henry Link, whose *The Return to Religion* came out in 1936, went so far as to say that the "desire to change the social order [is] one of the most common symptoms of an inferiority complex." Jesus, Link added, was certainly no "social reformer," but rather "a reformer of men." (Link also had a marked admiration for the American businessman: "The businessman, the employer, performs the daily miracle of converting water into wine. He converts raw materials into the means of a livelihood, and he converts undirected employees, individualists, into members of a team which has both direction and power.")

The ultimate statement of the identity of business and religion —the probable inspiration for much of the later work of the busy author, Dr. Norman Vincent Peale—was made by Barton, the son of a minister, and the cofounder of the advertising agency Batten, Barton, Durstine & Osborne. Barton's little book *The Man Nobody Knows* (1924) brought Jesus back to life again for 726,892 Americans directly, and probably millions more who read the book without buying it.

Under Barton's skilled ministrations, Jesus came to life as a hard-driving executive, a sport, a life-of-the-party extrovert, an inspired sales manager, an all-media adman, and ultimately as "The Founder of Modern Business." This Nazarene of bulging muscles, purposeful stride, and imperious manner ". . . picked up twelve men from the bottom ranks of business and forged them into an organization that conquered the world." Barton saw Jesus in six aspects:

As executive—"He believed that the way to get faith out of men is to show that you have faith in them; and from that great principle of executive management he never wavered."

As outdoorsman—"He was the type of outdoor man whom our modern thought most admires. . . ." He was unlike the "stern-faced" Jewish prophets who, in contrast to Jesus, "are not the kind of men whom you would choose as companions on a fishing trip."

As life-of-the-party—". . . he makes use of his mighty power [by turning water into wine] not to point a solemn moral, not to relieve a sufferer's pain, but to keep a happy party from breaking up too soon. . . ."

As sales manager—". . . every one of the 'principles of modern salesmanship' on which businessmen pride themselves, are brilliantly exemplified in Jesus' talk and work. . . . [Perhaps the most important of these principles is] 'putting yourself in step with your prospect.' "

As adman—"Jesus of Nazareth . . . would be a national advertiser today, I am sure, as he was the great advertiser of his own day. Take any one of the parables, no matter which—you will find that it exemplifies all the principles on which advertising text books are written."

As Founder of Modern Business—" 'Wist ye not that I be about my father's *business?*' he said. He thought of life as a *business.*"

Barton's culminating passage summed up the "Protestant Ethic" as it evolved in the 1920's. "Great progress," Barton wrote, "will be made in the world when we rid ourselves of the idea that there is a difference between *work* and *religious* work. . . . All work is worship; all useful service prayer. And whoever works wholeheartedly at any worthy calling is a co-worker with the Almighty in the great enterprise which He has initiated but which He can never finish without the help of men." [7]

· 2 ·

The extreme statements of these latter-day business religionists did not arise from sheer exuberance. They were new versions of what once were more elevated sentiments. By examining some of their early predecessors' views it may be possible to learn something of value in assessing the moral and philosophical equipage of the modern prime vested interests.

To go back to the beginning, Hebrew belief, under the Mosaic

law, tried to promote equality of wealth for the good of Hebrew
society as a whole. Usury was forbidden between members of
the tribe. As Deuteronomy said:

> Thou shalt not lend upon usury to thy brother; usury of money,
> usury of victuals, usury of any thing that is lent upon usury: Unto a
> stranger thou mayest lend upon usury; but unto thy brother thou shalt
> not . . . [Deut. 23:19, 20].

The Jew, as Haney notes, "came to regard the trader with a considerable degree of contempt, calling him 'Canaanite.' " [8] As the
book of Hosea said, "He is a merchant, the balances of deceit are
in his hand: he loveth to oppress" (Hosea 12:7).

The Bible emphasized again and again the obligation on the
strong to take care of the weak: of society to protect the poor and
to keep them safe from exploitation; to provide interest-free loans
and charity as means of maintaining solidarity among a limited
group of "God's chosen." The New Testament reflected the broad-
ening of such charitable admonitions to all mankind in accordance
with the teachings of Jesus.

The Judeo-Christian economic ideals were, of course, merely
minor themes in a broader context. The end was to live a godly
and righteous life, and wealth was a mere means that was often
considered a barrier to moral perfection. In any event, matters of
economics were marginal in societies that were essentially agrarian
and in which barter predominated.

The rise of Rome put new emphasis on private property and
the agency of contract to effect the purchase and sale of property.
As Haney says, "Roman law lent itself to the tendency to make
economics a science of exchanges determined by the working of
impersonal laws." [9] He also notes "the separation of the non-per-
sonal elements in [Roman economic thought and] law from the
personal, and the emphasis placed upon the former." The ethical
overtones of stoicism exerted restraint on the pagan lust for
gain by urging resignation to the dictates of nature. Marcus Aurelius, for one, urged, " 'Love your trade, however humble,' and
find in it refreshment. Spend life's remainder, as one who with

his whole heart has committed his all to the gods, and is neither tyrant nor slave to any man." [10] And later, Aurelius asked,

Have you ever seen a dismembered hand or foot, or decapitated head, lying severed from the body to which it belonged? Such does a man, so far as he can, make himself, when he refuses to accept what befalls, and isolates himself, or when he pursues self-seeking action. You are cast out from the unity of nature, of which you are an organic part; you dismember your own self.[11]

The Judeo-Christian economic ideas thus merged with the Roman mixture of monetary-property sophistication and the ideal of stoic withdrawal. The amalgam has gone under the name "natural law." In the Middle Ages, the Roman Catholic Church brought these doctrines into unity in the notion of *justum pretium,* the "just price." That price was based on "natural" value under a system of accounting in harmony with "natural law." To sell something for profit was contrary to natural law and was considered sinful.

The works of Albertus Magnus and especially of Thomas Aquinas helped solidify the Church's position on this and other economic rules of conduct. Usury came under particularly heavy attack, apparently in rough proportion to the growth of a money economy. The Church based its views on interest payment directly on Aquinas (who had in turn drawn on the Greek, Hebrew, and early Christian works). Time belonged to everyone, the reasoning ran. It was a gift from God and it could not be bought or sold, which is what seemed to happen when money was lent at interest.

Thus, on a very sketchy glance, it can be seen that by the time of the Renaissance and the rising of the humanism of that day, the Church had taken its stand in opposition (as it developed) to the spirit of commerce. It may say something for the force of the latter that it overcame sixteen centuries of fixed antipathy.

As the historian Henry Charles Lea demonstrated in *The Inquisition of the Middle Ages,* the Roman Church found itself arrayed against heresy that had close and discernible links with what might be called the commercial instinct. The Spanish medieval proverb, in fact, noted that "a little heresy is good for business," and the hotbed of heresy was France, which later was to spawn Calvinism, and the north of Italy, which was later to blossom forth with the Renaissance. The Church was in effect accumulating large quantities of capital under the Inquisition. As Lea noted:

> The blighting influence of [the distrust caused by the Inquisition] . . . upon the development of commerce and industry can readily be perceived, coming as it did at a time when the commercial and industrial movement of Europe was beginning to usher in the dawn of modern culture. It was this, among other incidents of persecution, which arrested the promising civilization of the south of France and transferred to England and the Netherlands, where the Inquisition was comparatively unknown, the predominance in commerce and industry which brought freedom and wealth and power and progress in its train.[12]

Although the Church unquestionably was corrupted and estranged from its own ethical ideals, it still represented the unfulfilled goal of Christianity, a goal that has come under strong attack from some of the most popular varieties of modern Protestantism.

Before Protestanism raised its several heads, humanism had provided much of the intellectual foundation for the revolt against Roman Catholicism by reviving classical learning and thereby erecting a pagan authority equally august to the sacred authority of Rome. As the Ottoman Turks overran Byzantium in the fifteenth century, they sent scurrying before them a large group of scholars who were the trustees of classical learning in a day when the West had all but forgotten its classic ancestry. The Eastern scholars fled mostly to Italy. Their knowledge and their ancient manuscripts fed the new interest in antiquity. They became the catalysts to the Renaissance. Pagan sentiment spread rapidly in the succeeding century through the upper classes everywhere in Europe. Latin and Greek scholarship flowered anew; national literatures emerged; and art flourished, as did science and technology. The new learning acted to weaken the fealty of the upper classes to the Church.

In many ways the epitome of the age was Desiderius Erasmus, the Dutch scholar. Erasmus published a new translation of the New Testament, which exposed many errors in the official Church Testament (the Vulgate). He furthermore attacked the rigidity of Church scholarship with graceful wit in *Praise of Folly* (1509).

The new point of view represented by Erasmus led to a climate of opinion in which a Martin Luther was almost necessary. As one contemporary wag put it, "Erasmus laid the egg; Luther hatched it." [13] It might not be off the point to suggest that Erasmus laid and Luther hatched the egg, and that Calvin brought the issue to market.

· 3 ·

If, as some have said, the Renaissance represented the upper-class revolt against Roman Catholic authority, the Reformation represented the revolt of the middle class.

That revolt was at first moderate enough. Luther was interested primarily in purifying the Church, not in demolishing it. His initial approach was that of a man wielding a feather duster, not a mace. When on Halloween of 1517 he tacked his Ninety-five Theses on the side door of Castle church in Wittenberg, he imagined that nothing more was afoot than an academic exchange of views; that a grateful pope would be pleased that the Church had been alerted to corruption in the sale of indulgences. Within a short time, however, all Germany was exercised over the audacious challenge to papal authority. What Luther had started, others more zealous and radical threatened to finish in a paroxysm of violence. Under the forces thus loosed, the peasantry revolted in 1525 and petitioned its lords for relief. In "The Twelve Articles of the Peasants," the princes were asked to grant local election of pastors, reductions in tithes, an end to serfdom, "brotherly" co-operation in the problem of crop-eating game, rights to gather firewood on common lands, and relief from rack-rents and exorbitant dues. At that point, Luther had the unhappy choice of speaking for the princes or for the peasants. Princely support had undoubtedly spared him from Rome's retribution, while the radical ideas circulating in the peasantry might well have provided comfort to Rome by weakening the princes' authority. Luther spoke up in a tract *Against the Murdering, Thieving Hordes of Peasants*. In it he said, "Let every one who can smite, slay and stab, secretly or openly, remembering that nothing can be more poisonous, hurtful or devilish than a rebel. It is just as when one must kill a mad dog; if you don't strike him, he will strike you, and the whole land with you." [14] To contain such dangerous radicalism, Luther and Lutheranism looked to "the magistry" of princes who ruled "our Germany."

Politically conservative as Luther and his prime associate Melanchthon were, their Reformation nevertheless opened the way for a widespread reaction to all constituted authority. The right wing of that reaction remained docile to civil authority (with, no doubt, a sure sense of self-preservation). The left wing, especially as it was represented by the Swiss Anabaptists, called for immediate separation of Church and State. They wanted nothing less than to shed themselves of the authority of Rome and of local magistracies simultaneously. This Anabaptist movement seems to have been something of a lower-class phenomenon in its origins. As Fosdick has written: "Commonly springing from the depressed and the poor, they [the Anabaptists] appealed to motives which were powerful in the rank and file. All the more, however, because their popularity was dangerous, they were persecuted with a ruthlessness which in the end almost obliterated them." [15] Thus until the rise of Calvin, the Reformation had avoided many of the dangers of extreme rebellion; in the process of breaking away from Roman Catholic traditionalism it had been obliged to attack the more extreme Protestants to secure the good wishes of temporal rulers on whom the survival of the Reformation depended. Once having made its break with Catholicism, Lutheranism counseled obedience to civil authority. Furthermore, Lutheranism remained basically a German denomination.

The emergence of John Calvin some years after Luther posted his Ninety-five Theses marked a new element in Protestantism that was more activist and radical, and (as it developed) far more influential in the long run. It was Calvin who girded the Reformation with rigid logic. It was Calvin who made the break with Rome more deep and unbridgeable than had either Luther or Zwingli. Of Calvinism, R. H. Tawney has written:

As a way of life and a theory of society, it possessed from the beginning one characteristic which was both novel and important. It assumed an economic organization which was relatively advanced, and expounded its social ethics on the basis of it.[16]

Historians of the Reformation have ranged the great reformers from Luther, the conservative, to Calvin, the radical, with the Swiss theologian Zwingli somewhere in the middle as to his view of society. Even Zwingli, however, seemed to have retained a medieval world view; to him, private property originated in sin. As Tawney said:

. . . Calvin, and still more his later interpreters, began their voyage lower down the stream. Unlike Luther, who saw economic life with the eyes of a peasant and a mystic, they approached it as men of affairs . . . . Like early Christianity and modern socialism, Calvinism was largely an urban movement. . . .[17]

To some, Calvin was "the only gentleman among the reformers." He was born to solid circumstances in Picardy in 1509 and from early youth was noted for his scholarship. He first prepared for the priesthood but later (to please his father, some said) he veered to the law. As Fosdick recounts, Calvin was known to his fellow students by the nickname "the accusative case."

Like Augustine twelve hundred years earlier, Calvin was acutely aware of the sense of sin. So similar was his own view of the human condition to that of Augustine that some scholars have likened the early Calvinism to Augustinianism. The two owned striking similarities: they emphasized the corruption of human nature occasioned by the fall of man; the resulting thralldom of the will; predestination and election; and several less memorable themes.

In his twenty-seventh year, Calvin published the most influential document of the Reformation (with the possible exception of Luther's theses), the *Institutes of the Christian Religion*. Like a perpetual storm cloud, the knowledge of man's wickedness hung over the great work. As the first chapter of the second book of the *Institutes* said:

. . . original sin is seen to be an hereditary depravity and corruption of our nature, diffused into all parts of the soul. . . . For our nature is not merely bereft of good, but is so productive of every kind of evil that it cannot be inactive. . . . to sum it up briefly, . . . the whole man is in himself nothing but concupiscence. . . .

In the short version of the *Institutes* called *Instruction in Faith*, Calvin asked of sin and death, "What can we expect in the face of God, we miserable ones who are oppressed by such a load of sins and soiled by an infinite filth, except a very certain confusion such as his indignation brings?" [18]

One can expect nothing except the certitude that some few are "elect," that is, recipients of God's grace, while the rest are damned. Under the heading "Election and Predestination," Calvin explained:

For, the seed of the word of God takes root and brings forth fruit only in those whom the Lord, by his eternal election, has predestined to be children and heirs of the heavenly kingdom. To all the others (who by the same counsel of God are rejected . . .) the clear and evident preaching of truth can be nothing but an odor of death unto death. Now, why does the Lord use his mercy toward some and exercise the rigor of his judgment on the others? We have to leave the reason of this to be known by him alone. . . . We acknowledge, therefore, the elect to be recipients of his mercy (as truly they are) and the rejected to be recipients of his wrath, a wrath, however, which is nothing but just.[19]

Instead of the Lutheran admonitions of obedience to civil authority, Calvinism's writ (under the heading "The Magistrate or

Civic Officer") reiterated that princes and magistrates were lieutenants of God, empowered by divine sanction to rule. Subjects and citizens were urged to "submit willingly":

> But from obedience to superiors we must always except one thing: that it does not draw us away from obedience to Him to whose edicts the commands of all kings must yield. . . . If men command us to do something against him, we must do nothing, nor keep any account of such an order. On the contrary, let rather this sentence take place: that it is necessary to obey God rather than men. . . .[20]

From these principles, Calvin drew daily in the theocratic canton of Geneva. There he ruled as priestly dictator until his death in 1564, combining theory with action, abstract truth with concrete necessity. To Calvin there was nothing inherently evil in usury if it did not exceed legal limits. High interest exacted from the poor who needed the money for consumption was reprehensible; high interest charged the rich who would use the money for production was not. Nor were profits reviled as the evil fruits of chicane. "What reason is there," asked Calvin, "why the income from business should not be larger than that from landowning? Whence do the merchant's profits come, except from his own diligence and industry?" [21]

Cut loose from the rigid limitations of traditionalism, the successive generations of Calvinists were armed with the idea that they (or some of them, anyway) were elect, chosen people; that blind obedience to rulers was not as important as conformity to the wishes of God; that each man, in effect, was on his own with his Maker; that industriousness and frugality were prime virtues, while their contraries were sins; that austere forbearance in spending money should accompany diligent discharge of worldly labors. For the gloomy overtones of pervasive sin and inevitable damnation, men of affairs had little use. To be sure, there were continual struggles within "the Piety," as it was called. Down to very recent times the battle raged between the Augustinian center (those concerned for the maintenance of the "pure" spirit of Calvinism) and the liberal fringes (those preoccupied with worldly gain). But the result, viewed in retrospect, has favored the latter. The positive thinkers have largely prevailed over the negative thinkers. That is not to say that this inherent tension is forever relaxed; it is on the contrary still much in evidence, as I shall try to demonstrate later.

As the new faith spread from Switzerland throughout western Europe and into Britain, the Calvinists found themselves a small minority in a non-Calvinist world. They were in this one important respect in a position similar to the historic condition of the Jews: they were professional outsiders who believed themselves to be specially chosen by God. They were different from others, and they knew it; from their sense of isolation they derived great strength, but not in a way that Calvin might have expected or approved. As they were in a minority, there was no hope in Europe of erecting a theocratic state such as Calvin himself had ruled in Geneva. Thus, instead of resulting in a rigid moral censoriousness enforced by the state, Calvinism gave rise to pressures for religious toleration and to a solemnly pious individualism that came to memorable flower in seventeenth century England and thereafter in America.

An idea common to Hebrew culture and to the English Calvinists (who came to be known as Puritans for their zeal to "purify" the Anglican Church of its vestigial Catholic trappings) was the covenant—the contract between man and magistrate, the formal agreement endowed with God's sanction. From that idea came the development of the ideal of constitutional limitations on the rights of rulers. Instead of Germanic obedience in the mold of Lutheranism, the far more subtle notion of constitutionalism deriving from Calvinism became one of the most significant outgrowths of the Reformation; "It is necessary to obey God rather than men," as the *Institutes* had said.

In the unsettled days of the English Interregnum, the Calvinists in their various wings (Presbyterians, Congregationalists, and the radical left sects that were nearly Anabaptist in outlook) gained great power, and briefly ruled under Oliver Cromwell. Yet so deeply ingrained was the ideal of the covenant, the constitutional sanction, that in the 1640's, barely a century after the *Institutes'* publication, there is the record of Cromwell's revolutionary army democratically soliciting rank-and-file opinion through regimental representatives appearing before the Army Council, from which emerged "The People's Agreement."

As Lee Cameron McDonald has pointed out, the tradition of such covenanting among Calvinists carried with full force to America, beginning with the Mayflower Compact of 1620, continuing in the New England town meeting, and culminating in 1789 in the Constitution of the United States. As McDonald observes, the Calvinist was suspicious enough of human nature, pessimistic enough about man's perfectibility, that he was led to the conclusion that "a constitutional balance of power might be a necessary restraint on man's sin." [22] From such pragmatic judgments on the limits of probability grew the governmental structure that in America gave such scope to the productive energies of men.

The development of modern industry owed still deeper debts to Calvinism; not only did the new creed help create the institutions under which manfacturing flourished; it also armed those professional outsiders, the later heirs of Calvin, with the intellectual weaponry for temporal success. To the development of this psychology of achievement and to the development of Calvinism in America I now turn.

· 4 ·

Calvinism removed the magic from religion and put method in its place. In the form that Calvinism took, salvation was to be won not by the intercession of a priest-magician but by strict devotion to one's worldly calling, by diligent work. As the German scholar Max Weber wrote in *The Protestant Ethic and the Spirit of Capitalism:*

. . . naturally the whole ascetic literature of almost all denominations is saturated with the idea that fruitful labour, even at low wages, on the part of those to whom life offers no other opportunities, is highly pleasing to God. In this respect Protestant Asceticism added in itself nothing new. But it not only deepened this idea most powerfully, it also created the force which was alone decisive for its effectiveness: the psychological sanction of it through the conception of this labour as a calling, as the best, often in the last analysis the only, means of attaining certainty of grace.[23]

Weber used the term "Protestant Ethic" to describe this peculiar outlook of the workers and entrepreneurs who created modern capitalism. His evidence, later confirmed by other examples, showed that early Protestants (specifically the Dutch Reformed, French Huguenots, and English Puritans) far surpassed their Roman Catholic contemporaries as business leaders. Furthermore, as Professor Harry M. Johnson has noted, ". . . to a considerable extent the Catholics have not caught up yet [that is, in 1960]. The leading capitalistic countries are predominantly Protestant. More striking is the relative success of Protestants even within Catholic countries." [24]

Weber observed that the greed for gold is "as old as the history of man" and that it is a condition quite independent of capitalism. However, capitalism under the influence of the Protestant Ethic greatly modified the ancient and generalized lust for material gain by identifying greed with duty. The ascetic overlay to greed provided by Calvinism, Weber suggested, resulted in a willingness among the pious to restrict present consumption in the interests of greater future consumption. Furthermore, the Spirit of Capitalism did what no force had ever done before: It made an equation of wealth and goodness, yet it also stressed the sanctity of constant diligence and the evil effects of extravagance. It created forbearance in spending wealth. It stressed the virtual holiness of having money rather than the things money buys. Money itself became the end, and its expenditure a betrayal of fundamental righteousness. "Money can beget money," as Benjamin Franklin said, "and its offspring can beget more, and so on. . . . He that kills a breeding-sow, destroys all her offspring to the thousandth generation. He that murders a crown, destroys all that it might have produced, even scores of pounds." [25]

Therefore, as Weber suggests, the Spirit of Capitalism inspired vigorous greed with the object of expanding opportunities for still more greed; it inflamed the passion for money but gave that passion no outlet except in activities that produce still more passion and still more money; in sum, it made the ability to consume more pronounced but the propensity to consume less pronounced. This spirit, then, gave greed a new time scale. It elongated a man's perspective. It gave his life order and method. It militated against the spontaneously enjoyed pleasure and the impulsive expenditure. It made possible the ultimate accumulation of sums great enough to cause economic structure to undergo a revolutionary change.

By fastening a man's affection on worldly pursuits and therefore on money (rather than on the things money buys), the Protestant Ethic accomplished still another useful end: It made for honor among those possessed of the Ethic. Thus, a workman would work hard because that was the way to serve God. And an employer would exploit the diligent workman because that was also the way to serve God. As Weber pointed out, Germany prospered through the honesty and reliability of its workingmen, whereas the Italian laborers' "lack of *coscienziosita* . . . is one of the principal obstacles to . . . [Italy's] capitalistic development."

The Protestant Ethic under its Calvinist impetus steeled an entire class (if it did not in fact create that class) to overthrow the agrarian overlords' control of a static marketplace, to introduce instead a dynamic marketplace, and thereby to end the reign of traditionalism. It was not flippancy for Tawney to call Calvin the Marx of the middle class.

The Ethic flourished in several major forms, as Weber pointed out: Calvinism, Pietism, Methodism, and the "sects growing out of the Baptist movement." The early Reformers as well as later leading sectaries seemed to sense that they were setting loose revolutionary forces. John Wesley, for example, who in the eighteenth century led the last of the significant puritanical movements in England by founding Methodism, wrote:

I fear, wherever riches have increased, the essence of religion has decreased in the same proportion. Therefore I do not see how it is pos-

sible, in the nature of things, for any revival of true religion to continue long. For religion must necessarily produce both industry and
frugality, and these cannot but produce riches. But as riches increase,
so will pride, anger, and love of the world in all its branches. How
then is it possible that Methodism, that is, a religion of the heart,
though it flourishes now as a green bay tree, should continue in this
state? For the Methodists in every place grow diligent and frugal;
consequently they increase in goods. Hence they proportionately increase in pride, in anger, in the desire of the flesh, the desire of the
eyes, and the pride of life. So although the form of religion remains,
the spirit is swiftly vanishing away. Is there no way to prevent this—
this continual decay of pure religion? We ought not to prevent people
from being diligent and frugal; we must exhort all Christians to gain
all they can, and to save all they can; that is, in effect, to grow rich.[26]

That passage illuminates an inner contradiction in Protestantism
that has been a continuing phenomenon. The great debates within
American Puritanism defined in large measure the opposed views
of worldly ambition and "pure" religion. As Wesley had predicted,
"pure" religion did not prevail. It was successively watered down.
Its harshness was tumbled smooth. Its gloomy preoccupation with
judgment was effectively removed.

In the 1700's this conflict of the worldly and the spiritual elements of American Protestantism took its color from a "Great
Awakening," as it was called, in which the leading role was played
by Jonathan Edwards, who for a time ran a virtually theocratic
state in the Connecticut Valley. It was Edwards who staged the
first revival and it was he who gave hell-fire and brimstone its
greatest advocacy. Edwards was a reformer, that much was clear.
What may not have been equally clear was the long line of reform
movements that followed in the same general pattern.

The division between the worldly and the spiritual communi-
cants of the early New England church, as Professor Perry Miller
has noted, provided an "irreconcilable" polarity. "It also provides
a theme," Miller adds, "probably the basic and sundering theme,
of American literature." [27]

The man often contrasted with Edwards as representative of
worldly Calvinism has been his far more famous contemporary,

Benjamin Franklin—the man, as the Chase Manhattan Bank once said in a window poster, who "gave Free Enterprise its soft and persuasive voice: Advertising." As Professor Miller has said,

This duel [of ideals between Edwards and Franklin] was all the more eloquent, not because the two met in open debate, as did Jefferson and Hamilton in the 1790's—they showed little or no awareness of each other's existence—but because they started in their contrary directions from the same parent stock, the Puritanism of New England. . . . As they divide the heritage between them, Franklin and Edwards expose the inner tensions . . . [that] all Protestant immigrants—the Dutch and Scotch-Irish Presbyterians, Baptists, Quakers, German Calvinists and Lutherans, and eventually the Methodists—brought to these shores. They make wonderfully clear how this incipient civil war within the piety could be brought into the open only by conditions of this new world. . . .[28]

To mention the less familiar of these two American Calvinists first, Jonathan Edwards came to a position of prominence in 1729, when he took the pulpit in Northampton. The backsliding tendencies among New England Calvinists were already in evidence. People were moving away from the pure doctrines as the science of Newton and the philosophy of Locke leavened the religious climate in America.

The original intellect of Edwards fashioned a restatement of Calvinist doctrine that incorporated the new learning, yet permitted a revival of the dwindling fervor of Puritanism. His method was to write learned tracts and to preach terror sermons that reduced his hearers to quivering incoherence and horrified resolutions of renewed piety. In 1735 a "Great Awakening" resulted from Edwards' inspired preaching:

. . . imagine yourself to be cast into a fiery oven, all of a glowing heat, or into the midst of a glowing brick-kiln, or of a great furnace, where your pain would be as much greater than that occasioned by accidentally touching a coal of fire, as the heat is greater. Imagine also that your body were to lie there for a quarter of an hour, full of fire, as full within and without as a bright coal of fire, all the while full of quick sense. What horror would you feel at the entrance of such a fur-

nace! And how long would that quarter of an hour seem to you! . . .
But what would be the effect on your soul, if you knew you must
lie there enduring that torment to the full for twenty-four hours! . . .
for a whole year . . . a thousand years! O then, how would your heart
sink, if you thought, if you knew, that you must bear it forever and
ever! That there would be no end! That after millions and millions of
ages, your torment would be no nearer to an end, than ever it was;
and that you never, never should be delivered! [29]

Benjamin Franklin, as his life and works demonstrated to his
lasting fame, was not interested in eternal damnation but in
temporal reward. While Edwards raged against backsliding in
the Connecticut Valley (and was finally cast from his pulpit for
his troubles), Franklin was perfecting his personality in the hope
of making his mark in the world of practical affairs.

I had been religiously educated as a Presbyterian; and tho' some of
the dogmas of that persuasion, such as *the eternal decrees of God,
election, reprobation, etc.*, appeared to me unintelligible, others doubtful, and I early absented myself from the public assemblies of the sect,
Sunday being my studying day, I never was without religious principles. . . .
Tho' I seldom attended any public worship, I had still an opinion of
its propriety, and of its utility when rightly conducted, and I regularly
paid my subscription for the support of the only Presbyterian minister
or meeting we had in Philadelphia.[30]

Instead of attending to the admonitions of his church—keeping
the Sabbath holy, reading the Scripture, going to church, and the
like—Franklin set forth thirteen virtues he intended systematically
to cultivate. He devised a boxscore for himself so that he could
chart each day's progress in temperance, silence, order, resolution,
frugality, industry, sincerity, justice, moderation, cleanliness, tran-
quillity, chastity, and humility. The last one gave him trouble. As
he noted, "I cannot boast of much success in acquiring the *reality*
of this virtue, but I had a good deal with regard to the *appearance*
of it." He purposely avoided any sectarian bias in his self-improvement campaign as he hoped to publish his system under the title
The Art of Virtue, and he did not wish to "have any thing in it
that should prejudice any one of any sect, against it."

In a preface to his *Poor Richard's Almanac,* under the title "The Way to Wealth," Franklin collected many of Poor Richard's maxims. In them the worldly aspects of asceticism were heavily emphasized. Positive thought suffused his aphorisms: "So what signifies *wishing* and *hoping* for better Times [?] We may make these Times better if we bestir ourselves. *Industry need not wish,* as Poor Richard says, and *He that lives upon Hope will die fasting. There are no Gains, without Pains.* . . . And as Poor Richard likewise observes, *He that hath a Trade hath an Estate, and He that hath a Calling, hath an Office of Profit and Honour.* . . . *If we are industrious we shall never starve.* . . . *Industry pays Debts, while Despair encreaseth them,* says Poor Richard. . . . *God gives all Things to Industry. Then plough deep, while Sluggards sleep, and you shall have Corn to sell and to keep.* . . .

Franklin also warned against sloth (it "makes all things difficult"), excess sleep ("time enough for sleep in the Grave"), gluttony ("a fat Kitchen makes a lean Will"), and extravagance and debt ("he that goes a borrowing gets a sorrowing").

These two aspects of American Calvinism—of what may be called broadly the negative thought of Edwards and the positive thought of Franklin—are, as Miller has said, " . . . the Gemini who share the same soul, one occupying it while the other sleeps. . . ."

· 5 ·

The convenient labeling of the opposed strains of Calvinism as positive and negative is not wholly satisfactory, for it tends to obscure another element in the evolution of American Protestantism in the nineteenth and twentieth centuries. That element, for want of a better term, is the sense of conscience.

The Puritan owned not a social but an individual conscience. The rigid Puritan hated sin more than he loved generosity, as Parrington said.[31] But under the influence of the French romantic optimism (specifically that of Rousseau) about human nature, a new kind of radicalism sprang from the Calvinist well of innovation. The Unitarians, as they came to be known, stripped away a great deal of the doctrinal overhead of Calvinism, and advanced the notion that God did not abhor the crawling worm of a man pictured by Calvin; that instead God loved the perfectible man portrayed by the more modern French philosophers of the Enlightenment. The belief emerged that an inherently good man who was fully worthy of God's love was rendered less than good by society and its institutions. From this new excitement within the piety grew an eagerness for social reform that made its presence felt in the antislavery agitation of New England Abolitionists.

In succeeding years, the "Social Gospel" became the scripture of the new left wing of Protestantism, while the hell-fire and brimstone of "fundamentalism" marked the right wing. In the center, somewhere, and commanding an apparent majority of the available affection, were the spiritual heirs of Franklin, the believers in the God of business enterprise. The liberal Protestants concerned with social justice came into direct collision with what may be called the Franklin-Barton-Peale Protestants as the rising power of industry caused new and painful dislocations. The former supported labor unionism and the various reforms of the Progressive Era, while the latter quite naturally urged the churches to stick to scripture and to leave political action to the men of affairs. The chilling reception that the chairman of United States Steel, Judge Gary, gave the committee of ministers who hoped to mediate the 1919 strike and to gain a fair settlement for labor was fairly typical of the attitude of industry to the more liberal strains of Protestantism.

One index of the rising center of American Protestantism (and the clergy's consequent decline in power and prestige) was the relative number of clergymen and businessmen on the governing bodies of universities and other nongovernmental institutions. In 1860, one study has indicated, clergymen constituted 39 percent of the trustees of nongovernment institutions. By 1935 the figure was closer to 9 percent. Businessmen, on the other hand, accounted for 28 percent of the trustees in 1860 but 47 percent by 1935.[32]

The declining prestige of the clergy and the growing importance of the businessman reflected the changed relationship of religion and business, a change of which Barton was well aware in the 1920's. Said he, "Some day some one will write a book about Jesus. Every business man will read it and send it to his partners and his salesmen. For it will tell the story of the founder of modern business. Finally the man said to himself, 'I believe I will try to write that book myself. And he did.'" The book, as noted earlier, was *The Man Nobody Knows,* and it was a huge success. It was another small index of the new balance of influence between industry and organized religion.

The fundamentalist wing of Protestantism, as I said above, has had substantial success in gaining new membership among the lower classes. Sects like the Pentecostal Holiness and Jehovah's Witnesses have made wide gains among the urban poor, particularly by emphasizing otherworldly reward. Liberal and neo-orthodox Protestantism, meanwhile, has continued to attract much of the best religious scholarship; and in such centers as the Union Theological Seminary in New York, it continues to work significant influence on American letters and education. The liberal and neo-orthodox Protestants have been active politically also, playing a key role in forming the Liberal party in New York State and in the Americans for Democratic Action group within the Democratic party.

The business Protestants seem to have veered somewhat in the direction of the fundamentalists. Paradoxically, the business Protestants have also adopted a kind of anticlericalism toward the liberal Protestant clergy, with occasional curious results. Their anticlericalism seems to reflect their wish that the Church forget whatever else it may be doing and concentrate on fighting Communism. Those ministers who see their mission as a more affirmative one than anti-Communism, whose interests remain with the social aspects of Christianity, have come under steady attack from the businessmen. The National Council of the Churches of Christ, for instance, has borne a steady stream of calumny and ill wishes from conservative and fundamentalist Protestants largely because of its continuing concern for social reform and its belief that civil rights and economic legislation are proper church concerns.

Specific anti-Communist organizations within Protestantism have enjoyed wide support from the businessman. Moral Rearmament is one example. That organization urges "absolute honesty, purity, unselfishness, and love." It seeks to convert new members to its cause by means of large rallies and newspaper advertisements. It runs a large hotel in Caux, France, as its European headquarters and it also has quarters in Michigan. It is somewhat vague in its doctrines, and its critics say that it is sometimes loose with the truth about its own accomplishments. (It claims to have saved Japan, Brazil, and Western Europe from Communist revolution.) It talks about "total war" with Communism and it affects a rather shrill belligerency in its public pronouncements in its newspaper advertisements. Various extreme right-wing sects of fundamentalist Protestantism also provide a fertile ground for anti-Communist evangelism. The Christian Anti-Communist Crusade is one such organization. For whatever reasons, the vested interests contribute heavily to these groups.

· 6 ·

By a long and perhaps circuitous route, hopefully the point is now reached at which the themes discussed earlier seem to fall into a visible relationship. The essential Protestant belief in work has accompanied industrial development as the world knows it today. From the related scorn for idleness and poverty has come a continuing harshness in dealing with the victims of industrialization (and attempts to link concern for those victims with Communism). From the belief in positive thought has come such modern developments as administered optimism and the consequent unwillingness of Americans to acknowledge their most serious economic problems.

The relationship of religion to the prime vested interests is not tenuous and difficult to discern but pervasive and highly visible. The success in past years of these doctrines has resulted in the creation of a view of life that marks not only Protestant America but Catholic and Jewish America as well. This view especially colors middle- and upper-class attitudes. It informs their political and economic opinions and it provides them their air of self-congratulation.

Of vested interests and religion it is fair to say that the rise of manufacturing industry has accompanied the weakening of traditional religion, yet the old tension between the values of organized industry and organized religion continues. Where the differences are harmonized and explained away, as in the popular Protestant literature, the result is a religious view of great utility in sanctifying the business life. Some, however, regard such affirmations of moral excellence as the fruit of sustained and extreme heresy. This continuing battle of ideals between the "worldly" and the "spiritual" explains much of the criticism and revulsion toward the prime vested interests. The adaptation of religion to the needs of industry (specifically, the religious sanction of the kind of avarice without which such industrial development is probably impossible) has caused deep and lasting ambivalence —even in the citadels of industry itself. It might be possible to say that this particular ambivalence—this continual lurching between positive thought and negative thought—provides a key to the phenomenon of the business cycle in the United States.

These Gemini, one sleeping while the other is awake, may provide a useful clue to the impact of religious and moralistic ideals on economic psychology. The heirs of Franklin and Edwards in the popular literature, as one might expect, are different from their apparent intellectual progenitors, but they are recognizable, nevertheless. The Gemini of the 1950's were represented by two men owning common cultural roots in American Calvinism. One, Norman Vincent Peale, offered handy tips on getting ahead along with bursts of affirmation. The other, Vance Packard, inveighed against slipping moral standards and larded his books with expressions of moral horrification. One told us to affirm, the other told us to smite the rascal affirmers. One counseled a positive and aggressive preparation for the future, the other a semiretreat to the simplicity of the past. One sold books by the hundreds of thousands, the other only by the tens of thousands. In that relative statistic there was no doubt a lesson.*

These fluctuations in the American's opinion of himself may yield useful information on the apparent modern relationship of vested interests and religion: of the middle-class Organization and the moral climate; of investor psychology and popular Protestantism.

The relationship of America's Puritan heritage to the modern phenomena of business cycles, stock valuations, capital investment, unemployment, administered optimism, conservative politics, and reform movements is too complicated for any easy explanation to suffice, and I doubt that I have done more than suggest what some of those relationships may be.

This extended excursion into the intellectual roots of some aspects of modern capitalism will have accomplished its task if it has demonstrated where some of the dominant attitudes of the middle class came from and what ends these attitudes seem to serve today.

A subject of such importance to the prime interests deserves further attention. The succeeding chapters will therefore try to examine these attitudes in their various guises outside the confines of organized religion, but within the vested interests' enclave itself.

* One part of the lesson seems to have been that large corporations have been in the habit of buying the Peale books by the thousands to give away to their employees. (U.S. Steel once paid for 250,000 subscriptions to the Peale magazine *Guideposts*—one for each employee.) On the other hand, the Packard books have to make their way sale by sale, for the most part.

The Ideology of the Enclave

⊓⊔⊓⊔⊓⊔⊓

As earlier chapters have indicated, the large enclave of affluence in America has been created and is maintained by the prime interests. Broadly speaking, those inside the enclave walls are the well off and the well educated; those outside are the poor and the ignorant.

Those deepest inside the enclave are quite at ease in their secure universe. Among the enclave dwellers closer to the walls, however, one can detect less ease of manner, more anxiety over continued solvency, and a somewhat more militant—some would say nasty—attitude toward outsiders. Insiders who aren't sure of themselves try to prove to the old-timers that they are worthy residents of the enclave; therefore they often speak vehemently against outsiders.

In many ways these who are relatively close to the gates are the most interesting of the insiders. To these of uncertain status the continued exclusion of the poor from the enclave seems to be a reassertion of morality and virtue rather than an act of rejection.

The economic attitudes marking the middle class have grown directly from American Puritanism's characteristic way of looking at life. The middle-class American associates diligent labor with piety, wealth with virtue, and positive thought with right thinking. The typical American is armed not only with these positive views but with their contraries: lack of diligence in work (or even lack of a job itself) is associated with godlessness, poverty with immorality, negative thought with defeat and disaster.

Not all the affirmative elements of the Protestant Ethic have been maintained with equal force. The work-worship equation, for example, has undergone particular modification because hard work pursued on an individual basis quite often conflicts with the norms of socially approved behavior. The emphasis in the corporate mode of organizations is unquestionably more on "getting along" than on isolated achievement. As William H. Whyte, Jr., argued in *The Organization Man,* the "social ethic" has come into prominence in the twentieth century, while the Protestant Ethic has receded somewhat in importance. It would be a mistake, therefore, to conclude that the Protestant Ethic has been amended past recognition. Only a narrow view of the Ethic could make such a conclusion possible. The Ethic is not a single idea; it is instead at least three ideas (as has been said above): work-worship, wealth-goodness, and positive thought. Not all of these parts have suffered equivalent changes by any means.

· 1 ·

A glance at the media that support this ideology will help illuminate the special attributes of the middle-class point of view. The media I have in mind are basically the print media, and especially the American magazine. These organs seem to nurture and advance the middle-class ideology more systematically and effectively than do the broadcast media, whose mass audiences include most of the lower classes. Newspapers, meanwhile, being localized in impact, do not seem to have the vast influence of the magazines as far as shaping social-economic attitudes.

· 2 ·

As a starting place, consider the weekly picture magazine *Life.* In 1962 it boasted more than 7 million subscribers, a probable

20 million weekly readers, and advertising revenues greater than all but 400 of the nation's biggest manufacturing corporations. As an instrument of cultural dissemination, it was without a doubt one of the most influential organs that this nation had ever seen. Therefore certain of the ideas treated by *Life* during the 1961–1962 period give, I believe, a particularly authentic glimpse of the middle-class ideology as reflected in print. Specific ideological themes that seem to have had particular significance in that connection were poverty, "national purpose," and public charity.

The 1961–1962 period, to digress a moment, is of interest because it was then that *Life* lifted its own face with a major redesign in hopes of stopping the leakage of advertising revenue to television and other media. June 2, 1961, was the first issue of "the new *Life*," and for sixteen weeks thereafter I, for one, read the magazine closely (on the theory that thereby I would witness the emergence of a new cultural medium, or at the very least that I would be able to see to what degree the public taste had changed in *Life* editors' estimation).

I got a line-count gauge, kept a running content tally, and used a slide rule to compute percentages—what proportions, specifically, of each issue were devoted to which general subjects. My attention had been caught especially by the two-part "Aim of *Life*" that the publishers set forth for themselves and their countrymen on June 2nd. The first aim was to win the cold war, the second to "create a better America." In addition to these goals, the magazine still had its sizable audience to keep interested. For that reason it should have come as no surprise that during that same period the four major editorial appeals, in order of importance, were entertainment, inspiration, education, and acquisition.* [1]

What *Life* did to poverty deserves extended examination. In the first place, to an enclave dweller, poverty is clearly not an American domestic problem, and therefore if a mass magazine is to discuss poverty, it will properly be poverty in a foreign setting

* For details on the method I tried to follow in this analysis, see p. 271, note 1.

as there simply is no domestic poverty worth noticing. In this instance, Latin America was the scene.

Poverty in Latin America was a big problem because it provided a breeding ground for Communism, *Life* explained. Beginning in June, 1961, and continuing at two-week intervals, "The Crisis in Our Hemisphere" unfolded. The series told the middle-class American in easy-to-take doses how he should think about poverty and Latin America, Communism and winning the cold war. Symbolically, at least, *Life* and its readers wound up the series by wiping out poverty in Latin America, and therein seems to lie an important element of the enclave ideology: poverty does not exist wherever the American system has prime influence.

Before getting down to a detailed description of *Life*'s symbolic conquest of poverty, it is first necessary to quote from the larger philosophy behind that conquest. "We must win the Cold War," the magazine explained in an editorial in the issue that started off the Latin American series (June 2, 1961). "Liberty," *Life* explained, was pitted against "tyranny." It was that simple. "And the love of excellence," *Life* added, "both in mind and in virtue, should be both shield and sword against the infidel." Readers thus learned that the enemy was someone special, an "infidel." He was apparently worse than George III, the Kaiser, or Hitler, in *Life*'s estimation. "For the first time America has a capital-E Enemy. . . ." *Life* said.

After that short guide to current events, readers were ready two weeks later for the magazine's symbolic assault on poverty. What made poverty particularly notable, as the headline on the Latin American series pointed out in the June 16, 1961, number, was that it was "Freedom's Fearful Foe." Happily, *Life*'s literate liberty lovers were alert to the problem. As the symbol of the Foe, the magazine focused on a Rio de Janeiro slum. Unrelieved misery and filth filled 11½ pages. Even death stalked there, in the eyes of a twelve-year-old boy who was presented as the bell-wether of a family of seven. The family was beaten. "It would be nice to believe that this labor of love and courage will triumph. But it won't," *Life* confided. Liberty was finished.

Or was it? *Life*'s readers hoped not. Hopes soon translated themselves into action. "Presented here," said the magazine three weeks later, "is a sampling of the story's mail as both a human document and the splendid answer to a tragic cry for help" (July 7, 1961, pages 15–16). Thus, by saving the boy and his family, the readership of *Life* became heroic itself.

"Flavio's Rescue: Americans bring him from Rio slum to be cured," *Life*'s cover proclaimed on July 21. Inside, the headline said, "The Compassion of Americans Brings a New Life for Flavio." And, "A Brave Boy, Symbol of Impoverished Millions, Is Rescued from a Rio Slum." There were twelve pages of photos of the now happy boy, the new family home in Rio, the new clothing the boy got from his benefactors, the lavish medical care he got in America, and the warmth of the greeting from the little boys in his Colorado home-away-from-home. "A Happy Start in a Friendly World."

The week before the slum boy's rescue, there had been a discussion of the rising Mexican working class and the declining Peruvian oligarchy. There were two photos of the working class and they were in black and white; there were seven photos of the oligarchy and they were in color.

Just as poverty was necessarily a foreign problem, wealth and solvency had curiously familiar forms wherever they were found. As a Peruvian magnate told *Life,* "Lima society is like Long Island society. A man who does not work is looked down on here—now." (July 14, 1961, p. 88). There were photos of the magnate and his wife taking their ease around the family mansion, a picture of the wife water skiing, and a picture of the husband at work at his own anchovy meal plant. But *Life* was not forgetting, amid all the lush color photographs, that poverty was a continuing problem (the rescue of Flavio was still a week in the future). As the magazine said of the Peruvian millionaire:

The main difference between Rafael's society and its counterpart in the U.S. is not a matter of behavior. Nor is it something for which Rafael himself can be held directly responsible. While he lives as he does, over 200,000 men, women and children live in Lima's slums, wasted by disease, some even foraging with pigs in the city's garbage heaps.

By the end of July, 1961, *Life* was openly delighted with the way poverty and the Latin American series were going. In an extended essay called "Aim and Response" in the July 28th number, the magazine's publisher described how *Life* had made itself even greater as an instrument of national grandeur. He concluded with a summary of the lengths to which his magazine's good influence had extended:

. . . most heart-warming of all was the response which came to *Life*'s report on poverty in Latin America, and the moving story of the child Flavio. As we reported in the issue just preceding this one, the wholly spontaneous reaction of *Life*'s audience has rescued Flavio from the grip of the *favela*. Even more important to the larger human drama, *Life*'s readers seem to have set in motion a broader scale assault on the twin problems of poverty and disease by their own efforts and by the efforts of the South Americans. . . . [July 28, 1961, page 1.]

It all more or less went to show what private initiative could accomplish in the way of solving problems. Later on in that issue, *Life* had still another go at the Latin American problem. That article, called "The Races and the Terrain, a Mixed-up Inheritance," turned out to be mostly about the terrain, which proved ideally suited to four-color photographs: rivers, mountains, jungles, coffee fields, a "gaudy macaw," bubbling oil, and finally a photo of the garbage dump with the people and pigs rooting around it. Then came the text of "The Staggering Problem," as *Life* called it that week. It was a problem "dangerous to life, limb and sanity for anyone who fools around" with it, the magazine said. Later on it explained: "What are needed are the tactics of full-scale psychological warfare, for we are dealing not only with an information gap but with an empathy gap. . . ." What the magazine hoped for, as it turned out, was more cultivated goodwill in the manner of many American corporations who had introduced "such old U.S.-tested reliables as cleaner washrooms, free coffee, and financial sponsorship of the local equivalent of the Little League."

That was just about where *Life* left Latin America. On the verge of cleaner washrooms. Other problems were growing more interesting, anyway.

All was not well with the boy Flavio nor with the magazine *Life* nor even with the heart-warming story of Latin American poverty conquered by the American middle class. A few months later a Brazilian equivalent of *Life* called *O Cruzeiro* complained that the *Life* story was basically false. By way of retaliation, *O Cruzeiro* sent its own photographers and reporters to Harlem, where they did a similar photo essay on a Puerto Rican family named Gonzales. One photo showed cockroaches crawling over the face of a child. *Time* magazine, *Life*'s sister publication, claimed that the Gonzales family had been paid to pose for the pictures and that the cockroaches were dead ones carefully propped in place by Brazilian photographers. The Brazilian magazine responded by charging that *Life* had fabricated its Rio slum story; that a baby shown in a picture crying because a mad dog had bitten it had in reality been slapped by its father for some small mischief; that a dead girl in a coffin surrounded by candles was still very much alive in the Rio slum streets, and that *O Cruzeiro* knew where *Life* had bought the coffin. The controversy faded out and was soon forgotten, as were poverty, Latin America, and *Life*'s long series.

· 3 ·

The ideology of the middle class as reflected by the above descriptions of *Life*'s contents is particularly visible when relief and welfare come under discussion. A case in point was the Newburgh Affair (see page 96). In its first mention of the city's plan (June 30, 1961, page 43), *Life* approvingly said that the little city had "seceded from the welfare state and set up some stringent new rules." The magazine went on to note that a few states and other cities had done likewise. In its next notice of Newburgh,

Life ran an editorial in praise of the city's tough stand (July 28th) that said: "Newburgh has shown real guts. . . . The great American tradition of generosity to the unfortunate must continue. But Newburgh provides a healthy example of local government assuming due initiative and responsibility" (page 36B). Finally, in September (September 4th, page 4), the magazine took another swipe at the problem of organized charity. It heaped scorn on those who give as well as on those who receive:

If free food thus contributes to unemployment, there are nevertheless some offsetting benefits. Employment increased in New York City, where Welfare Commissioner Dumpson added 39 civil service employees to his department (at a cost of $136,500 a year) to handle the stocks of food. Obviously, this job could not be done by people on relief, since they could scarcely carry their own groceries home while handing them out to others.

Thus the enclave American had substantial reinforcement for his cherished belief that poverty is badness, that it is un-American, that it is unable to exist where the middle class has major influence. Furthermore, there was a related notion advanced time and again by *Life*, namely, that government is inherently more wasteful than any other form of enterprise. The subtle message was conveyed in the passage quoted above by saying that there would be $136,500 more a year paid out in salaries of civil servants. An average salary for the thirty-nine new employees, that is to say (although *Life* did not say so), of $3,500.

· 4 ·

Life was by no means the only definer of the middle-class sense of values; nor, for that matter, was it even the most energetic. The *Reader's Digest* seemed to own the distinction of being the organ of *the* militant middle class.

Before I suggest how the *Digest* and *Life* complemented each other in this respect, it bears saying here that both magazines sprang directly from the mainstream of American Puritanism in a way that undoubtedly helped fix their hostile attitudes toward the American poor. Both were founded by the sons of Presbyterian ministers. Henry Luce (*Life's* founder) was the son of a Presbyterian missionary in China; De Witt Wallace (the *Digest* founder) was the son of an American-based Presbyterian minister-teacher. From this common heritage of moral judgment, worldly asceticism, and positive thought came the remarkable outpouring of articles that distinguished *Reader's Digest* even more than *Life*.

It hardly requires my evidence to establish that the *Digest* formula has varied little from month to month or year to year. As a rule there is in a typical issue a bit of smut, some health hints ("The Miracle of the Clavicle," or some such title), wildlife lore, positive thought, patriotic boosting, and generalized scolding of some sort. Leaving aside the least memorable of these themes, the positive-thought and tongue-clucking elements are of particular relevance just here. Thus, in a representative issue (November, 1961), there was a standard positive-thought article by a standard positive thinker (Norman Vincent Peale). In "You Are Tougher Than You Think" came this message: "You can if you think you can."

As for tongue-clucking, the burden was borne in that issue by an article that told the "shocking truth" about "children without fathers" who drained welfare funds provided by taxes paid by solid citizens everywhere. The Aid-to-Dependent-Children program, the *Digest* pointed out, encouraged "illegitimacy and fraud, and it has stifled individual initiative toward moral or financial self-improvement." (The proximity of "moral" to "financial," of course, was a natural enough apposition.) As the *Digest* editor who wrote the article said:

I have traveled from coast to coast in the past year, interviewing local welfare workers and following four state-government investigations of the [Aid-to-Dependent-Children] program. On the basis of this accumulation of evidence it can only be concluded that the federally subsidized ADC relief rolls are contributing to debauchery and fostering a demoralizing dependency on government handouts.

There you had it. An editor left the *Reader's Digest* estate one day and began his coast-to-coast wandering in search of truth.

Reluctantly, as the evidence piled up, he was forced to the painful conclusion that depravity was a way of life for many because the government was encouraging depravity. Generation after generation of chiselers were attaching themselves to the public trough, while decent people continued to live their upright lives, pay their taxes in full and on time, and depend for *their* eroticism not on shockingly immoral and casual alliances with passers-by but by reading the little laugh lines in their favorite monthly magazine, among other things. What to do about it? Get tough! Compel parents "to accept responsibility for their children." "We must curtail this burgeoning dependency, instead of creating more. We must stop coddling parents at the expense of the children. . . ." We must, should, ought, have to . . . Injunctions and imperatives ran through the article, as did a generalized wish for a "decent, moral" climate in which the young might grow up.

It was never said in so many words, but that article was about Negroes. By leveling that oblique attack on the outside Americans, the *Digest* was doing its part to keep taxes down for the inside Americans. It was furthermore giving the middle-class American still another reinforcement of the dearly held belief that lack of solvency and lack of virtue are really just about the same thing; that "moral and financial self-improvement" was just another way of saying that poverty makes for badness, or—in the ultimate shorthand—if you're poor, you're bad.

Elsewhere in the world of popular magazines this middle-class belief got equally subtle but pervasive advocacy. The *Ladies' Home Journal's* Summer (July–August) number in 1962, for example, asked on its cover: "17 Boys from Good Families: Why Did They Steal?" An interesting question. But more interesting was the question, What, exactly, is a "good" family?

This boy was 18, the only son of well-to-do parents, and he owned his own car. The other two boys were 16 and 17 years old, and they, too, were from reputable, high-income families [page 72].

Again the apposition "reputable" and "high-income." That, as most everybody knows, is what makes a "good" family. *This*

Week magazine made the definition explicit in 1959. It published a survey undertaken by two sociologists (from Harvard and St. Louis universities) that listed distinguishing attributes of "good" and "bad" families. There was a pretense spiritedly maintained throughout the article that there were in fact some determinants of "goodness" and "badness" other than money. The "good" family had a "ring of friendship"; it also belonged to various organizations and societies and acted according to middle-class norms. The "bad" family, on the other hand, was isolated. It had no ring of friendship; it produced school dropouts in disproportionate numbers; it was likely to produce a broken home, also; and it was likely to be generally antisocial. The real conclusion was inescapable: the "bad" families were the poor families.

Thus throughout the magazines that come to the middle-class American runs the fine filament of bias reinforcing itself in a thousand subtle ways. That filament helps tell the reader that his conceptions of the good life, the moral and decent human condition (and his righteous indignation with "coddling"), are not narrow and bigoted viewpoints but are on the contrary the attitudes of the moral leaders of the nation, of the nice people of good backgrounds who guard the walls of their enclave against the depraved outsiders. "Good" comes to mean "college-bred, middle-class, solvent"; "bad" comes to mean "uneducated, lower-class, poor."

It does not seem overstatement to say that the middle class in America spends a great deal of its time manipulating symbols to prove its solvency and its consequent goodness. "Wealth-equals-virtue" exerts such wide influence that it oftentimes effaces every other idea; it becomes the fulcrum of existence, the sole lodestar of the baccalaureate mass.

In Westchester County, New York, an enclave within the enclave, the identity of solvency and virtue is particularly plain. One example is provided by the *New York Herald Tribune*'s Mount Kisco radio station, WVIP. "Better programing for the Best People" is the station's slogan.

· 5 ·

As suggested earlier, the activity of the public scolds helps
to define the mood of the enclave and perhaps it even influences
the development of the business cycle. It would be misleading,
however, if the foregoing discussion has suggested a monolithic
structure to the enclave way of thinking. That mode of thought
is not monolithic but is on the contrary surprisingly diverse, ac-
commodating both the residual Franklinists and the remaining
Edwardians. It ranges from the highly conservative (Moral
Re-Armament, for example) to the highly liberal (Arthur Schlesinger, Jr.) A great variety of public scolds shares the common,
basic perspective of the dominant American middle class. No
matter what conclusion this starting place may point to, the beginning premise is that the middle class abounds (or should
abound) in moral excellence; that its prudence and stability
equip it (or should equip it) for great tasks; that it is (or should
be) an admirably empowered moral judge. The middle class,
right and left agree, has that practical wisdom and that agree-
ably sober cast of mind that conduce to moral virtue and intellectual splendor. The judgmental and commercial possibilities
proceeding from that belief are myriad.

· 6 ·

At the outset of this chapter I observed that those deepest
inside the enclave (in the sense that they were most secure in
their positions) had an outlook distinct from those of more am-
biguous status (nearer to the enclave wall). American political
history has borne out that observation time and again. Men born
to riches are disposed to compassion (if they are not preoccupied with consumption and bodily comfort). Those born to poverty (and later enriched) seem to be convinced that one's own
unaided efforts are all one needs, that charity under government
auspices is almost worse than no charity at all. It is a fact worth

repeating that Alexander Hamilton, Herbert Hoover, and Dwight Eisenhower were all born relatively poor but grew rich in their maturity; that Thomas Jefferson, Franklin D. Roosevelt, and John F. Kennedy were all born rich and that they grew compassionate in their maturity.

Whatever light that distinction may throw on the enclave ideology, the observer can avail himself of other signs if he wishes. For example, he can be reasonably sure that he is hearing the enclave ideology expressed when words like "ought" and "should," "must" and "have to" recur. The onlooker may likewise be certain he is hearing the insiders' talk when tongue-clucking about depraved and immoral outsiders is bandied about.

Time and again the listener can hear the simplistic complaints and the reflex responses of the middle class; time and again he can discover that there is almost nowhere to hide from them.

T E N

The Wisdom of the Enclave

⎍⎍⎍⎍⎍

The ideology of the middle class obviously shapes the wisdom of society at large. It is to this common fund of wisdom that this chapter turns. Rather than attempting a comprehensive catalog of middle-class views, however, all that I can do here is to cite a few examples of enclave wisdom and attempt to list a few of the more intriguing paradoxes that grow from it.

· 1 ·

The wisdom of the middle class, on its most basic level, consists of familiar aphorisms, of folk sayings. On a higher plane of sophistication, this sound thought is represented by a common inventory of adjectives that has a kind of brand-name relationship with various sensitive words—"property," "wealth," "unionism," or "management," among others.

To take the folk sayings first, consider these examples: "You can't get rich quick," and "You can't get something for nothing." On their face, both statements are more expressions of moral judgment than descriptions of real-life probability. The common theme that gives them similarity is the abhorrence of sudden or new wealth that they reflect. By means, then, of enclave folk wisdom, "quick riches" or "new money" become terms to describe the nonhonorific kind of capital gains, the capital gains won by those who have not had much money hitherto. Quick riches (in the absence of some ancestral residue of pelf) are regarded as tainted. Riches gained without proper effort or without some sacrifice are considered equally suspect.

This brief citation illustrates one of the curious truths about middle-class wisdom. Such wisdom is not concerned to describe reality or to solve real problems but rather to convey some sort of moral judgment. Such wisdom attempts, therefore, to interpose a creed between the real world and the onlooker trying to make sense out of that world. Thus standard enclave thought tacitly confers or withholds approval as a means of enforcing a particular scheme of values on the population at large. Something of the effectiveness of middle-class orthodoxy is demonstrated by the general belief that these two patent falsehoods are true.

It may be worthwhile to delve a bit deeper, into several of the associated idea clusters that hover near these two aphorisms. At bottom, the view of life expressed by these sentiments is one and inseparable from that clause of the Protestant Ethic that equates wealth and morality. Quick riches implicitly carry the connotation of quickly gained riches unsanctified by earlier riches. To see how little logical weight is carried by the notion that quick riches are impossible, it takes no more than a brief glance at the stock market.

Somewhere equally close to the core of that canon of enclave wisdom is the fable of the deserving rich, variant Number One —the savers and the spenders. The fable, briefly restated, is that since time began, there have been savers who carefully nurtured their substance, repressed errant lusts and desires, shunned luxury, and put by a little something for the future. Then there have been spenders who have been extravagant profligates, squandering their substance, living riotously, giving never a care for the morrow. Thus, by goodness—frugal foresightedness—the rich have become rich; and by badness—extravagant nonchalance— the poor have become poor. Wealth therefore is but saving grown great, poverty but spending run wild. In any event, saving takes

time. Therefore "quick riches" can be seen in their true light as
a contradiction in terms.

Accordingly, a man cannot get rich quick; richer, yes; rich, no.

· 2 ·

On a more complex level, consider the pattern of reasoning
widely used by the American middle class, the "brand-names"
mode. This mode, as the term suggests, depends on fixed names
for fixed values. The commercial analog of this sort of thought
process is provided by the branded products sold by national
advertisers, particularly in package goods that carry small price
tags, take up little shelf room, and are therefore sold in myriad
retail outlets—namely toothpastes, foodstuffs, patent medicines,
cigarettes, and soaps. Once a customer has acquired loyalty to
Colgate-Palmolive, Del Monte, Anacin, Chesterfield, or Lux, the
hope is that he will not stray thereafter. After a time, a natural
inclination in people to affirm comes into play. A buyer—imagine
it is you—relaxes his suspicions. You forget the rigors of analysis
because your favorable disposition to the brand name in question has been reinforced so many times that further suspicion and
analysis would be so much wasted time. From a manufacturer's
standpoint, such loyalty provides him insurance against lost sales
resulting from lower quality. If you have engraved on your mind
a loyalty to Del Monte brand prunes and Del Monte has a sour
year, you will perhaps charge off the difference to sourness in
yourself, not in the prunes. Therefore if reality changes, your
perception of reality need undergo no disruptive equivalent
change. Change thereby can be successfully ignored, and the inevitable stresses and tensions that accompany change can likewise be avoided.

That is the method of the brand-names mode of thought, and
those are some of its advantages and disadvantages. A cerebral
onlooker would be tempted to observe that brand-names thought,
less than being thought, seems more a cheerful readiness to sum-
mon the appropriate slogan for whatever key word or phrase

needs adornment. Thus, the onlooker might go on to say that, for example, as when "prunes" is said, the response is "Del Monte"; when "American business" is the phrase, the antiphon will be "free enterprise"; when "manager," "hard-working"; "union," "dictatorial"; and "wealth," "hard-earned." Thus a package-thought approach to current problems unquestionably frees much of the populace for the full enjoyment of the fruits of an abundant society. It has its more noxious effects at the same time, however.

The question then is, "At what point does the estrangement from reality that such thought encourages become a serious threat to a person's welfare?" It is a difficult question to respond to because at this point the discussion begins to trail into metaphysics. Who is to say where danger begins or when a society begins to suffer serious weakness because of its inability to see reality as it is, not as some creed says it is? A human being cannot simply jettison every illusion he has. Without illusions, life would be impossible. But at the same time, with too many illusions, life becomes unlivable.

Mass illusions, views held in common with many other people, assume the status of what Professor Galbraith has called "conventional wisdom," and what I have chosen to call "secular piety": the view held by most of the populace, either actively or without demurrer. A word on this secular piety seems to be appropriate here.

The usual conversation of polite, informal society abounds with the cadences of secular piety, and one would be hard put to deny that just these views represent the fine network of truths that keep society together, that they represent a cement of great utility. As it happens, the average man finds the illusions that I am talking about in this book marginal to his main interests. That is, he believes in free enterprise, in the sanctity of property, and in the grave danger of centralized government without particular passion, yet with a certain tenacity; he wears these truths lightly because they are abstractions, after all, and of limited immediate application. At the same time, this believer in secular piety is anxious to be liked, and in the interests of being thought a good fellow, he will endure a mild swindle by a TV repairman, or submit to the pleas of an encyclopedia salesman. He will be tolerant of the petty sharp practices of commerce, and his illusions will emerge unshaken. It does not seem overstatement to say that the American would rather be shorn of his sugar-bowl money than stripped of his marginal illusions.

How can a man's essential beliefs remain unshaken by events? The answer (or at least part of it) is to be found in the practice of "reinforcement." That term has come into prominence within the past few years in educational circles, where it is central to the theory of teaching machines and related methods of imparting great amounts of information swiftly and accurately. "Reinforcement" is the technique of saying "that's right" by mechanical means a split second after a student has learned something. In its adult applications, reinforcement is a method of long standing in keeping standard illusions intact. It is most effectively in use wherever a high degree of organization exists—in a garden apartment by virtue of its layout, in a corporation by virtue of necessity and tradition. Corporation management, an enclave within the enclave, provides a notable example of secular piety practiced on a high plateau of intensity and reinforced by outstandingly effective means: Because management tends to be a closed loop in which the disposition to say "that's right" is well marked, it is within this segment of society that secular piety often seems most secure.

From his first days in the pay of a corporate industrial employer, the management trainee begins his novitiate that points him toward moral perfection, as it is understood in the enclave. Although standards of piety change according to the needs of each age, the detailed methods of reinforcement (essentially precept and admonition followed either by a pecuniary or ceremonial reward) apparently remain unchanged. A reading of Henry Charles Lea's *The Inquisition in the Middle Ages*, Max Weber's essays on bureaucracy, and William H. Whyte's *Organization Man* suggests more similarities than dissimilarities through the ages in creating and maintaining an intraorganizational climate of assent. In the medieval Roman Catholic church, the epoch of T'ang Dynasty China, and in the milieu of the modern corporation, the devices of inspiration and reward seem surprisingly constant.

The kind and gentle reproof, the soft-spoken guidance of the novice manager, these are the methods that secure the young man's orthodoxy and that help him perfect his skills at living in a new kind of society. Bit by bit he grows more aware of the conflicts that rise between his own inclinations and the wishes of his new chosen corporate society. He learns, if he survives, the methods of harmonizing those conflicts. Thus, he becomes more secularly pious in several respects, but in none more prominently than in his vocabulary. It is almost possible to set down a glossary of pious terms in common use, and that is what I have attempted below.

I have listed here a dozen terms that are ideologically sensitive and that consequently are important to an orthodox point of view. Next to each word is a list of variant attributives. Secular piety, I maintain, has these and other similar sets of word associations for its principal instruments:

WORD OR IDEA	APPROPRIATE ADJECTIVES	
Management and the Corporation	Democratic	Practical
	Professional	Realistic
	Savvy	Responsible
	Progressive	Aggressive
	Hardheaded	Alert
Labor and Unionism	Featherbedding	High-Pressure
	Irresponsible	Complaining
	Dictatorial	Destructive
	Negative	Bullheaded
	Disruptive	Divisive
Government	Wasteful	Regimented
	Inefficient	Shortsighted
	Bureaucratic	Nosy
	Highly Centralized	Welfare Statist
	Dangerous	Backbreaking

WORD OR IDEA	APPROPRIATE ADJECTIVES	
Taxation	Murderous Inequitable Ruinous Excessive Frightening	(or any other adjective suggesting death, dismemberment, or intolerable pain)
Wealth	Hard-Earned Honestly Gained Incentive-Sustaining	
Profits (of one's own corporation) *for public consumption:*	Pitiful Vanishing Elusive Paltry Weak	
for internal consumption and for security analysts:	Rebounding Gratifying Adequate	
Property	Sacred Vital Fundamental Inviolable	
Economic Theory *Classical:*	Sound Precise Practical Realistic	
Keynesian-Modern:	Woolly Collectivist Irresponsible Atheistic	
Poverty (in America)	Illusory	
Civil Rights	Diversionary	
Depression	Impossible	
Recession (or "Rolling Readjustment")	Mild	

This list could, of course, be expanded well past its present limits, but further examples do not seem so worthwhile as a summary of the elements reflected above. Secular piety, in a shorthand rendition of the major points above, resolves itself into this brief creed:

Management works hard, deserves reward and honor, can save country.

Labor featherbeds, grabs more than fair share, gripes and complains.

Government intrudes, pokes nose in where it doesn't belong, taxes ruinously, wastes money grievously, advocates woolly policies, advances incorrect economic doctrines.

Status quo: generally good, should stay.

Changers, spenders, complainers: bad, probably don't believe in God.

· 3 ·

One is almost constrained to regard enclave wisdom with mixed emotions. As philosophy it isn't much. Even as simple description of what happens in the real world it is defective. But as ideology it meets the basic requirement. It gives society the illusions needed for complacent survival. One can expect very little more from any body of public cant.

As ideology goes, secular piety isn't all that noxious. Nevertheless, its practitioners seem constantly in danger of blotting out alternate patterns of behavior, of stifling their countrymen with their ritual beliefs, and of rendering the spirit of innovation too weak for the public good. Ideology becomes overbearing if it has things too much its own way, and that is basically what is wrong with enclave wisdom.

ELEVEN

Corporate Culture and the

Vested Interests

лплплплпл

In previous chapters the discussion has repeatedly come back to corporations in their various activities. It takes no exhaustive argument to establish that the corporate mode of organization is one of the most visible manifestations of the vested interests.

The five hundred largest manufacturing corporations maintain the pattern of life that increasingly comes to mark the American civilization, and it is a bureaucratic pattern. The word "bureaucratic" is customarily reserved for reference to Federal government, yet that same word applies with full force to the modern corporation.

The German sociologist Max Weber set forth the distinguishing attributes of bureaucracy in this fashion: [1]

Bureaucracy has for its essential characteristics the principal of fixed and rule-bound functions and channels of authority, stable transmission of power by strict regulations, and "methodical provision for the regular fulfillment of . . . duties. . . ." Hence the growth of office hierarchy, elaborate files, expert incumbents, and the like that Weber characterized as typical of bureaucracy, and hence the perfection of "rational matter-of-factness" as a mark of the career bureaucrat and administrator. These qualities therefore come to be associated with bureaucracy: order, stability, continuity—in sum, precision at a leisurely pace.

· 1 ·

The corporation and its constituency is not so simply labeled and filed away. For under the seemingly placid exterior of any bureaucracy churns a struggle for preferment, which provides an energizing climate and a cross-purpose at the same time. That cross-purpose is the little-understood but real enough contest between production and ceremony, between what may be classified as methodical and magical activities. As always, method contends with magic.

As it happens, bureaucracy encourages both such "rational" and "irrational" activities. Therefore expertness in administration becomes in many instances a matter of sacerdotal excellence, of holding the mysteries of office procedure much as a priest holds the mysteries of the Eucharist: ready to be shared willingly once the ceremonial prerequisites have been met. An expertness in sales or manufacturing, productive skills, may elevate a man to an important hierarchic post, and it will be a "rational" promotion. It will be a methodical advancement if he has no notable ceremonial skills (he is blunt, for instance) but wins his post simply on the basis of his knowledge of how to sell wide-flange I-beams.

The discussion is unrealistic, because it has been pursued so far as if a man is either productive or ceremonious. Of course, the adept bureaucrat can be both. To be a successful producer, common sense confirms, a man must be skillful at ceremonial activities; at least he cannot be gauche. Likewise, a ceremonially accomplished administrator cannot, except in rare instances, be wholly without productive skills. Skills tend to run in sets anyway. The man who can do one thing well can usually do many other things well also. With that understanding of the limitations of the analysis I am pursuing, the discussion can move on to a more detailed examination of the conflict between productive and sacerdotal bureaucracy.

In the spring of 1961, the American Society for Public Administration met in Philadelphia, and the discussion turned to the tensions between elected officials in various local, state, and Federal government posts, and the career administrators. A panelist at the discussion offered the opinion that career bureaucrats are too often "smug, know-it-all administrators who revel in expertise." As *Business Week* magazine reported the meeting:

The "experts'" use of specialized language tends to insulate them from the elected officials, who speak a language "much closer to that of the people," according to one panelist. . . .

There's a tendency for some bureaucrats to become so proficient at handling certain problems that they don't want them solved.

During the Period of Feudal States in China (200–600 after Christ), Weber recited, a tradition of similar divergence between priestly and productive roles of bureaucratic labor prevailed:

Only the adept of scriptures and of tradition has been considered competent for correctly ordering the internal administration and the charismatically correct life conduct of the prince, ritually and politically. In sharpest contrast to the Jewish prophets, who were essentially interested in foreign policy, the Chinese literati-politicians, trained in ritual, were primarily oriented toward problems of internal administration, even if these problems involved absolute power politics, and even though while in charge of the prince's correspondence and of the chancellery they might personally be deeply involved in the guidance of diplomacy.[2]

Weber tells of one particular instance that illustrates the clash of productive and ceremonial skill in ancient Chinese bureaucracy:

In the feudal state of Wei, a proved general—U Ki, the alleged author of the textbook in ritually correct strategy which was authoritative until our time—and a literary man competed for the position of first minister. A violent dispute arose between the two after the literary man had been appointed to the post. He readily admitted that he could neither conduct wars nor master similar political tasks in the manner of the general. But when the general thereupon declared himself to be the better man, the literary man remarked that a revolution threatened the dynasty, whereupon the general admitted without any hesitation that the literary man was the better man to prevent it.[3]

A survey made by the *Harvard Business Review* among four thousand subscribers in 1961 indicated that businessmen who were docile, in the image of the Chinese literatus, proved more attractive to their superiors in top management than men who, like the feudal general, had earmarks of the innovator: argumentativeness, intolerance, rebelliousness. Hence "organization men" were seen as more desirable subordinates than men with a greater independence of spirit.

It does not seem off the point, then, to pursue this question for a bit. Does ceremonial bureaucracy impair in any important way the evolution of the economy or of industry? That is, are the costs of ceremonialism worth worrying about, or are its results in themselves worthwhile?

Before any such question can be answered, it should be noted that if there is such a thing as an organization man, he will—by definition—be ceremonially adept: intent on maintaining the order and stability of his organization. Armed with similar job goals was the feudal Chinese literatus. Here is how Weber enumerates the skills of that early bureaucrat: Knowledge of scriptures (from which tradition may be discerned) and a knowledge of the calendar and of the stars (from which divine will may be known). The modern corporate administrator, by comparison, will know his corporation's history and particularly his department's recent history (from which precedents may be discovered); he will also have a knowledge of the whims of the various men within who have the tacit right of sabotaging his proposals for action. Hence the ceremonially adept bureaucrat can, in his way, cast a horoscope and announce what favorable signs his experienced eye detects.

· 2 ·

There have been those who have argued that the rise of sacerdotal bureaucracy, of organization men, or of what have elsewhere been called antimanagers,* threatens to choke off the sources of invention, hence of economic growth, and thus of continuing well-being. Is it true? If so, the costs of ceremonialism seem extraordinary. One way to measure the validity of such charges is to examine the events surrounding recent important inventions.

In the first place, invention cannot be wholly separated from development, so at the outset the myth of isolated creativity has to be reconsidered. The evidence at hand suggests that without some sort of bureaucratic apparatus, the fifty most important inventions of the recent past would have been impossible, for the most part. They would have failed for financial, manufacturing, marketing, or simple technical reasons. Development of an idea to a point of commercial self-sufficiency is usually far more complicated work than the original hatching of the idea, as the history of the safety-razor blade forcefully demonstrates. In truth, without the developmental support of a complex organization many inventions would assume no more reality than most of the vague ruminations that go on in original minds.

As related in the book *The Sources of Invention* by John Jewkes, David Sawers, and Richard Stillerman,[4] many if not most contemporary inventions have represented the confluence of two distinct skills: creation and administration. The case histories of inventions, to be sure, also demonstrate that corporations have often proved barriers to swift innovation (catalytic cracking of petroleum and continuous casting of steel are two examples). These case histories also suggest that outsiders, or men who have not fully respected the *bona-fides* of reigning administrators, often prove themselves more correct about the technical possibilities of

* See *Men Who Make Us Rich*, pp. 185–200 *et passim*.

prospective innovations than the experts (Bakelite, hydrogenated fats, insulin, jet engines, color film, long-playing records, and inertially guided rockets all provide examples). Nevertheless, the handmaid of invention, development, is revealed again and again as the honorific word for what can otherwise be termed "administration." Consider the invention and development of xerography.

Chester Carlson, a schoolboy with a love of science, took to printing his own magazine for amateur chemists. He thereby learned of the vexations of typography. He resolved to improve type reproduction methods if he could. He went to the California Institute of Technology, graduated as a physicist, and then went to work for Bell Laboratories. There he grew interested in patents. Carlson studied for the bar, became an attorney, and began to practice patent law. In 1934 he started a systematic search for a fresh approach to the problem of swift, inexpensive duplication of printed material. He steered clear of chemical processes on the theory that the big companies like Eastman Kodak would have explored every feasible avenue there. Thus the way pointed to a photoelectric approach. Initial experiments proved fruitless. As the inventor himself later wrote, "I realized that I would have to go deeper into the subject in order to understand the subject matter better and, if possible, to discover some phenomena in the literature which had been overlooked by previous inventors." [5]

He spent four years in the New York Public Library reading technical books and magazines. At length, the possibility of using an electrolytic process suggested itself, but the obstacles seemed overwhelming. It would require far too much current, Carlson discovered, to duplicate by the general method he wished to use. The young inventor then recited to himself the difficulties along with a possibility that occurred to him:

. . . if the low voltages and high currents of electrolytic processes could be replaced by high voltages and low currents, the same amount of light could control a greater amount of energy. With the problem so sharply defined, the solution came almost as an intuitive flash. I was aware that a previous inventor had used powder to develop electrostatic images. By combining that with my concept of an electrostatic

light-sensitive plate, the invention was complete and it only remained
to search the literature to see whether a suitable photoconductive material was known.[6]

The year was 1937. A patent application was filed right away,
even though no exact experimental basis for proceeding had yet
been devised. Years passed, and it happened that Carlson (who
in his duties as a patent attorney called on various research organizations) persuaded Battelle Memorial Institute, a large non-
profit research institution, to undertake development of xerography. Carlson ceded his patent rights in return for a large return on future proceeds from developmental refinements. By
1946 these refinements were largely perfected, and industry at
last began to express interest. It wasn't until 1950, however, that
the Haloid Corporation of New York brought the invention to
market; that was the year of the first Xerox copying machine in
office use. Growth thereafter was swift and widespread, inspired
in no small degree by the keen interest of the United States Signal
Corps, one of the most important of Xerox license holders. As *The
Sources of Invention* sums it up:

An outsider [from the photocopying field] was responsible for the
basic invention in this case. Development work proceeded along many
channels; a non-profit research organization made the initial advances,
then a small firm pushed the commercial development along rapidly,
and, finally, the Army and large and small firms participated in the
development.[7]

There is, then, a mixed record: where *invention* is the goal, individual or small group effort seems to be the ideal; where *discovery*, much the same scale of ideal operation suggests itself.
But where *development* is involved, there group effort on a fairly
large scale seems to play the key role, particularly in complex
chemical or electromechanical inventions. In these latter cases,
in other words, bureaucracy comes to bear on the task with significant contributions.

At the same time, bureaucracy in its sacerdotal aspects unquestionably can stifle the inventive spirit. The dismal record of the American steel industry in opposing technical innovations such as the continuous casting mentioned above suggests what can happen in extreme cases. The strange insularity of the steel-industry leadership (as discussed in Chapter 3) seems to point to a dysfunctional measure of sacerdotal ascendancy over productive instincts.

With a few notable exceptions, the manufacturing corporation in the United States avails itself without hesitation of the fruits of invention and even helps to sustain the climate in which development can go forward in part by means of fairly regular changes in command. Professor Oscar Grusky has observed that while bureaucracy helps soften "the disruptive aspects of succession . . . [a]t the same time, because of their predispositions for stability, bureaucracies require periodic succession at the top if they are to adapt adequately to their environment. Without frequent succession, bureaucracies tend to lose that degree of flexibility which they especially need." [8] However that may be, there are real problems here that probably will not improve spontaneously.

Meanwhile, as the economy matures, and as the dramatic spurts on the scale of the industrial growth of the 1870–1920 period become rarer, industrial bureaucracy becomes more attuned to gatekeeping than to roistering out after new conquests. Much the same subtle change in goals (and hence in bureaucratic style) has become visible in the military establishment, also. As the United States Naval Postgraduate School described the new style, the army has become more attuned to a long-drawn-out cold war, to an actionless existence from the standpoint of military experience. As the army bureaucracy becomes more resigned to such sedentary activities as long-range planning, the ceremonial elements of the officer corps intensify while, of necessity, the productive elements atrophy. Thus the naval school observed that the change in General Staff outlook from "action-orientation" to "routine-orientation" has caused some anguish among old-line officers.

It has given rise to the feeling that "bookkeepers are running the army." [9]

· 3 ·

In assessing the effects of corporate life, one is struck time and again by the ambivalence that typically marks the employees of corporations themselves. They obviously prosper by the stable nature of corporate life. Their whole private existence is built on installment debt, mortgage payment, and fixed obligations that take most of their paychecks. Nothing makes for docility like high fixed costs. They would be severely embarrassed financially should instability come to mark America's dominant corporations in even the modest degree to which such instability marks Madison Avenue advertising agencies. Yet at the same time, corporate managers are acutely sensitive to the drawbacks of their office existence; they know in a thousand ways that they have sacrificed much of their individuality in the interest of survival within a tightly knit group.

The bargain that the corporate manager has struck is not really far different from the bargain most of the middle class has struck for the privilege of living in a complex, urbanized society in which the division of labor has been pushed close to its ultimate refinement. The benefits of stability and prosperity are in some measure bought by accepting severe limitations on one's freedom and by accepting highly repetitive work in all but the most creative occupations.

The luxuriance of sacerdotal ritual in a corporation comes as something of a relief, then, from the drab sameness of most productive labor. Ceremonial observances are concerned in one sense largely with the complicated economic psychology of psychic wealth and psychic income, which is infinitely varied and which in fact often makes office routine highly exciting.

Such economic psychology is by nature a subject in which there is not much hope of discovering anything concrete. What

I have to say, then, is more in the vein of conjecture. I am tacitly asking, "Is it this way?" at each full stop that follows.

There is probably some substance to the view that bureaucracy deliberately arranges itself for what lawyers call "adversary proceedings." That is, two sides constitute themselves and then agree to disagree for a while, after which they agree to agree. Thereby will a proposal get a rounded examination. Under such circumstances it often occurs that decisions are not made but rather that they accrete. While that method wins scant approval from academic management theorists, it has its own logic and its own considerable benefits, not least of which is that adversary proceedings are labor-intensive. More men are needed to staff this kind of ceremonially biased bureaucracy than its contrary, the productively biased bureaucracy.

Where a complex bureaucracy comes into being it often has similarities to the familiar world of retail commerce. Just as merchants in the same neighborhood compete for customers to come into their stores (yet need each other's proximity to maintain the total attraction of their shopping center), so ceremonially adept bureaucrats compete for petitions from among the lower reaches of the hierarchy. This sort of competition is quite subtle for the ranking administrator secure in his position, less subtle for the executive who is going downhill in status, but real and pervasive for all conditions of administrative employees. One's volume of mail, under this regimen, is as good to the bureaucrat as checks from charge-account customers are to retail merchants. Likewise, the quantity of incoming telephone calls, memoranda, and telegrams serves to indicate how the gross psychic income of an office is being allocated.

Corporate managers who have a strong productive bent often express the opinion that they could do most of their work at home at far less man-hour cost to the corporation. These men argue for a pattern of administration, which, aside from whatever benefits it may boast, has one cardinal drawback: it is directly anticeremonial in its net effect. Were administrators to scatter to their homes to pore over their documents in solitude, the sacerdotal observances and rituals would fail for want of the requisite number of celebrants and observers. A ceremonial anarchy would ensue, and in the nature of bureaucracy, such a development would be intolerable. No committees could meet, no conferences convene. No casual corridor conversation could take place. Hence a swarm of problems that would never have arisen would arise (and they would require written solutions). Most important, the ceremonial marketplace in which gross psychic income is allocated would simply cease to exist. Under such circumstances, one could as well expect to run a modern industrial economy without a Wall Street as to run a corporation without its ceremonial marketplace. No central planning can fully substitute either for the public marketplace or the corporate psychic marketplace.

The dimensions of this marketplace and some of the psychic arbitrage that goes on there are revealed by a glance at the committee, an institution within an institution. A principal task of a committee is to emphasize the rank differentials of the participants. Committee meetings tend to proliferate, moreover. Goodyear Tire & Rubber Company, in fact, set up a special committee in 1960 expressly to deal with the problem of too many committee meetings. Their first step was to call a new series of meetings to discuss the problem of too many meetings.[10] Thus the ambivalence of one corporation toward its own allocation of resources between productive and ceremonial labor led to an apparently insoluble problem: the company had to have ceremonial sanction to moderate ceremonial time expenditure. Framed that way, such a proposition need not detain us for speculations on its ultimate prospects for success.

Another symptom of ceremonial growth and development is the common industrial complaint about too much paperwork. The invention of xerography discussed above makes any reduction in paperwork unlikely. Wider sharing of productive information by such fast and inexpensive duplication methods means that productive information increasingly comes to be used for ceremonial purposes. The excess of informative paper in circulation also calls into being new ritualistic refinements. No longer do judgments come with insouciance from intuitive impulses; now that analytical information is available as never before, an expert board will sit down to consider its possible applications. Without prolonging this discussion, it is enough to say that no one can have serious intentions to reduce paper work, despite frequent protests to that effect. New allocations of paper, yes. Absolutely less paper? Not likely. Such a development would be directly contrary to the nature of priestly bureaucracy.

It does not seem exaggeration to say that sacerdotal bureaucracy has every prospect of becoming more, not less, preeminent in the United States and in other industrialized nations. The trend in industrial management seems clearly toward ceremonial cooperation, not productive freewheeling. That may simply be another way of saying that each of us is more dependent on society than ever, less able to survive without the aid and support of others, and accordingly, our institutions, with their tendency to caricature, follow the requirements of the times. Such ceremonial enhancement does not seem cause for breast-beating, however. It does not seem likely that the sources of invention will dry up or that the living tissues of corporate society will become gangrenous. It simply argues that a new and more subtle type of behavior is beginning to typify American industry and that sometimes the results may not be wholly what we expect or want.

· 4 ·

There are two types of corporate leadership that provide either a productive or a ceremonial climate. There are, therefore, two basic conditions that give the institutional metabolism its rhythms and its essential tone. There is on the one hand the innovative, informal climate typical of rapid growth that usually accompanies charismatic leadership. On the other hand there is the more restrained, highly structured climate that emerges with economic maturity and that is accompanied by the evolution of a new kind of leadership, archonic leadership. The term "charismatic leadership" was first used systematically by Max Weber in "The Sociology of Charismatic Authority."

Charismatic leaders are, in Weber's words:

> The "natural" leaders [who]—in times of psychic, physical, economic, ethical, religious, political distress—have been neither office-holders nor incumbents of an "occupation" in the present sense of the word, that is, men who have acquired expert knowledge and who serve for remuneration. The natural leaders in distress have been holders of specific gifts of the body and spirit; and these gifts have been believed to be supernatural, not accessible to everybody. The concept of "charisma" is here used in a completely "value-neutral" sense.[11]

The archonic leader, on the other hand, is the creature of orderly succession founded on expertness of knowledge and long service in lower positions within the corporate hierarchy.

Generally speaking, the charismatic leader presides over the smaller corporation that is undergoing forced-draft growth, while the archon is more the administrator of a large, stabilized corporation. While it oversimplifies considerably the distinct roles of the two kinds of leaders, it is reasonably accurate to say that the charismatic leader is a productive leader concerned with accomplishing certain concrete ends. The archonic leader, by contrast, is a ceremonial leader. He is concerned with means, not ends.

The charismatic leader on the scale of a Billy Durant gives way to leaders in an archonic mold like Harlow Curtice in a corporation such as General Motors. It was Durant who put the giant organization together, Curtice who ruled at the peak of postwar sales in 1955. It is almost as if the charismatic executive is a hunter and gatherer who proceeds by flashes of intuition to his great decisions, while the archon makes far more deliberate progress. The archon has his committees of expert advisers whom he consults before reaching decisions. Once again, method succeeds magic. Or does it? The new scheme of decision-making is more rational, more "scientific" than the older style of intuitive management. But on second glance, it may be more accurate to say that a new kind of stylized group magic (sacerdotal bureaucracy) has succeeded the earlier, individualized magic (charismatic leadership).

Let me carry the distinction between charisma and archonry one step further by saying that, broadly speaking, charismatic leadership rises from (or perhaps creates) a zealous productive spirit that sometimes borders on religious dedication. Hence some of the elements that have been associated with a patriarchal society founded on ancestor worship may be said to mark, also, the charismatic style of development. Archonic bureaucracy, on the other hand, comes more and more to be associated with ceremonial luxuriance. No other reasoning seems to make sense in explaining why there has been such sizable growth (estimated at 44 percent in the 1949–1959 decade alone) in "upper executive" ranks; why, for example, Borg-Warner Corporation has forty chairmen and presidents (one for each division); why the growth of high titles has taken on much of the semblance of an inflationary spiral in status payments.

These signs of greater status emoluments reflect the belief that a modern manager can be motivated by good wishes, by psychic income, by honor and esteem granted in a formal way. Many anomalies of modern corporate bureaucracy, it appears, can best be understood if viewed within the context of love being sought, being found, or being exchanged. Take the need for fealty (a typical mark of a charismatic regime) contrasted with the need for emulation and ritual deference (a typical pair of attributes of the modern, archonic organization).

International Business Machines Corporation has provided a memorable example of charismatically oriented fealty (as mentioned earlier, in Chapter 2). Thomas J. Watson, the guiding genius of the company's years of greatest growth, received vows of fealty from his protégés in various anthems that IBM executives used to sing at company sales meetings. Here is a sample of the relevant verses from the IBM Songbook: *

* A rare document, this songbook is no longer in use in the company. An IBM public-relations executive suggested once that the corporation apparently doesn't like its outmoded hymnal to circulate, as he himself had tried repeatedly to see the book without success.

From "March on With IBM," a couplet in the introductory verse goes:

> With T. J. Watson guiding us,
>   we lead throughout the world,
> For peace and trade our banners are unfurled,
>   unfurled. . . .

In "Hail to the IBM," the phenomenon of identity of charismatic leader and his organization is particularly evident. The syntax here suggests that one is simply another aspect of the other, that man and institution are interchangeable:

> Lift up our proud and loyal voices,
>   Sing out in accents strong and true,
> With hearts and hands to you devoted,
>   And inspiration ever new;
> Your ties of friendship cannot sever,
>   Your glory time will never stem,
> We will toast a name that lives forever,
>   Hail to the IBM.
>
> Our voices swell in admiration;
>   Of T. J. Watson proudly sing;
> He'll ever be our inspiration;
>   To him our voices loudly ring;
> The IBM will sing the praises,
>   Of him who brought us world acclaim,
> As the volume of our chorus raises,
>   Hail to his honored name.

The identity is almost as clear in "Ever Onward," the second chorus of which appeared earlier. This "IBM Rally Song," as it is alternately known, has the following first verse:

> There's a thrill in store for all,
> For we're about to toast
> The corporation known in every land.
> We're here to cheer each pioneer
> And also proudly boast
> Of that "man of men" our friend and guiding hand.

The name of T. J. Watson means a courage none can stem:
And we feel honored to be here to toast the "IBM."

EVER ONWARD—EVER ONWARD! . . . etc.

In this sort of ritual fealty, the fatuous can never be far away. Even an organization as sensitive to the fitness of things as IBM could not contain its enthusiasm. In the "IBM School Song," the fourth verse represents a further attempt at charismatic fealty:

> With Mr. Watson leading,
> To greater heights we'll rise
> And keep our IBM
> Respected in all eyes. . . .

Finally, in the "IBM Country Club Song," the attempt at fealty begins to yield fast-diminishing returns:

> Stand up and cheer for our fine
>   Country Club
> Where recreation is the theme.
> We thank you, T. J. Watson,
>   The leader of our team.

Critics can easily poke fun at those songs, but critics cannot so easily dismiss the spirit that they reflected or the unprecedented corporate growth that the singers of those songs created. By rendering such songs at company rallies, the IBM manager told the company founder that there was a bond of love between them, a bond of mutual respect, if you prefer. Hence the charismatic leader got reinforcement for his general style of leadership; he was formally granted a psychic windfall as an inspiring mentor, a friendly guiding hand, and as team leader. There is reason to believe that without such support, without the love and respect of his followers, Watson could not have done the job he did; that IBM would not have emerged with such swiftness to a position of world leadership and influence. By singing such songs, his men were saying in a ritually convenient manner, "That's right, Boss;

you're doing fine." Such, then, are the ways of bureaucratic ritual, at least as they have been practiced by industry in the twentieth century.

When the great energizing atmosphere of rapid growth dissipates, however, the songbooks and their equivalents apparently disappear also. Instead, subtlety begins to mark the newer forms of ritual. Fealty as such seems to languish and in its stead comes symbolic conformity: love and respect for archonic leadership indicated not by spontaneous or uncomplaining *esprit de corps* but by emulation of archonic personality and sartorial traits.

· 5 ·

To further the distinction between charismatic leadership and archonic leadership, I should say here that the charismatic leader seems far more concrete a personality than does an archon. The archon is sort of an ultimate abstraction of power, a man whose power derives from his orderly succession to leadership, not a man whose natural gifts and accomplishments have compelled his —and no one else's—elevation by acclamation.

One effect of the abstract eminence of archonic leadership is occasionally evident in the creation of what may be called reflex toadyism. In its extreme manifestations such toadyism grows almost to the status of a fixed pattern of managerial behavior. To the degree that an archon permits himself to be eulogized and fawned on, the practice of eulogy and fawning becomes an established part of a corporation's daily life. In most extreme cases there arises a fawning competition among all ranks of management: a kind of organized unrequited brotherly love. Upper-middle management prostrates itself before top management in the art of exaggerated deference; middle-middle does likewise in its relation to upper-middle; and lower-middle with middle-middle. The whole practice threatens to collapse of its own weight in proportion as the chief executive has no charismatic qualities to legitimatize the ritual deference he receives. If the whole tableau is merely a sustained gesture of respect for power, it threatens to become demeaning, not ennobling (as genuine expressions of fealty evidently can be). Hence when the General Electric Supply Company, as was its occasional custom, "devoted" the appliance sales of a particular month to the president of General Electric, the parent organization, even though the president had no particular distinction as a salesman, the act was commonly described by the sales managers down the line as "ass kissing" by their district-manager superiors, not at all a sign of appropriate loyalty. What made the practice particularly transparent was the vagueness of "devoting" sales; no one could ever figure out exactly what, if anything, was being devoted. Outwardly, however, the sales managers competed with each other in their enthusiasm for the votary offering.

No doubt the limited terms of office of archonic leadership (on averages, about the same as college presidents—seven years) helps keep such toadyism in check.

Natural emulation of archonic leadership is a more typical and probably a more sincere method by which the priestly bureaucracy symbolizes its hierarchic structure. In some instances, the result of such emulation is as openly visible as whether a man wears brown shoes or black. The object, whatever color finally is worn, is to follow the leader.

The career prospects of a member of the middle management in an archonic regime depend in no small measure on his skills in this narrow application: how well he emulates the men who will select top management in his generation of candidates. The symbolic conformity that arises in response to such needs is too complex for extended examination here. All I can do is to try briefly to sketch several of its aspects.

The middle manager's ultimate success in his quest for an archonic position depends on three things: luck, ceremonial skill, and productive skill (and probably in that order). Of the first and the last there is little that can be said here. Of ceremonial skill, however, what can be said is that the manipulation of symbols is essential to its perfection. In career-escalation, such manipulation depends on emulating the general attributes of the incumbent leadership: clothing, style of life, discourse, attitudes, even background. To accomplish such emulation, a large head start is probably essential. Hence it is probably easier to be a Yale man than to act like one by *ex post facto* symbol manipulation. Yet imposture is not exactly diamond-rare in modern executive suites. Sacerdotal bureaucracy, in fact, seems to create a wide market for polished candidates, and therefore puts something of a premium on the outer attributes (for ceremonial purposes) more than on the inner capabilities (for productive performance). Therefore it seems germane here to examine briefly some of the structural aspects of facades in contemporary use.

There seems to be something of a hierarchy of symbols that ranges upward from verbal symbolism to aural (in the sense of "subtle emanation," not in the sense of "audible") symbolism. Thus the hierarchy falls into three parts: verbal, material, aural. It encompasses under the heading "verbal" such things as words and the things words suggest; under "material" such things as autos, houses, and the like; and under "aural" such things as suave elegance of address. Emblematic (or material) symbols tend to excel verbal symbols in their credibility, while aural symbols, being fixed in large degree by a person's ancestry, surpass even emblematic symbols in believability. What this means, in short, is that verbal symbols can be counterfeited more easily than either of the other types of symbols. Consequently, these symbols are somewhat suspect, with one important qualification: Those who make a living manipulating verbal symbols seem hesitant to seize on and expose verbal humbug, no doubt out of a sense of professional courtesy. Intellectuals, diplomats, admen, pundits, priests, journalists, writers, and lawyers remain active consumers of well packaged verbal symbolism, and they seem willing to go to greater lengths than other members of the middle class to credit such symbolism at face value.

Owing to the important weaknesses in verbal symbolism, skilled symbol manipulators in corporate environments often shun verbal means and embellish their own status instead by their preference for material and aural symbols; but this course has its difficulties, as these latter types of symbols are resistant to tampering.

Given the hazards and difficulties of manipulating the various kinds of symbols, it is a matter of common observation that there are nevertheless a number of skillful practitioners at large. In some degree, these manipulations are but another aspect of the quest for love and respect within the institutional walls. If a man can establish by symbolic manipulation that he has enjoyed a lovingly lavish childhood and adolescence, he in some mystic but real way seems a worthy candidate for new windfalls of esteem under the psychic equivalent of the rich getting richer. Therefore those who may not have been overloved in their earlier lives go to whatever lengths they can to give the impression of an affluence of love in the past, on the correct supposition that such an impression will be useful in the future. In many ways it will be, but in none more specifically than in making the ceremonial novice seem similar as a type to the archon. A few specific examples of the powerful effects of symbols in conferring the aura of the natural bureaucratic leader are listed below.

One humble instance that falls between the "aural" and "material" classifications, yet illustrates some of the power of each, is the shoeshine a man maintains. Its aural aspects may be viewed with the knowledge that a man's superiors within an organization will probably not go far wrong in judging his degree of commitment to the established order if they equate his commitment to the gloss on his shoes. They know that this symbol, marginal though it is, suggests subtle emulation of the uppermost members of the organizational hierarchy. For these and other reasons, the high shine is generally accepted at face value, and, by way of comparison, it is commonly accorded more reliability as an index than any half-dozen aphorisms of conventional wisdom. (Good as they sound, they are still verbal, and therefore inherently less credible than other symbols.) Although admittedly a trivial symbol, the shoeshine deserves further attention, first by examination of its contrary. An ostentatiously bad shine, or a pair of battered, heel-worn, and curled-up shoes is symbolic of at least a latent contempt for accepted norms of polite behavior. (One need only note the characteristic condition of a beatnik's footwear to satisfy himself on this point.) As for the shoeshine's material symbolism, it may well be that a good shine is esteemed especially because it confirms the expenditure of labor, probably someone else's. Therefore it may not be farfetched at all to assign to a well shined pair of shoes a receipt-like quality in that the shine confirms that its owner has paid something to keep his place in the social order outwardly visible, and that he thereby has done his bit to keep that order fixed. That he may stride the corridors with resplendent shoes, some member of the lower class must bend over a shine stand with sullied fingers and deep bow. By availing himself of a shine boy's services, a man does his part to keep the boy at his work, off the public dole, and out of mischief. Furthermore, the buyer of the shine announces in his finished appearance that he has done his daily task in maintaining this small buttress of the *status quo*.

The shoeshine suggests a parallel example of material symbolism that is in some way related through the physical act of shining. Although I digress to pursue the matter, perhaps the detour will seem to have been worth it. A family striving for *haute bourgeoisie* stature can no doubt speed its elevation if, while the husband attends to his daily shoeshine, the wife keeps on display in the home large amounts of brightly polished sterling. Whether she herself keeps it polished or a maid performs this function is not nearly so important as the appearance of the shined silver; the belief that hired help keeps it polished tends to occur to the visitor without prompting. It need hardly seem surprising, then, that silver owes some of its value and charm to the fact that it requires continual labor to keep it shined and that it thereby possesses the power to evoke admiration for its owner in much the same way and for much the same reasons as does a well shined pair of shoes. Whether these matters render the symbol of a shoeshine simply a matter of emblem shuffling or perhaps elevate it to the realm of aura-creation is a difficult question to answer with certainty.

Equally difficult to classify firmly as material or aural is the matter of clothing. For reasons similar to the effect of a shoeshine or of polished silver, a man can maintain an aura of reliability and soundness by pursuing certain effects in his attire no matter what his real cast of mind. There seems to be only one proviso, and that is that he show a sense of sumptuary restraint. Such restraint begins with the selection of gray or dark blue for clothing. Light colors suggest volatility, a condition of personality unsuited to ritually correct norms of behavior. The knife-sharp crease in a man's trousers is a material symbol, which, if pursued with some eye to subtlety, can become a matter of aural symbolism. For example, a worsted or gabardine fabric will hold a crease longer and better than a tweed or flannel. Because most people are aware of such fabric properties, a worsted or gabardine-clad person with a sharp crease manipulates merely an emblematic symbol. Let him instead wear tweed or flannel, and let him keep continually sharp creases in such trousers, and he will have graduated to aural symbolism. That is to say, the awareness of continual labor in maintaining those creases confers on the wearer at least a small increment of distinction such as is almost always conferred by unostentatious but visible expenditure.

If these speculations be accurate, then the whole object of symbol manipulation comes down to just that: tangible proof of expenditure. If that is so, then the various symbols may be regarded as so many receipts for goods or services bought, and the more imposing a man's symbolic receipts for money quietly spent, the greater respect and honor become his due. For his money, his parents' money, even his grandparents' money, spent quietly but tellingly, he reaps a high (if psychic) regard. It is in this particular connection that aural symbolism establishes its credentials as the most convincing and therefore the most useful symbolism of the three varieties. An aural-symbolic receipt of the very highest negotiability is that of physiognomy. Because regular features suggest generations of outlay for such goods and services as protein and orthodontia, good looks become at least a rough index of ancestral expenditure; furthermore, the best looking young women tend to consort with and wed the more wealthy young men, and generations of such selective breeding by solvent males at last makes its mark. Height, while probably less exacting as an index of expenditure, still suggests excellence of diet for some generations (an excellence generally available to Americans, and therefore of more dubious validity than physiognomy, but nevertheless of some significance).

Voice level, mannerisms, and gestures, on the other hand, no doubt would prove, if subjected to precise investigations, to have a discernible relationship to present-generation expenditure on "culture" and education. The well modulated voice, the unhurried turn of the head, and the open but not rudely expansive gesture may all be taken as receipts for sizable parental (not ancestral) expenditure on such things as dancing lessons, musical recitals, long tours, leisurely visits to art galleries, and private school education. No doubt such attributes can furthermore stand as receipts for any number of dollars spent in arranging, attending, or graciously evading cocktail parties, coming-out parties, fraternity and eating-club initiations, country-club dances, cruises, and the like.

At this point it becomes clear that aural symbols are also related to verbal symbols in some particulars, just as in other particulars (as indicated above) aural and material symbols overlap. The use of oral language in so far as the sound (not necessarily the content) is concerned has deep aural utility. Mispronunciation has the same effect here as would an ill-concealed belch in a cotillion receiving line.

There are few verbal symbols that cannot be faked, but even fakery has its costs. Elocution lessons or accent coaching do not come cheap. Therefore, in that sense, the sound of educated discourse is as good as the real thing, so far as it may represent a receipt for expenditure. Acceptable verbal symbolism requires a fair admixture of polysyllables, and complete sentences seem to be the rule. A fairly high level of abstraction also seems to mark this sort of discourse where the upper middle class is concerned, while colorful figures of speech or obvious bombast are kept to a bare minimum. The language itself, as distinguished from its manner, seems to approximate the clothing worn by a petitioner to the *haute bourgeoisie*. That is, it tends toward gray. Beyond these general observations it is difficult to venture without producing in the reader the same general drowsiness that this kind of talk itself brings on. Should he imagine himself in need of further insight into such speech, however, let him creep up on anyone boasting an outstandingly fine shoeshine and attired in gray and let his ears guide him from there, guarding the while against a telltale yawn that might betray his presence.

· 6 ·

The symbols of corporate ceremony are nothing but means to the end of love and respect—in a word, to the elevation of status. Although the artifices of the middle class are substantial, there are occasional revelations that show in particularly clear fashion how pitiable are those who have been stripped of the psychic wealth that a bureaucratic civilization bestows. Lose a title and you have lost a great deal. For example, in Long Island, New York, the craftsmen employed by the Nassau County Civil Service Commission complained bitterly when their distinctive titles (electrician, plumber, carpenter, painter) were taken from them and the generic "maintenance man" was conferred instead. These county employees were deeply stung. They petitioned the Civil Service Commission, saying that "maintenance man [as a title] signifies a man of no particular abilities, save those of working a broom and closing doors." Their letter also observed, "Since the medieval guilds men have had to study, train and then prove their abilities before earning the privileges of title. Today, much of a man's status in his community depends on the title of his job." Nevertheless, the letter went on, a private consulting firm had urged the county to strip away the craft titles of its employees as part of a civil service reclassification. "[We] have [been] made . . . an indistinguishable unit in a mass society, which is the same as being dead in a living world," the men protested.[12] The county agreed to study their protest.

Ceremonial crises of that sort are a great deal rarer in the culture of large corporations, largely because of the general upgrading of job-title nomenclature since World War II. Vice presidents are no longer rare. What *is* more common is the productive crisis, the feeling within management itself of disaffection, of estrangement from corporate goals, despite the outward appearances.

One example helps make the point. In 1961–1962, General Foods Corporation commissioned an attitude survey among its headquarters executives and middle managers. The survey consisted of an exhaustive questionnaire. It was conducted in such a way as to measure what dissidence there might be without trying in any way to discourage true expressions of feelings. After spending at least $20,000 on the survey, top management discovered a good deal of frustration and a general feeling of purposelessness among these executives. Said one executive, who later described the survey to me: "I spent one whole day filling out the answers, and I tried to be as honest as I could. I was amazed when I was finished at the hostility of my responses. But it was done anonymously, to encourage frankness. A few months later I saw an abstract of the survey's conclusions. I was really surprised. I found out that my own views weren't very far out at all. In fact, my own feelings, as it turned out, were fairly typical."

Similar expressions of vague unhappiness, of lack of understanding of what (if any) productive purpose the executive cadre is performing, arise in many, perhaps most, corporations. As the old-line army generals complain that bookkeepers have taken over the standing army, so many of the newer executives in industry are complaining that the paper-shufflers have taken over their corporations. The problem of cross-purpose remains an important one, in many ways the central internal worry of the contemporary vested interests.

T W E L V E

Conclusion

ЛЛЛЛЛЛЛЛ

If I have accomplished what I set out to do, the foregoing chapters will have conveyed something of the scope of vested interests in their origins, their development, and their behavior.

I have argued that a twentieth century enclosure movement is afoot and that it is being actively furthered by the vested interests. This new enclosure is evidenced by the continuing high level of domestic unemployment and by the massive proportions of American poverty. Accompanying the movement toward an economy that showers its riches only on nice people ("nice people" in its usual sense of solvent people) is the phenomenon of sound thought and the closely related secular piety. I have advanced the observation that the point of view suggested by these phrases is fairly representative of the vested interests' prime beneficiary, the middle class. I have also tried to establish that the effects of this kind of thought have been noxious, on the whole, ever since 1914. (Before that, such narrowness of mind may well have been a contributing factor to capital accumulation in the era of the Robber Barons.)

The growth of interests has also been examined within an evolutionary framework with hunting-gathering and advertising-consumerism representing the extremes of primitive and sophisticated economic organization. As for the day-to-day operations of vested interests, the histories of two industries (textiles and petroleum) have been examined in fairly close detail. The political devices by which these interests have won special privilege like-wise have been explored at some length.

After that, I tried to illuminate the relationship among the Establishment, the vested interests, and the poor. The conclusion that I reached was that the Establishment plays the sometime role of tribune of the poor, while the vested interests act the part of hostile adversary to the poor. To alleviate the condition of the poor, in brief, would raise the interests' costs more than would be tolerable, the archons seem to believe.

Thereafter the discussion turned away from the hard and know-able world of specific economic pressures and political responses. It moved toward the diffuse world of ideas. I tried to explain the psychological-economic basis of organized optimism, and to chart its rather astonishing growth in the United States. I then sought the roots of reflex optimism in popular religion. The rela-tionship of vested interests and religion brought the discussion back time and again to the principle of the deserving rich. As ideology, that principle has given long and distinguished service, and it has been amplified anew by various mass magazines. Thus the religious origins of the reigning American ideology sanctify what might otherwise seem to be just a series of justifications for predatory behavior. The wisdom of the enclave, viewed close up, turns out to be a set of slogans that have ingrained themselves into the public psyche in a thousand ways. The perceptions of enclave dwellers nevertheless have importance because they can enhance or diminish settled valuations. Let the enclave begin viewing with alarm the state of public morals, and a full crisis of solvency may soon be on the whole populace. I argue that the oscillating estimates of morality have curious similarities to the oscillating estimates of business prospects that mark the business-man's view of his world.

The last point that was made concerned the prime institution of the contemporary vested interests, the corporation. I tried to establish as a basic mutation in the corporate style the rise of priestly behavior that has accompanied the culmination of productive abilities. Productively adept executives find ritual and ceremony consuming more and more of their time. The duality of production/ceremony has its analog in the opposed personality types of the charismatic leader and the archonic leader. One, the argument goes, is concerned with making a product or creating a service, while the other is interested largely in corporate housekeeping. I have tried to assess the costs of the continuing refinement of sacerdotal bureaucracy, but I have come away convinced only that the accounting system that might help find such an answer has yet to be invented. What seems to give conventional accounting methods the greatest test is the growing suspicion that priestly behavior may be just what the economy needs to keep unemployment among college graduates to a minimum, and as such it may prove far less costly than welfare support of surplus bachelors of arts.

· 1 ·

In an earlier attempt to sum up the effects of automation on present institutions I sketched a picture that even now, just a few years later, in some particulars seems to have been too pessimistic. Developments within middle management, particularly, support the view that the excess of middle-echelon managers will probably continue to inspire ceremonial luxuriance rather than status degradation (as I had earlier suggested).

Nevertheless the effect of the contemporary vested interests and the impact of archonic leadership are creating the walled enclave that was described earlier. Under archonic direction, manufacturing industry has centralized its decision-making to a great degree, and it has won control over natural resources, production, investment, research and development, markets, and prices. It has effectively separated ownership and control, thus making possession of office (in distinction to ownership rights) the real basis of power. Under the archonic regime, capital accumulation is by forced draft in the sense that most manufacturing capital comes from special, tax-sheltered depreciation reserves; therefore, in effect, the system makes for investment at the command of top management. The consumer invests involuntarily by having an increment added to the price of products he buys. The price he pays includes his contribution to new plants and equipment whether he wants to contribute or not. Pay for a new Chevrolet and you are also paying your part for a new Chevrolet assembly plant that is still on the drawing boards.

This archonic system is notable for its persistent cost-push inflation, which in part reflects the inefficiencies of the system—inefficiencies that are paid for by consumers and by taxpayers by various subterfuges.

As it happens, the forces that might be expected to balance and neutralize the thrust of the manufacturing interests have scant prospects of effective life. Middle management, despite its selective dissidence, remains largely docile and content. Lower management is already beginning to fear its own technological unemployment because of the encroachment of computers. Therefore it is not disposed to challenge top management's line of decisions in any way at all. As for hourly workers, they and their unions are rapidly losing their powers as automation expels the unskilled and the semiskilled from the plant. Private property, which has always been credited with protecting private citizens from arbitrary exercises of power, has become so modified as to be almost unrecognizable. As for government, it acts the role of half-brother to industry, a role particularly visible in the military-industrial complex that is the biggest single industry in the nation or in the world.

That leaves the political force of aroused public opinion as the ultimate weaponry against abuses of industrial power. Of archonic power, Professor Horace M. Gray has observed that

. . . its own excesses and the falsity of its pretensions arouse the latent hostility of public opinion to the point of action. When that time comes, as it invariably has in American history, the awesome power of the Archons will stand revealed for the artificial, parasitic thing it really is. A few deft surgical strokes—abolition of some privilege, dissolution of some combine, introduction of new competition, modification of some institution—will suffice to sever the roots which sustain and nourish the systems; the power of the Archons will wither and economic freedom will revive.

Once the institutional sources of power are identified and society is resolved to act, the reduction of concentration, which formerly appeared impossible, becomes relatively easy. . . .[1]

Whether that optimistic an estimate of political progress is warranted or not, the progressive impulse, to be sure, is a familiar and recurring theme in American history.

· 2 ·

Perhaps as likely a denouement of excess archonic power as political reaction will be an economic evolution toward a society aligned with the needs of a new kind of vested interest, advertising-consumerism. Many signs point in that direction, and therefore a brief glance at the implications of such a development seems in order here.

The tension between manufacturing and advertising, as suggested earlier, is becoming more prominent. This tension has for one of its symptoms the alternate uses to which resources are allocated if manufacturing industry is preeminent or if advertising-consumerism attains the status of prime vested interest. Manufacturing, if we take its largest single industry as its vital center, is largely concerned with military production. Advertising, on the other hand, again judging from its most lively sector, is largely concerned with so-called package goods (soap, cigarettes, prepared foods, patent medicines, and the like). These package goods are the essence of civilian consumption and of mass-merchandising techniques: they are typically indistinguishable from their competing products; they carry low price tags; they are physically small enough to fit into shelves of hundreds of thousands of small retail outlets (but their preferred arena is the large supermarket).

The balance struck between these competing interests sets the tone from which daily life draws its rhythms. Under the military-industrial ascendancy, much of the nation's consumption is socialized consumption. In a narrower view, such a style of consumption seems to be largely without rational basis, to be witless. Suffice it to say that the launching of a large missile can consume raw materials and man-hours in substantial quantities. The electronics industry alone sees three-quarters of its output go into rocketry. Obsolescence in missiles is not only planned, it is often instantaneous, and such products do not compete in any easily discernible way with civilian industry.

Highly competitive conditions prevail in the world of advertising-consumerism, on the other hand. Were the nuclear-missile race to stabilize in the near future, and were peace to be assured, the slack in the economy that would have to be taken up would almost of necessity cause a huge growth in the impact of advertising.

If, then, the path of evolution is into the world of still higher mass consumption, as it seems to be, the cultural costs are likely to seem very high to many observers. Still higher mass consumption means that package-goods concepts of advertising will probably set the basic tone, just as large-scale military-goods production means that defense concepts provide the basis of development under the dominion of manufacturing interests.

If these assumptions are accurate, the ascent of advertising-consumerism will mark a day of still greater uniformity in products, of further attempts to mold public opinion by chemical and electromechanical means (negative ion dispensers and especially Musak are already in wide use across the country), and by increasing pressures on the educational system to redouble its already considerable course load of consumer education.

Under such circumstances the American nation promises to become even more the "land of happy monotony" that Lord Bryce saw emerging in the 1880's. A widely admired advertising leader has explained why monotony has frequently been an element of package-goods advertising:

A famous dental cream campaign has been running for twenty-two years and has kept this brand in first place in spite of massive onslaughts from its competitors. A famous bread campaign has been running for sixteen years, and the branches continue to proliferate. A great mouthwash campaign ran for thirty-three years. A cigarette campaign ran for eleven years. A campaign for a deodorant soap ran for over twenty-five years. A candy campaign, with a relatively small budget, has been running for seven years and has one of the highest penetrations in the United States. A great headache remedy ran the same campaign unchanged for over twenty years. One drug company, now a giant corporation, founded its business on a single product—and ran the copy unchanged for thirty-one years.

There are many examples.

Three great basic principles of advertising reality emerge from our research:

1. Changing a story has the same effect as stopping the money, as far as penetration is concerned.

2. Thus, if you run a brilliant campaign every year, but change it every year, your competitors can pass you with a campaign that is less than brilliant—providing he does not change his copy.

3. Unless a product becomes outmoded, a great campaign will not wear itself out.[2]

In a climate of advertising-consumerism predominance, the mature population will perhaps learn to its dismay of a new kind of tyranny. As the demands of package-goods promotion intensify, the mass media will concentrate even more than they do today on the most likely audience. As the president of the ABC-TV network has said, "We're programming for the younger, larger families—the ones with more teeth to brush, more bodies to bathe, and more hair to shampoo." Hence the tyranny of the young, the tyranny that has transformed most popular culture (movies, light fiction, television, and popular music) into loud and hackneyed entertainment useful largely in stimulating erotic behavior—useful, that is to say, in the creation of new consumers.

High cultural costs seem to mark the birth of any new prime interests. If such a birth is now taking place, the costs will not be without their benefits. If consumerism does rise to preeminence, the United States may find its remedy to the "high-level under-development," in which 7 percent are unemployed and 15 percent of the industrial capacity is unused, which has come to typify the American economy since the Korean War. The sheer pressure for more consumption may force by political-economic processes real concessions to the potential consumers in the nation who could do more, proportionately, than anyone else—the poor. Thus the grip of the archonic leadership may be weakened and the way made ready for a new kind of order.

· 3 ·

Yet the archons and the entire business mentality that they represent continue to have a kind of divine right to sabotage political innovation by virtue of their close relationship to spontaneous optimism. It is one of the ironies with which we all live that the man among us who represents Organization and Method, the supposed enemies of spontaneity, nevertheless presides in some ill-understood way over the urge to action, the "animal spirits," as Lord Keynes called them, that conduce to economic growth and development. It is this man who has it in his power to make the enclave less formidable. It is this man who makes a vested interest the lordly thing it can be. But at the same time, as Professor Schumpeter said, "A genius in the business office may be, and often is, utterly unable outside of it to say boo to a goose. . . ." [3]

Notes

ЛЛЛЛЛ

Notes to chapter 1

VESTED INTERESTS AND SOUND THOUGHT

1. A. A. Berle, Jr., *Economic Power and the Free Society* (New York: The Fund for the Republic, 1957), quoted in Francis M. Carney and H. Frank Way, Jr., eds., *Politics 1960* (San Francisco: The Wadsworth Publishing Co., 1960), pp. 172–174.

Notes to chapter 2

THE EVOLUTION OF INTERESTS

1. Josephson, *The Robber Barons*, p. 367. See bibliography for further details.
2. Thorstein Veblen, *The Theory of Business Enterprise*, p. 17.
3. Quoted in Henry Demarest Lloyd, *Wealth Against Commonwealth*, p. 467.
4. Arthur Schlesinger, Jr., *The Coming of the New Deal*, p. 491.
5. Max Radin, *Handbook of Anglo-American Legal History*, p. 362.
6. *IBM Songbook*, undated, p. 6.

Notes to chapter 3

AMERICA'S MAJOR INTERESTS

1. See Sigmund Diamond, *The Reputation of the American Businessman*, especially pp. 177–182.
2. John Kenneth Galbraith, *The Affluent Society*, p. 122.
3. George Katona, *The Powerful Consumer*, p. 173.

Notes to chapter 4

HOW THE INTERESTS WORK

1. E. H. Cameron, *Samuel Slater, Father of American Manufactures*, p. 59.
2. *Ibid.*, p. 170.
3. *Southern Textile Bulletin*, Vol. 1, No. 1, March 2, 1911, pp. 11–12.
4. Quoted in John Greenway, *American Folksongs of Protest*, pp. 130–131.
5. "Almost Unbelievable," Textile Workers Union of America, New York, January, 1961, p. 40.
6. *Ibid.*, p. 54.
7. *Ibid.*, p. 51.
8. Robert Engler, *The Politics of Oil*, p. 84.
9. *Ibid.*, p. 353.
10. *Ibid.*, p. 89.

Notes to chapter 5

THE POOR AND THE VESTED INTERESTS

1. *The Other America*, p. 6.
2. *Ibid.*, p. 120.
3. Jacob Oser, *The Evolution of Economic Thought*, p. 10.
4. *Studies in Housing and Minority Groups*, edited by Nathan Glazer and Davis McEntire, pp. 73–80.
5. The following events are described in complete detail in A. J. Liebling, *The Press*, pp. 78–89, on which this account is based.
6. *Ibid.*, p. 81.
7. *Ibid.*, p. 88.

Notes to chapter 6

VESTED INTERESTS AND GOVERNMENT

1. From Frank Moore, ed., *The Rebellion Record, Supplement* (Washington, 1869), XII, 362–368. Quoted in Leonard W. Levy and Merrill D. Peterson, eds., *Major Crises in American History: Documentary Problems*, Vol. I, 1689–1861, pp. 473–474.
2. John Marshall, *Life of Washington*, II (1850 edition), pp. 99 ff., quoted in Charles A. Beard, *An Economic Interpretation of the Constitution of the United States*, pp. 297–299.
3. Bertrand Russell, *A History of Western Philosophy*, p. 637.
4. *Congressional Record*, 63rd Congress, 1st Session, Vol. 50, Pt. 1, p. 130, as quoted in Louis M. Hacker, ed., *Major Documents in American Economic History*, Vol. II, pp. 28, 29.

5. *Subsidy and Subsidylike Programs of the U.S. Government*, 86th Congress, 2nd Session (Washington, D.C.: United States Government Printing Office, 1960).

6. *The Ideologies of Taxation*, p. 63.

7. Arthur M. Schlesinger, Jr., *The Crisis of the Old Order*, pp. 62, 63.

8. Eisenstein, *op. cit.*, p. 65.

9. Ross M. Robertson, *History of the American Economy*, pp. 564–565.

10. Herbert Hoover, *Addresses Upon the American Road, 1941–1945* (New York, 1946), p. 229, quoted by Arthur M. Schlesinger, Jr., in *The Politics of Upheaval*, p. 333.

11. Schlesinger, *ibid.*, p. 334.

12. Eisenstein, *op. cit.*, p. 46.

13. *Ibid.*, p. 130.

14. *Ibid.*, p. 124.

15. *Ibid.*, p. 45.

16. Gustavus Myers, *History of the Great American Fortunes*, pp. 709–710.

17. John C. Davidson, "Tax Rate Reform to Control the Spending Trend," National Association of Manufacturers (New York, 1960), pp. 1, 2, 4, and 5.

18. Eisenstein, *op. cit.*, pp. 180–181.

19. Harcourt, Brace & Co., 1959.

20. Berle, *Power Without Property*, pp. 36–37.

21. Peter L. Bernstein, "Paradoxes of Taxation," *The Nation*, March 24, 1962.

22. *The Share of Top Wealth-Holders* . . . , p. 52, Table 24, "Estimated Estate Wealth of Both Sexes, by Estate Size and Type of Property, 1953."

23. Engler, *The Politics of Oil*, p. 195.

24. Must Man Starve? (New York: Abelard-Schuman, Ltd., 1957), p. 183.

Notes to chapter 7

THE RISE OF ADMINISTERED OPTIMISM

1. *A Treatise on Money*, II, 151 n.

2. Miriam Beard, *A History of Business*, p. 437.

3. *Op. cit.*, II, 149.

4. *The Theory of Business Enterprise*, p. 75.

5. *Ibid.*, p. 203 n.

6. *The Theory of Economic Development*, p. 97.

7. Veblen, *op. cit.*, p. 67.

8. On May 9, 1918; quoted in L. Levy and M. Peterson, *Major Crises in American History*, I, 303.

9. In *Niles' Weekly Register*, Nov. 20, 1819, quoted in Levy and Peterson, *op. cit.*, I, 306.

10. Thomas Ford, *A History of Illinois*, cited in Levy and Peterson, *op. cit.*, I, 310.

11. Frederick Lewis Allen, *Only Yesterday*, p. 270.

12. *Ibid.*, p. 276.

13. John Kenneth Galbraith, *The Great Crash, 1929*, p. 126. Other "fundamentally sound" quotations above are from the same source, pp. 111–126, *passim*.

14. Quoted in George R. Terry, *Principles of Management*, p. 466. The document appears in this book under the caption "an excellent creed for developing a favorable attitude."

15. Sinclair Lewis, *Babbitt*, p. 161.

16. "A Message to American Industry," McGraw-Hill Publishing Company, Feb. 1, 1961.

17. *New York Times*, Oct. 17, 1961, p. 38.

18. Sec. IV, Nov. 19, 1961.

19. Nov. 25, 1961, p. 769.

20. *New York Times*, "Eisenhower Calls Spending a Factor in Stock Decline," June 2, 1962, p. 1 and runover.

21. *New York World-Telegram and The Sun*, "Advisers Wrong Again," Henry J. Taylor, June 4, 1962, p. 25.

Notes to chapter 8

VESTED INTERESTS AND RELIGION

1. Indianapolis: Bobbs-Merrill Co., 1927, pp. 207–208.

2. Pp. 63–64.

3. Charles and Mary Beard, *The Rise of American Civilization*, p. 700.

4. University of Chicago Press, Chicago, 1958.

5. Schneider and Dornbusch, *op. cit.*, pp. 104–105.

6. *Ibid.*, p. 88.

7. *Op. cit.*, pp. 179–180.

8. Lewis H. Haney, *History of Economic Thought*, p. 48.

9. *Op. cit.*, p. 75.

10. Aurelius, *To Himself*, Rendall translation, iv, 31 (p. 38).

11. *Ibid.*, viii, 34 (pp. 100–101).

12. Henry Charles Lea, *The Inquisition of the Middle Ages*, Margaret Nicholson abridgment, p. 248.

13. Ferdinand Schevill, *A History of Europe*, p. 98.

14. Harry Emerson Fosdick, ed., *Great Voices of the Reformation*, p. 72.

15. *Ibid.*, p. 283.

16. *Religion and the Rise of Capitalism*, p. 91.

17. *Ibid.*, p. 92.

18. Fosdick, *op. cit.*, p. 219.

19. *Ibid.*, pp. 222, 223.

20. *Ibid.*, p. 238.

21. Quoted by Troeltsch, *Die Soziallehren der Christlichen Kirche*, p. 707, and cited by Tawney, *Religion and the Rise of Capitalism*, p. 93.

22. *Western Political Theory: The Modern Age*, pp. 45–51, 66.

23. Scribner Library ed., p. 178.

24. *Sociology: A Systematic Introduction*, p. 447.

25. Quoted in Weber, *op. cit.*, p. 48.

26. Quoted in Weber, *op. cit.*, p. 175.

27. Miller, General Editor, *Major Writers of America*, I, 85.

28. *Ibid.*, I, 83–84.

29. Jonathan Edwards, "The Future Punishment of the Wicked Unavoidable and Intolerable," quoted in Miller, *op. cit.*, I, 153–154.

30. Benjamin Franklin, *Autobiography*, quoted in Miller, *op. cit.*, I, 109–110.

31. Vernon Louis Parrington, *Main Currents in American Thought*, II, 339.

32. Hubert Park Beck, *Men Who Control Our Universities* (New York: King's Crown Press, 1947), pp. 55–56, 178.

Notes to chapter 9

THE IDEOLOGY OF THE ENCLAVE

1. My classification system was as follows: I included under "entertainment" any article or part of an article that struck a reader on grounds of spectacle, sport, show business, exoticism, cheesecake, general prurience, or news treated within an entertainment framework (the New York City mayoral contest, for instance). Under "inspiration" I put such things as "National Purpose" articles, popular religion, adventure, and general ideological or propagandistic articles. "Education" included such things as an article on Chinese art in addition to straight news that aimed to inform rather than titillate, and articles with an attempted cultural impact. "Acquisition" included such things as articles dealing with consumer durables, soft goods, consumption of leisure products (like bathing suits, swimming pools, and suntan lotion), fashion, food, services, tourism, and celebrity articles in which consumption seemed to be the organizing principle.

Where possible, articles having more than one basic appeal were allocated in pages (or fractions thereof) to each relevant category. Hence a 10-page article on the Berlin crisis (August 25, 1961) was allocated 9 pages to education-news, one page to inspiration, although a 7–3 allocation could certainly have been made with fairness. Rather than to err toward the direction my natural suspicions suggested, however, I tried to allocate pages in the most neutral manner possible, hoping thereby to balance out whatever bias I had myself. (I think that is the only possible explanation for "education" holding third rather than fourth place in the hierarchy of editorial appeals. "Acquisition" would clearly have edged in third with a less rigid classification system.) Lastly, letters, tables of contents, indicia, and some few hybrid articles were unclassified. The total of unclassifiable material did not come to more than 2 percent of the nearly 1,000 pages of editorial matter that were classified in these issues.

According to this method, entertainment came out first with about 40 percent of the total, inspiration second with about 35 percent, education-news was third with about 15 percent, acquisition fourth with 8 percent, and unclassifiable matter took up the balance, or 2 percent. Of course, these rough proportions were not fixed from week to week but sometimes fluctuated widely. Thus the July 28, 1961, number was heavy on entertainment (particularly spectacle-prurience and show business and sport) but notably light on inspiration and acquisition. A week later, only 6 percent of the total pages were taken up with entertainment, over 50 percent with acquisition-consumption. A special twenty-eight-page photo article on summertime accounted for most of the acquisition lore.

The presumed relationships that my small sample indicates, I should add, are not susceptible to hard and exacting proof without expenditure of more time and effort than the project seems to be worth.

Notes to chapter 11

CORPORATE CULTURE AND THE VESTED INTERESTS

1. *Wirtschaft und Gesellschaft,* Part III, Chap. 6, pp. 650–678, translated as *From Max Weber,* p. 196.

2. *From Max Weber,* p. 418.

3. *Ibid.*

4. New York: St. Martin's Press, 1961.

5. Jewkes, *et al., op. cit.,* p. 406.

6. Jewkes, *et al., op. cit.,* p. 407.

7. P. 408

8. Oscar Grusky, "Corporate Size and Managerial Succession," *The American Journal of Sociology,* November, 1961, LXVIII, 3.

9. "Cold War Seen Bringing Army Nearer to Civilian Management Methods," *Business Week,* September 23, 1961, p. 168.

10. *Men Who Make Us Rich,* p. 191.

11. "The Sociology of Charismatic Authority," in *Wirtschaft und Gesellschaft,* Part III, Chap. 9, pp. 753–757, *From Max Weber,* p. 245.

12. "Long Island Craftsmen Protest Loss of Titles as Decline in Status," *New York Times,* Jan. 6, 1962, p. 21.

Notes to chapter 12

CONCLUSION

1. *The Progressive,* November, 1962, p. 48.

2. Rosser Reeves, *Reality in Advertising,* p. 32.

3. Joseph Schumpeter, *Capitalism, Socialism and Democracy,* pp. 137–138, quoted by John Robinson in *Economic Philosophy,* p. 20.

Bibliography

ⅉⅉⅉⅉⅉⅉⅉⅉ

Some works that I have drawn on are listed solely in the notes, as they were magazine or newspaper articles or quotations from books that I never read. The works listed below were all read: most of them wholly, others partially, a few hardly at all. A reader who wanted to familiarize himself with American social history and some of its intellectual roots might find here as good a starting place as any.—E. Z.

ALLEN, FREDERICK LEWIS. *Only Yesterday*. New York: Harper & Brothers, 1931.

————. *Since Yesterday*. New York: Harper & Brothers, 1940.

ANONYMOUS. *The IBM Song Book*. New York: privately printed, no date.

ANTONINUS, MARCUS AURELIUS. *To Himself*, Rendall Translation. London: Macmillan & Co., Ltd., 1907.

ARNOLD, THURMOND. *The Folklore of Capitalism*. New Haven: Yale University Press, 1937.

————. *The Symbols of Government*. New York: Harcourt, Brace & World, Harbinger ed. 1963.

BARKER, LUCIUS. "The Offshore Oil Case," in *The Third Branch of Government*, C. Herman Pritchett and Alan F. Westin, eds. New York: Harcourt, Brace & World, 1963.

BARTON, BRUCE. *The Man Nobody Knows*. Indianapolis: Bobbs-Merrill, 1924.

————. *The Book Nobody Knows*. Indianapolis: Bobbs-Merrill, 1926.

BEARD, CHARLES A. *The Economic Basis of Politics*. New York: Vintage Press, 1957.

BEARD, CHARLES A. *An Economic Interpretation of the Constitution of the United States.* New York: The Macmillan Company, 1961.

BEARD, CHARLES A. and MARY. *The Rise of American Civilization.* New York: The Macmillan Company, 1930.

BEARD, MIRIAM. *A History of Business.* Ann Arbor: The University of Michigan Press, 1962.

BERLE, A. A. *The 20th Century Capitalist Revolution.* New York: Harcourt, Brace & Co., 1954.

————. *Power Without Property.* New York: Harcourt, Brace & Co., 1959.

————. *The American Economic Republic.* New York: Harcourt, Brace & World, 1963.

BRINTON, CRANE. *The Shaping of the Modern Mind.* New York: New American Library, 1953.

BRYCE, JAMES. *Reflections on American Institutions* (from *The American Commonwealth*). New York: Fawcett Publications, Inc., 1961.

CAMERON, E. H. *Samuel Slater, Father of American Manufactures.* Portland, Me.: Bond Wheelwright, 1960.

COCHRAN, THOMAS C., and WILLIAM MILLER. *The Age of Enterprise: A Social History of America.* New York: Harper & Brothers, Torchbooks ed. 1961.

COMMONS, JOHN R. *Institutional Economics,* 2 vols. Madison: The University of Wisconsin Press, paper ed., 1959.

CONANT, JAMES B. *Slums and Suburbs.* New York: McGraw-Hill, 1961.

COTTRELL, FRED. *Energy and Society.* New York: McGraw-Hill, paper ed., 1958.

DAVIS, JOHN P. *Corporations: A Study of the Origin and Development of Great Business Combinations.* New York: Capricorn Books, 1961.

DIAMOND, SIGMUND. *The Reputation of the American Businessman.* Cambridge: Harvard University Press, 1955.

DOANE, ROBERT R. *World Balance Sheet.* New York: Harper & Brothers, 1957.

DUE, JOHN F. *Government Finance,* rev. ed. Homewood, Ill.: Richard D. Irwin, 1959.

EISENSTEIN, LOUIS. *The Ideologies of Taxation.* New York: Ronald Press, 1961.

ENGLER, ROBERT. *The Politics of Oil.* New York: The Macmillan Company, 1961.

FAULKNER, HAROLD U. *American Economic History,* 8th ed. New York: Harper & Brothers, 1960.

FOSDICK, HARRY EMERSON, ed. *Great Voices of the Reformation.* New York: Modern Library, 1954.

FOULKE, ROY A. *The Sinews of American Commerce.* New York: Dun & Bradstreet, 1941.

FOURASTIE, JEAN. *The Causes of Wealth.* Glencoe, Ill.: The Free Press, 1960.

GALBRAITH, JOHN KENNETH. *The Great Crash.* Boston: Houghton Mifflin Co., 1956.

———. *The Affluent Society.* Boston: Houghton Mifflin Co., 1958.

———. *Economics and the Art of Controversy.* New York: Vintage, 1959.

GEORGE, HENRY. *Progress and Poverty.* New York: Modern Library, no date.

GERTH, H. H., and C. WRIGHT MILLS, eds. *From Max Weber: Essays in Sociology.* New York: Galaxy Books, Oxford University Press, 1958.

GLAZER, NATHAN, and DAVIS McENTIRE. *Studies in Housing and Minority Groups.* Berkeley and Los Angeles: University of California Press, 1960.

GOFFMAN, IRVING J. *Erosion of the Income Tax Base in the United States and Canada.* Toronto: Canadian Tax Foundation, 1961.

GREENWAY, JOHN. *American Folksongs of Protest.* New York: A. S. Barnes, Perpetua Ed., 1960.

GRIER, EUNICE and GEORGE. *Privately Developed Interracial Housing.* Berkeley and Los Angeles: University of California Press, 1960.

HACKER, LOUIS M., ed. *Major Documents in American Economic History,* 2 vols. Princeton: D. Van Nostrand Co., Inc., 1961.

HAMILTON, ALEXANDER, *et al. The Federalist,* on the New Constitution. Hallowell: Glazier, Masters & Smith, 1837.

HANEY, LEWIS H. *History of Economic Thought,* 4th ed. New York: The Macmillan Company, 1949.

HARRINGTON, MICHAEL. *The Other America.* New York: The Macmillan Company, 1962.

HARTZ, LOUIS. *The Liberal Tradition in America.* New York: Harcourt, Brace & Co., 1955.

HAYEK, FRIEDRICH A. *The Road to Serfdom.* Chicago: Phoenix Books, University of Chicago Press, 1944.

HAYS, SAMUEL P. *The Response to Industrialism, 1885–1914.* Chicago: University of Chicago Press, paper ed., 1957.

HAZLITT, HENRY. *Economics in One Lesson.* New York: Macfadden, 1962.

HUXLEY, JULIAN. *Man in the Modern World*. New York: New American Library, 1948.

JEWKES, JOHN, DAVID SAWERS, and RICHARD STILLERMAN. *The Sources of Invention*. New York: St. Martin's Press, 1961.

JOHNSON, HARRY. *Sociology: A Systematic Introduction*. New York: Harcourt, Brace & Co., 1960.

JOSEPHSON, MATTHEW. *The Robber Barons*. New York: Harcourt, Brace & Co., 1934.

JUENGER, FRIEDRICH GEORG. *The Failure of Technology*. Chicago: Henry Regnery Co., Gateway ed., 1956.

KATONA, GEORGE. *The Powerful Consumer*. New York: McGraw-Hill, 1960.

KEMMERER, DONALD L., and C. CLYDE JONES. *American Economic History*. New York: McGraw-Hill, 1959.

KEYNES, JOHN MAYNARD. *Treatise on Money*, 2 vols. New York: Harcourt, Brace & Co., 1930.

————. *The General Theory of Employment, Interest, and Money*. New York: Harcourt, Brace & Co., 1936.

LAIDLER, HARRY W. *Concentration of Control in American Industry*. New York: Thomas Y. Crowell, 1931.

LAMPMAN, ROBERT. *The Share of Top Wealth-Holders in National Wealth, 1922–1956*. Princeton: Princeton University Press, 1962.

LASSWELL, HAROLD. *Politics: Who Gets What, When, How*. New York: Meridian Books, 1958.

LAURENTI, LUIGI. *Property Values and Race*. Berkeley and Los Angeles: University of California Press, 1960.

LEA, HENRY CHARLES. *A History of Sacerdotal Celibacy in the Christian Church*, 4th ed. London: Watts & Co., 1932.

————. *The Inquisition of the Middle Ages*, Margaret Nicholson abridgement. New York: The Macmillan Company, 1961.

LEKACHMAN, ROBERT. *History of Economic Ideas*. New York: Harper & Brothers, 1959.

LETWIN, WILLIAM, ed. *A Documentary History of American Economic Policy Since 1789*. Garden City: Doubleday Anchor Books, 1961.

LEVY, LEONARD W., and MERRILL D. PETERSON, eds. *Major Crises in American History*, 2 vols. New York: Harcourt, Brace & World, 1962.

LEWIS, SINCLAIR. *Main Street*. New York: Harcourt, Brace & Co., 1920.

————. *Babbitt*. New York: Harcourt, Brace & Co., 1924.

LIEBLING, A. J. *The Press*. New York: Ballantine Books, 1961.

LLOYD, HENRY DEMAREST. *Wealth Against Commonwealth*. New York: Harper & Brothers, 1894.

LUNDBERG, FERDINAND. *America's Sixty Families*. New York: Citadel Press, 1960.

LYND, ROBERT S. and HELEN M. *Middletown*. New York: Harcourt, Brace & Co., 1929.

———. *Middletown in Transition*. New York: Harcourt, Brace & Co., 1937.

McDONALD, LEE CAMERON. *Western Political Theory: The Modern Age*. New York: Harcourt, Brace & World, 1962.

McENTIRE, DAVIS. *Residence and Race*. Berkeley and Los Angeles: University of California Press, 1960.

MAYER, MARTIN. *The Schools*. New York: Harper & Brothers, 1961.

MILLER, PERRY. *The Puritans*. New York: American Book Company, 1938.

———, ed. *Major Writers of America*, 2 vols. New York: Harcourt, Brace & World, 1962.

MOSCA, GAETANO. *The Ruling Class*. New York: McGraw-Hill, 1939.

MULLER, HERBERT J. *The Uses of the Past*. New York: New American Library, 1954.

MUMFORD, LEWIS. *The Culture of Cities*. New York: Harcourt, Brace & Co., 1938.

———. *The City in History*. New York: Harcourt, Brace & World, 1961.

MYERS, GUSTAVUS. *History of the Great American Fortunes*. New York: Modern Library, 1936.

ORTEGA Y GASSET, JOSÉ. *History as a System*. New York: W. W. Norton, 1961.

OSER, JACOB. *The Evolution of Economic Thought*. New York: Harcourt, Brace & World, 1963.

PARRINGTON, VERNON LOUIS. *Main Currents in American Thought*, 3 vols. New York: Harcourt, Brace & Co., 1958.

PEALE, NORMAN VINCENT. *The Power of Positive Thinking*. Englewood Cliffs, N.J.: Prentice-Hall, 1952.

QUINN, T. K. *Giant Business: Threat to Democracy*, 3rd ed. New York: Exposition Press, 1954.

RADIN, MAX. *Handbook of Anglo-American Legal History*. St. Paul: West Publishing Company, 1936.

RAPKIN, CHESTER, and WILLIAM G. GRISBY. *The Demand for Housing in Racially Mixed Areas*. Berkeley and Los Angeles: University of California Press, 1960.

REEVES, ROSSER. *Reality in Advertising*. New York: Alfred A. Knopf, 1961.

RIESMAN, DAVID. *Thorstein Veblen*. New York: Scribner Library, Charles Scribner's Sons, 1959.

ROBERTSON, ROSS M. *History of the American Economy*. New York: Harcourt, Brace & Co., 1955.

ROBINSON, JOAN. *Economic Philosophy*. Chicago: Aldine, 1963.

ROSTOW, W. W. *The Stages of Economic Growth*. New York: Cambridge University Press, 1960.

ROVERE, RICHARD. *The American Establishment*. New York: Harcourt, Brace & World, 1962.

SANTAYANA, GEORGE. *Character and Opinion in the United States*. Garden City: Doubleday Anchor Books, 1956.

SCHEVILL, FERDINAND. *A History of Europe*, 6th ed. New York: Harcourt, Brace & Co., 1951.

SCHLESINGER, ARTHUR M., JR. *The Crisis of the Old Order*. Boston: Houghton Mifflin Co., 1957.

————. *The Coming of the New Deal*. Boston: Houghton Mifflin Co., 1958.

————. *The Politics of Upheaval*. Boston: Houghton Mifflin Co., 1960.

————. *Kennedy or Nixon: Does It Make Any Difference?* New York: The Macmillan Company, 1960.

SCHNEIDER, LOUIS, and SANFORD M. DORNBUSCH. *Popular Religion: Inspirational Books in America*. Chicago: University of Chicago Press, 1958.

SCHRIFTGIESSER, KARL. *The Lobbyists*. Boston: Atlantic-Little, Brown & Co. 1951.

SCHUMPETER, JOSEPH. *The Theory of Economic Development*. New York: Galaxy Books, Oxford University Press, 1961.

SHANNON, DAVID A., ed. *The Great Depression*. Englewood Cliffs, N.J.: Spectrum Books, Prentice-Hall, 1960.

SILK, LEONARD. *The Research Revolution*. New York: McGraw-Hill, 1961.

SMITH, ADAM. *Wealth of Nations*, 7th ed. London: A. Strahan and T. Cadell, 1793.

SPENCER, HERBERT. *Social Statics*. New York: Robert Schalkenbach Foundation, 1954.

STEFFENS, LINCOLN. *The Autobiography of Lincoln Steffens*, 2 vols. New York: Harcourt, Brace & Co., 1931.

————. *The Shame of the Cities*. New York: Hill and Wang, 1960.

SUMNER, WILLIAM GRAHAM. *Folkways*. New York: New American Library, 1960.

TARBELL, IDA M. *The History of the Standard Oil Company*, abridged ed. New York: Peter Smith, 1950.

TAWNEY, R. H. *The Acquisitive Society*. New York: Harcourt, Brace & Co., 1924.

————. *Religion and the Rise of Capitalism.* New York: New American Library, 1947.

TERRY, GEORGE R. *Principles of Management.* Homewood, Ill.: Richard D. Irwin, 1956.

TREVELYAN, G. M. *History of England,* 3 vols. Garden City: Doubleday Anchor Books, no date.

————. *English Social History.* London: Longmans, Green, 1920.

TREVER, ALBERT A. *History of Ancient Civilization,* 2 vols. New York: Harcourt, Brace & Co., 1939.

VEBLEN, THORSTEIN. *The Theory of Business Enterprise.* New York: New American Library, 1958.

————. *The Theory of the Leisure Class.* New York: Modern Library, 1934.

WEBER, MAX. *General Economic History.* New York: Collier Books, 1961.

————. *The Protestant Ethic and the Spirit of Capitalism.* New York: Scribner Library, Charles Scribner's Sons, 1958.

WHITEHEAD, ALFRED NORTH. *Adventures of Ideas.* New York: New American Library, 1955.

WHYTE, WILLIAM H., JR., *The Organization Man.* New York: Simon & Shuster, 1956.

WILSON, EDMUND. *The American Earthquake.* Garde City: Doubleday Anchor Books. 1958.

ZIEGLER, VINTON E. *The Protestant Churches and The Labor Movement.* Delaware, Ohio: Ohio Wesleyan University Master's Thesis, 1927.

Index

பாப்பாட்